THE AMERICAN PRIVATE EYE

RECOGNITIONS

detective/suspense

Bruce Cassiday, General Editor

THE AMERICAN PRIVATE EYE

The Image in Fiction

DAVID GEHERIN

FREDERICK UNGAR PUBLISHING CO.
New York

Designed by David Lunn

Library of Congress Cataloging in Publication Data

Geherin, David, 1943–
The American private eye.

Bibliography; p. 211
Includes index.
1. Detective and mystery stories, American—History
and criticism.   2. Detectives in literature.   3. American
fiction—20th century—History and criticism.   I. Title.
PS374.D4G39   1984   813'.0872'09   84-15251
ISBN 0-8044-2243-5
ISBN 0-8044-6184-8 (pbk.)

For Diane,
and for Chris, Pete, and Dan

Contents

Foreword

Galahad for Hire

For over sixty years, the private eye has been roaming the mean streets of America, looking for murderers and missing persons, for clues and criminals, for justice and, ultimately, for the truth. Along the way, he has been lied to, stabbed, sapped, and shot at, and his efforts have often resulted in frustration, discouragement, and disappointment. And for what? For twenty-five dollars a day, for the gratitude of a beautiful woman, for revenge, or simply because it's his job, or he has given his word, or it's all he knows how to do. Bruised but unbroken, this battered Galahad in a trenchcoat never abandons his mission, nor, as his continuing popularity attests, have his readers deserted him. Responding to the courage and dedication of this solitary brave man whose indomitable spirit strikes a responsive chord somewhere deep in the psyche, readers have made the private eye one of the most popular of all American heroes.

Although the term "private eye" dates back to the mid-nineteenth century when the detective agency founded by Allan Pinkerton used a wide-open eye and the slogan "We Never Sleep" as its trademark, the private eye we will be concerned with is the literary figure who came into being in the early 1920s in the pages of *Black Mask* magazine. Though there are similarities between the real-life detective and his fictional counterpart (after all, Dashiell Hammett, one of the creators of the literary private eye, was himself a former Pinkerton agent), it is important to remember that the private eye is a fictional rather than a real character. Anyone looking for a manual explaining how to be an actual detective would be well advised to look elsewhere than in the pages of a private-eye novel: but if one is interested in reading about a hero who exemplifies the highest standards of tough, courageous behavior, then the private-eye tale is for him.

Over the years, the private eye has enjoyed success in a variety of formats—in print, in films, on radio and television—and in the process he has become one of the most recognizable of American heroes, both at home and abroad, with an appeal that ranks him with that other native contribution to world culture, jazz. It is in print, however, first in the pulp magazines and later in hardcover and paperback books, that the private eye has made the greatest impression and it is this aspect of his existence that will be the focus of this study.

The chapters that follow will examine the works of over two dozen of the most important writers in the genre; along the way, a number of related issues will be taken up, including such matters as the conditions that led to the emergence of the private eye in the early 1920s, the various influences that shaped his development, the nature of the changes in his character over the years, and finally the many factors that have contributed to his enduring popularity.

A word about organization and selection of material. For the most part, the book follows a chronological approach. Each of the first six chapters roughly corresponds to a different decade beginning with the 1920s. Writers are generally assigned to the decade in which their private eyes began making their initial appearances. Chapter 7 offers some thoughts about the reasons for the private eye's longevity. With the exception of a few of the pulp writers whose work was largely confined to magazine publication and novelist Howard Browne, who published only four novels and a single short story about his detective, each of the writers included in this book created private eyes who appeared in series that lasted for at least five novels. The twenty-seven writers whose works are examined in detail were chosen on the basis of their influence on the genre, their enormous popularity, or, as in the case of several of the lesser-known writers, a desire to pay long overdue recognition to their creative contributions to the growth and vitality of the genre. This book is a tribute both to the private-eye hero and to all those writers—living and dead, famous and obscure—who contributed to the evolution and development of one of the most successful additions to American popular culture.

I would like to pay special thanks to several individuals whose assistance made my task easier: to Joel Lyczak, who among other things made his extensive collection of *Black Mask* magazines available to me; to Dave Lewis and Ken McDaniel, who provided me with photocopies of several rare pulp stories; to Rita Bullard of the Eastern Michigan University Center of Educational Resources and to Jannette Fiore and Anne Tracy of the Special Collections Division of the Michigan State University Library, who assisted me in obtaining hard-to-find materials; to Howard Browne and William Campbell Gault, who kindly answered my queries; to Loren Estleman, who shared with me his thoughts on the private eye and who gave me advance copies of his two perceptive essays on the hard-boiled hero; and finally to my editor, Bruce Cassiday, who provided advice and encouragement throughout this project.

1

Birth of a Hero

Although it is an American writer, Edgar Allan Poe, who is generally credited with inventing the detective story in 1841 with the publication of his tale, "The Murders in the Rue Morgue," it was eighty years before another American writer—actually a pair of American writers, Carroll John Daly and Dashiell Hammett—created the first authentic American detective hero, the private eye. Poe's detective, C. Auguste Dupin, significantly a Frenchman, not an American, appeared in only three stories—the others being "The Mystery of Marie Rogêt" in 1842 and "The Purloined Letter" in 1844—but his influence was profound for he provided the model for the world's most famous detective, Arthur Conan Doyle's Sherlock Holmes.

Like Dupin, Holmes was gifted with an extraordinary mind, one capable of discerning volumes of information from the tiniest bits of detail. In *A Study in Scarlet* (1887), the first Holmes story, his friend and biographer Dr. Watson quotes from an article Holmes wrote in which he set forth his belief in the value of careful observation and logical deduction:

From a drop of water . . . a logician could infer the possibility
of an Atlantic or a Niagara without having seen or heard of
one or the other. So all life is a great chain, the nature of
which is known whenever we are shown a single link of it.
Like all other arts, the Science of Deduction and Analysis is
one which can only be acquired by long and patient study.
. . . By a man's finger-nails, by his coat-sleeve, by his boots,
by his trouser-knees, by the callosities of his forefinger and
thumb, by his expression, by his shirt-cuffs—by each of these
things a man's calling is plainly revealed.[1]

For the next forty years, Doyle continued to write stories
that delighted millions of readers with Holmes's uncanny
ability to solve virtually any crime presented to him by applying the rules of careful observation and simple deductive
logic. To Holmes and his successors, detection was nothing
less than an exact science, an application of scientific principles to human affairs.

Sherlock Holmes became the prototype for virtually all
detective heroes created during the next few decades, and
the Holmesian tale became the model for the formal detective story, or whodunit, that remains popular even today.
Frequently eccentric in habit (Holmes played the violin and
injected cocaine), dilettantish in his interests (Holmes wrote
learned monographs on subjects ranging from tattoos to the
114 varieties of tobacco ash), and haughty in attitude toward
those less intellectually gifted than he, the Great Detective is
usually attracted to a case by the challenge and excitement it
offers. Usually an amateur rather than a professional, he successfully solves crimes that baffle the best minds on the
police force. His compensation comes in the sense of
satisfaction he gets in demonstrating once again his superior
intellectual skills rather than in any form of monetary
reward.

Following Holmes there came a veritable army of amateur
sleuths, some more foppish and irritating in manner than
Holmes but all sharing to some degree his reliance on careful

observation and logical methodology to solve crimes. In England there was E. C. Bentley's Philip Trent, Agatha Christie's Hercule Poirot (with his faith in his "little grey cells" as a way of solving crime), Ernest Bramah's Max Carrados (whose blindness was no obstacle to puzzling out solutions to crimes), H. C. Bailey's Reginald Fortune, R. Austin Freeman's Dr. John Thorndyke, Philip MacDonald's Colonel Anthony Gethryn, A. A. Milne's Antony Gillingham, Anthony Berkeley's Roger Sheringham, and Dorothy Sayers's Lord Peter Wimsey—to name only some of the brilliant sleuths created between 1907 and 1926. Despite the strongly British flavor to the genre, there were even some American cousins of Sherlock Holmes: Arthur Reeve's Craig Kennedy (called "The American Sherlock Holmes"), Jacques Futrelle's Professor S. F. X. Van Dusen (known as "The Thinking Machine," he once defeated a world chess champion only hours after having the rules of the game explained to him) and S. S. Van Dine's Philo Vance. Despite their individual eccentricities and methods, each of these detectives was portrayed as an intellectual giant whose problem-solving skills represented a celebration of the scientific method and a constant rebuke to evildoers.

As the mystery story developed, especially after the publication of E. C. Bentley's *Trent's Last Case* in 1913, it began to incorporate more and more features of the traditional English comedy of manners. Such conventions as stereotyped aristocratic characters, cozy country settings, a rigidly defined hierarchical society, and what can perhaps best be described as an English country-house style were borrowed from the same literary tradition that produced such nineteenth-century English masters of the novel as George Eliot, Jane Austen, George Meredith, and Anthony Trollope. Even when, as in the case of The Thinking Machine or Philo Vance or even the early Ellery Queen, the Holmesian detective was transplanted to America, he remained as aristocratic in attitude and as eccentric in habit as the stuffiest of his British counterparts.

But as George Grella reminds us in his excellent essay, "Murder and Manners: The Formal Detective Novel," "the whodunit assumes a benevolent and knowable universe,"[2] a world of cause and effect that, the sleuth is confident, can be forced to surrender a solution to any mystery if one diligently applies the laws of logic. A series of shattering events—social, political, and economic—began to occur, however, which would produce a radical disruption in the mystery story. The outbreak of World War I in 1914, for example, seriously challenged a number of widely held beliefs and comforting assumptions about man's ability to shape, by reason, his own destiny, about the inevitable progress of the human race, and about the inviolability of civilization itself. The reality of the war forced many thoughtful individuals to consider the very real possibility that the world was neither as benevolent nor as rationally ordered as had been previously assumed. This general disillusionment was exacerbated in the United States by the institution of Prohibition in 1920, which had the effect of suddenly transforming millions of law-abiding citizens into conspirators in illegal activities each time they took a sip of bootleg whiskey. Worse, because of the enormous profits to be made from bootlegging, American cities, large and small, soon came under the control of gangsters. Crime seemed to be everywhere. The final blow would come at the end of the decade, when the stock market crash of 1929 ushered in the economic suffering of the Great Depression. Social and economic disorder thus combined with philosophical disillusionment to produce what Raymond Chandler described as a "world gone wrong."

One of the most notable results of the general upheaval in society was a loss of confidence in reason as the solution to all man's problems. If the world was no longer perceived as rational but arbitrary and capricious, then man's intellect, no matter how fully developed, could not be depended upon to puzzle out all the answers. The Holmesian approach to crime-solving rests upon the belief that everything in the universe obeys the laws of logic and is therefore knowable. In a fundamentally irrational universe, however, reason becomes far less effective. One could no longer confidently solve a puzzle if he felt that some important pieces were missing, or if he were asked to put it together in the dark. Dashiell Hammett likens the confusion of the private eye to the actions of a "blind man in a dark room hunting for the black hat that wasn't there."[3]

The world of the classical whodunit also assumes a stable society, one in which crime is viewed as an aberration, a deviation from the norm that can be exorcised by the efforts of the detective, whose success in first identifying and then eliminating the criminal element makes possible the return to normalcy at the end of the story. But if crime and disorder are the rule rather than the exception, as they seemed to be in America in the 1920s, then no individual, no matter how brilliant, could be expected to restore order merely by discovering the identity of the criminal. The combination of these two elements—the displacement in the minds of many of a rationally ordered universe by one which seemed capricious and arbitrary; and the growing suspicion that crime was no longer a simple isolated phenomenon but rather an integral part of the very fabric of society—produced a profound change in the direction of mystery fiction. The emergence of the private eye is not, as some contend, "an imitation detective story which is based on a misunderstanding of the genre,"[4] nor is it, as Edmund Wilson said about *The Maltese Falcon,* simply an infusion of "the old formula of Sherlock Holmes with a certain cold underworld brutality" designed to give readers a "new shudder."[5] Rather it represents a fundamental reordering of perceptions and it produced, among other things, a radically new kind of hero, one far better equipped than the brilliant logician to cope with violence and disorder. Even though he was often unable to deduce solutions from bits of evidence or rid the world of evil at the end of the story, he did his best to combat it wherever he could by relying upon his fists rather than his wits, his brawn instead of only his brains.

The lack of verisimilitude in the formal detective story was also becoming more noticeable, especially in the light of recent world events. In his classic essay, "The Simple Art of Murder," Raymond Chandler complained about the arid formulas of the classical whodunits, observing that in order to fit the artificial patterns of the puzzle plot, which became the highest priority in such mysteries, characters were often little more than "puppets and cardboard lovers and papier mâché villains and detectives of exquisite and impossible gentility."[6] Too often, in Chandler's view, the crime in question, which he described as being typically "how somebody stabbed Mrs. Pottington Postlethwaite III with the solid platinum poignard just as she flatted on the top note of the Bell Song from *Lakmé* in the presence of fifteen ill-assorted guests,"[7] had no relevance to the world in which the readers actually lived. Many individuals, especially in the light of the war just ended, felt that death was too important to be treated as nothing more than an excuse for a puzzle. The times demanded verisimilitude, a leading proponent of which was Dashiell Hammett, whom Chandler honored for giving murder "back to the kind of people that commit it for reasons, not just to provide a corpse; and with the means at hand, not with hand-wrought duelling pistols, curare, and tropical fish."[8] Readers who preferred their murders "scented with magnolia blossoms" might have been put off by the realism of the new detective story, but those readers who understood that they did not inhabit a "very fragrant world" were drawn to the gritty and sometimes violent world that was being depicted in the tradition-shattering tales of writers like Daly and Hammett.

The formal detective story certainly did not disappear from sight as a result of the tribulations of the age; in fact, it entered what is called its Golden Age at about the same time as the upheaval began. Its new popularity can be seen less as evidence of the willful blindness of its readers and more as a tribute to the persistence of its strong nostalgic appeal, for

the neat logical conclusions to most such mysteries continued to celebrate the "cozy tea-and-crumpety-sense of
God's-in-His-heaven-all's-right-with-the-world"[9] assurance
that was noticeably missing from real life. What happened,
however, was that as the turmoil increased, the contrived
situations and cardboard characters that figured in such
books were forced to share the stage with mysteries that
more realistically reflected the anxieties of the age and that
featured heroes who were rough, tough, and frequently
violent.

The effects of post-World War I disillusionment were not,
of course, limited exclusively to the detective story. The
philosophical disturbances also produced such poetic
statements of disillusionment as William Butler Yeats's "The
Second Coming" (1921) and T. S. Eliot's "The Waste Land"
(1922), as well as the early stories of Ernest Hemingway,
which helped bring about a shift in style and attitude that
revolutionized American prose in the twentieth century. But
the change can perhaps be detected more readily in the
mystery novel because, for one thing, it represented such an
abrupt departure from what was the dominant (one is
tempted to say sole) form of the mystery story at the time.
Also, the shift can be clearly attributed to the combined efforts of two writers, Carroll John Daly and Dashiell Hammett, who almost simultaneously were creating the private-
eye hero in stories that began appearing in the pages of the
most important and influential of all the outlets for this new
type of writing, *Black Mask.*

It would be an exaggeration to say that either Daly or
Hammett set out deliberately to precipitate a revolution in
the detective story. Like many other writers at the time, they
were merely responding to the changes in values, or perhaps
more accurately to the loss of previously held values, and
were thus drawn to a kind of writing that would allow them
to reflect as realistically as possible a world which seemed to
them marked by disorder, uncertainty, and violence. In order to portray such a world, the first thing each

had to do was find a new hero, one who was more at home in this world than the infallible and omniscient sleuth, one better equipped to meet its severe demands.

Where did they find this new hero? His immediate predecessors were the popular heroes of the dime novels, such detectives as Nick Carter and The Old Sleuth and such Western stars as Buffalo Bill and Deadwood Dick, but in his essential characteristics his ancestry can be traced back even further, to such legendary nineteenth-century figures as Daniel Boone and Davy Crockett and to the frontier hero of James Fenimore Cooper's *Leather-Stocking Tales,* Natty Bumppo. The prototypical Western hero was a brave, resourceful individual who often found himself torn between society's dictates and those of his own conscience. Strictly speaking not a lawman, he nevertheless on his own initiative and for his own private reasons worked for the pursuit of justice, fairness, and dignity. As the United States was being transformed from a predominantly agricultural society into a predominantly industrial one in the early decades of the twentieth century, it was inevitable that the frontier hero would also soon become urbanized. What Daly and Hammett were able to do (albeit in significantly different ways) was to transplant this most authentic American hero from the plains to the city streets, giving new life to the Western hero in the form of the modern private eye.

Race Williams

(Carroll John Daly)

The initial step in the revolution occurred in the December 1922 issue of *Black Mask* when Carroll John Daly published a story entitled "The False Burton Combs," which featured an unnamed, self-styled "soldier of fortune" who was to become the prototype for the first private eye. Willing to accept any job, no matter how dangerous, provided the price is right—"I don't mind the risk, but I must be paid accordingly"—he agrees to spend the night keeping company with a frightened young man for a hundred dollars. The man, Burton Combs, confesses that he fears for his life and offers Daly's hero a tidy sum if he will agree to impersonate him for the rest of the summer on Nantucket Island. He agrees. Eventually he finds himself in a confrontation with three men who have come gunning for the real Burton Combs, but in a bloody shootout he manages to kill all three gunmen.

Daly's hero describes himself as "just a gentleman adventurer" who makes his living "working against the law breakers," not because of any commitment to justice but simply because in his experience they have proven to be the simplest sort to fleece. As fearless and as tough as any of the criminals he encounters—"I could shoot as good as any bootlegger that ever robbed a church. They're hard guys, yes, but then I ain't exactly a cake-eater myself"—he adopts whatever methods are necessary, including killing, in order to survive in his violent world. Although the local authorities are disturbed by his gunplay, he is acquitted in the killing of the three gunmen after his lawyer, defending his actions, convinces the jury that, "if that isn't self-defense and good American pluck I'd like to ask you what in heaven's name is?" In the end, the hero accepts an offer of a steady job from Burton Combs's father, and elects to settle down, get married, and retire from his dangerous profession.

Although Daly thus forsakes his soldier of fortune, he doesn't entirely abandon his basic character. He resurrects him, gives him the name Terry Mack and features him in "Three Gun Terry" in the May 15, 1923, issue of *Black Mask*. Like the unnamed hero in Daly's earlier story, Terry Mack occupies a shadowy area somewhere between the law and the criminal. "I ain't a crook, and I ain't a dick. I play the game . . . my own way." Like his predecessor, he is tough, fearless, and a bit trigger-happy. He carries three guns: two .45s and a .25 caliber pistol. Unlike his predecessor, however, he is by profession a private investigator who charges a flat rate rather than whatever the danger commands. He gets fifty dollars a day, plus a two-hundred-dollar bonus for each enemy corpse he produces.

But it was Race Williams, introduced in "Knights of the Open Palm" in the June 1, 1923, issue of *Black Mask,* who was to become Daly's most popular creation. Sales of *Black Mask* reportedly jumped 15 percent whenever a Race Williams story was featured. He became the true progenitor of the American private eye. Like Three-Gun Terry Mack, Williams is a fearless private investigator who will take any job, whether it be infiltrating the Ku Klux Klan ("Knights of the Open Palm"), ridding New York of the infamous Gorgon brothers, the most ruthless and powerful gangsters in the city (*The Third Murderer* [1931]), working to discover the identity of The Hidden Hand, the crime genius who is terrorizing all of Florida (*The Hidden Hand* [1929]), or trying to thwart a nefarious plot to plunge the United States into war (*Murder from the East* [1935]), as long as the price is right. "I ain't afraid of nothing," he boasts, "providing there's enough jack in it." Unlike Holmes and his descendants who were amateur sleuths drawn to a case by the intellectual challenge it offered, Williams is a professional who makes his living by chasing criminals, and he demands to be well paid for his efforts.

Williams isn't motivated by any noble desire to eradicate crime from the world; that would be bad for business. "I'm not a preacher against crime. I've made too much money out of criminals. They're my bread and butter." He is willing to sell his services to the highest bidder, although he draws the line at becoming involved in illegal activities. But despite all the talk about the financial angles of a case, it is the thrill of the hunt and the dangers of his profession that he finds equally rewarding. "If I couldn't still feel the lure of the man-hunt," he confesses, "I wouldn't be in the game." And, although he is reluctant to admit it for it would damage his image as a hard-hearted businessman, he occasionally becomes interested in a case for purely personal reasons. In both *The Tag Murders* (1930) and *Murder from the East,* for example, it is the kidnapping of a twelve-year-old girl that prompts his involvement.

Like his motives, Williams's methods are also radically different from those of the intellectual sleuths. He is a man of action, not thought, a man schooled in the laws of survival rather than the laws of logic. "Thoughts never got me any place. If ever a lad can figure things out wrong, I'm that lad. What I want is action—and what I get is action." His knowledge comes for the rough and violent streets of the city, not from dusty tomes. "Right and wrong are not written on the statutes for me, nor do I find my code of morals in the essays of long-winded professors," he declares. "My ethics are my own."[10] Unlike his Holmesian counterparts, he has little faith in the careful collection of clues as a method of solving crimes. Sherlock Holmes may have been an expert on the 114 varieties of tobacco ash, but to Williams "a burnt cigar ash only tells me that someone has smoked a cigar, and nothing more." His goal is not deducing the identity of the culprit or puzzling out a challenging problem; he is simply interested in bringing criminals to justice, which he often administers on the spot in his favorite way—by putting a bullet between the evildoer's eyes.

What Race Williams does share with Sherlock Holmes and others of his ilk is a confidence bordering on arrogance; so self-assured is he that he never doubts his abilities nor questions his frequently rash actions. "I'm not a lad who won't admit a thing is wrong, just because he did it," he declares in *The Third Murderer.* But then he adds, "If it was wrong it was just too damn bad. . . . Nothing I could do then would take a forty-four bullet and shove it back into my gun again. Why cry over it?" If he finds himself in a situation that calls for a bit of gunplay, he shoots without hesitation and with no apologies. If his violent actions happen to disturb his readers, that's too bad; "Truth is truth," he declares. "Call it murder if you like—a disregard for human life. I don't care. I'll run my business—you run yours."

Williams's swagger can be attributed to his fearlessness and his confidence in his marksmanship, neither of which he tires of trumpeting. When he learns that a $100,000 contract has been put out to "GET RACE WILLIAMS," he meets the threat with his own challenge: "COME AND GET HIM." As a man who lives in a rough and violent world, he knows he must be tough enough to meet its challenges and he prides himself on his reputation for he-man heroics. It not only puts fear into the hearts of the underworld, it's also good for business. On the day after an account of an incident in which he held off twelve men gunning for him appears in the newspaper, he receives twelve job offers. Williams's bold methods and fearless nature have kept him alive in a violent world that would quickly devour those effete eccentrics whose approach to crime is largely limited to poking about in ashtrays and deducing motives from actions whose significance is hidden from all but the most perceptive observer.

Although when it comes to criminals Williams's ethics are uncomplicated, boasting as he does, "My conscience is clear. I never bumped off a guy what didn't need it," it would be incorrect to conclude that he has no principles at all. While it seldom gives him pause to shoot a criminal in the back if the situation demands it, he will have nothing to do with a crooked racket, nor will he sell out a client to a higher bidder. Nor, even though it contains information that might be helpful, will he betray a client's confidence by reading a document he has been entrusted with in *The Snarl of the Beast*.

Nor, despite his generally hard-boiled attitude toward things in general—"I've seen so much that my heart is petrified to a granitelike hardness"—is he devoid of feelings. Moved by a client's story in *The Snarl of the Beast,* he reaches out and grasps his wrist in a gesture of sympathy. Although he's not what you would call chivalrous in his attitude toward the female sex, since he doesn't hesitate to bash a woman in the head with his gun in *Murder from the East* because "she had it coming to her," he does have a soft spot in his heart for certain women. Despite his claim that he wouldn't hang from a precipice in order to get her a rare flower, he is prepared to risk his life to save the beautiful Tina Sears in *The Hidden Hand* because she had earlier saved his life. But the woman who provokes most of his gentler feelings is Florence Drummond, known as "The Girl with the Criminal Mind" for her underworld activities and "The Flame" for her power over men. Williams first meets her in *The Tag Murders,* where she earns his gratitude for shooting a man who is about to gun him down. She turns up in several of the subsequent books, although Williams is never certain whether she has gone straight, as she claims, or whether she has reverted to her previous life of crime, as it appears. Williams's relationship with The Flame represents a crude attempt on Daly's part to introduce a romantic element into the series, thereby adding a much-needed human dimension to his two-fisted, trigger-happy hero.

It is obvious that Race Williams does not trace his ancestry to the Holmesian sleuth but to the rough-and-ready hero of the Wild West, to the daring gunfighter who relied on a quick eye and a steady trigger finger in his campaign to bring justice to a troubled frontier. In fact, an exchange in the very first Race Williams story sounds as if it might even have come from a dime-novel Western. Western elements were not inappropriate in *Black Mask,* which for many years advertised on its cover that it featured "Detective, Western, Stories of Action." Warned by a Ku Klux Klansman that he has twenty-four hours to get out of town, Williams tells him that he and his two henchmen have exactly twenty-four *seconds* to get out of his room. Nobody can push Race Williams around, just as no one dared to push the tough cowboy hero around either. The popularity of Race

Williams demonstrated that the brave frontier hero could effectively be transplanted to the streets of New York without any loss of daring or courage. Or audience.

Daly was an unlikely candidate as the pioneer of what came to be known as the hard-boiled school of detective fiction and an unlikely creator of such a rough and violent character as Race Williams. As a youth, he attended the American Academy of Dramatic Arts in New York, later worked as an usher and projectionist, and eventually owned and operated the first movie theater on the boardwalk in Atlantic City. When he subsequently turned to writing in his early thirties, he moved to White Plains, New York, and, unlike his brave hero, settled into an unadventurous, highly regulated life, never venturing out of the house during the winter. Daly's home environment was so rigidly controlled that he never even allowed the temperature of the house to vary more than two degrees. Nor did he share his hero's fearlessness, reportedly refusing his wife's entreaties to have his teeth fixed because of his fear of dentists. Daly saved all his heroics for his writing, to which he devoted himself each night during the quiet, lonely hours between midnight and dawn.

Nobody ever accused Daly of being much of a writer and readers looking for elegance of phrasing or subtlety of characterization will be disappointed. Daly had no ear for dialogue and his plots are threadbare, especially in the novels, which are little more than story sequences loosely patched together. *The Hidden Hand* is a typical example: in order to get to "The Hidden Hand," a notorious crime genius, Williams first has to confront each of his four associates, which he does in mechanical order one after the other. So much for plot development. Daly's idea of creating suspense is either to fill the page with dashes, aiming for a breathless quality that the action fails to generate, or else to have a character die just as he is about to reveal some crucial bit of information. Rather than developing characters in any detail, he relies on colorful sobriquets like "The Beast,"

"The Head Tag," "The Hidden Hand," "The Girl with the Criminal Mind," and "The Angel of the Underworld" to do all the work of characterization for him. Finally, the action in the stories is heavily melodramatic and overly repetitious. When Daly finds a scene to his liking, he uses it in novel after novel. Also, he seldom employs action as a way of revealing Williams's toughness, preferring instead to have his hero tell the reader how tough he is. The result is that the stories become little more than extended monologues in which Williams strikes he-man poses and brags endlessly about his courage and fearlessness.

Even though, as Michael Barson charges, Daly may have been a "third-rate word-spinner" who featured his "second-rate protagonist" in "fourth-rate productions,"[11] it isn't difficult to account for the enormous popularity of his work in the twenties. Race Williams represented a fresh new face, a new kind of hero who in his rugged individualism touched a responsive chord in his audience. In an essay on Daly's contribution to the development of the private eye, G. A. Finch argues that one reason for Williams's popularity was that in his brash new hero Daly managed to "translate the wishes of the non-thinking reader into action: the desire to overpower enemies without scruple or fear of retaliation; and to live in a world in which there are no obstacles to the quick elimination of chosen lawbreakers."[12] A hero like Race Williams was admired because his readers saw him as an ordinary man "who had what no ordinary man had and every common man wanted to some degree: autonomy of action—to do what was necessary to punish enemies without fear of reprisal."[13] While there can certainly be no denying that Williams's shoot-first-ask-questions-later philosophy pandered to the baser instincts of his audience, there are other equally important reasons for his quick acceptance. For one thing, the time was ripe for a new hero. It was Ogden Nash who once quipped that "Philo Vance needs a kick in the pance," but it was Race Williams who was the first to deliver a telling blow to the priggish intellectual sleuths like Philo Vance who dominated mystery fiction in the 1920s.

Between 1923 and 1934, Daly published some thirty-five Race Williams stories in *Black Mask,* including in one brief flurry between 1927 and 1932 six multi-part story sequences, all of which were subsequently published in hardcover as Race Williams novels. The first of these, *The Snarl of the Beast,* published in 1927, has the distinction of being the first private-eye novel ever published. After leaving *Black Mask,* Daly continued to turn out Race Williams stories for a number of other pulps (including a total of twenty-three for *Dime Detective*) and also created several other heroes (Vee Brown, Clay Holt, Satan Hall), none of whom ever caught on the way Williams did.

Daly never developed as a writer, however, and as more believable private eyes began to appear in the pulps in the early 1930s Race Williams's popularity waned. Although he continued to write for the pulps until their demise in the 1950s—the final Race Williams story didn't appear until 1955—Daly was never able to regain his audience. Despite the fact that Race Williams is remembered today largely for his historical significance, Daly's contribution to the development of the new mystery hero cannot be ignored for it was Race Williams who first set the example that an entire army of private eyes was to follow.

The Continental Op

(Dashiell Hammett)

The revolution that altered the shape of the mystery story in the 1920s involved more than the simple substitution of a new hero for an established one. Among other things it also resulted in a distinctly new atmosphere of realism and a powerful new style. Erle Stanley Gardner, commenting on the origins of the private-eye story, credited Carroll John Daly with developing the new type of mystery tale, but it was Dashiell Hammett whom he honored as the true originator of the hard-boiled style that was to become a trademark of the new detective fiction. Daly was a clumsy writer who relied on melodramatic devices and often wildly implausible situations for effect. Hammett adopted a much more realistic approach in his stories, employing a hard-boiled style that was not only an effective vehicle for embodying the toughness of his hero but also for capturing in grim detail the criminal milieu of urban America in the 1920s. By matching style to character Hammett demonstrated the possibilities for artistic development that eluded Daly.

Just four months after Daly introduced Race Williams, Hammett (writing under the pseudonym "Peter Collinson") published a story entitled "Arson Plus" in the October 1, 1923, issue of *Black Mask* in which he introduced a short, overweight, unnamed detective employed by the San Francisco branch of the Continental Detective Agency. The Continental Op, as he became known, eventually appeared in thirty-six stories between 1923 and 1930, all but two of them in *Black Mask* (included in this number are two four-part story sequences which were later published in hardcover form as *Red Harvest* [1929] and *The Dain Curse* [1929]). A hard-working, dedicated professional investigator, the Op offered a realistic alternative to the brash, swaggering Race Williams as the embryonic private-eye hero was beginning to take shape in the early 1920s.

Race Williams was little more than a fantasy figure created out of Daly's imagination, influenced by the popularity of the gunfighter hero of the Old West and colored by the violent tenor of the times. Hammett, on the other hand, spent many years himself as a private investigator for the Pinkerton Detective Agency. Two of his more celebrated

assignments involved gangster Nicky Arnstein and film star
Fatty Arbuckle. He drew upon his own experiences as
material for his stories. Although he acknowledged that the
Op was modeled on James Wright, assistant superintendent
of the Pinkerton Baltimore office for whom he once
worked, Hammett also confessed that the reason the Op was
never given a name was that he actually represented a number of private detectives he really knew: "He's more or less
of a type: the private detective who oftenest is successful:
neither the derby-hatted and broad-toed blockhead of one
school of fiction, nor the all-knowing, infallible genius of
another. I've worked with several of him."[14] Unquestionably, the verisimilitude that characterizes Hammett's
stories—a quality noticeably lacking in Daly's—was due to
his ability to draw upon his personal experience for his fiction.

Like Race Williams, the Op is a professional rather than an
amateur detective, but unlike Williams, who is motivated by
the love of thrills and the love of money, the Op is dedicated
to his work. Forty years old in the later stories, he has been a
loyal employee of the Continental Agency since the age of
twenty, about the same age Hammett was when he joined
the Pinkertons. He is not a free-lance operator like Williams
but a "hired man" bound by the strict regulations and
policies of his agency. He entertains no notion as Race
Williams does that there is anything heroic about his job:
"The idea in this detective business," he proclaims, "is to
catch crooks, not to put on heroics." He is a detective for a
simple reason: "I happen to like the work." Maybe he could
make more money in some other line of work, but as he can-
didly admits, "I don't know anything else, don't enjoy
anything else, don't want to know or enjoy anything else."
It isn't the money or the thrill of the encounter that gives
him pleasure; his satisfaction comes from "catching crooks
and solving riddles" and from doing his job as well as he can.
Even when he is fired from a job by a client, he continues on
the case until the end of the day since the client will have to
pay for his services for the full day anyway.

His methods also differ dramatically from those of Race Williams, who prefers violent confrontation with the criminal as a way of solving his cases. To the Op, "Ninety-nine percent of detective work is a patient collecting of details," and what success he has is usually the fruit of "patience, industry, and unimaginative plugging, helped out now and then, maybe, by a little luck." The Op is completely convincing in his methods of detection. In "The Whosis Kid," for example, he stakes out a house for nine hours simply because he is suspicious about someone he saw enter it. In "Zigzags of Treachery" he spends endless hours shadowing suspects, including one for an uninterrupted fifteen-hour stretch. In "The Scorched Face" he spends four days painstakingly compiling and then checking out a list of every woman in San Francisco who was recently murdered, committed suicide, or disappeared. In "The Girl with the Silver Eyes" he combs the newspaper files to learn which days during the past month were rainy, then checks the records of the three largest cab companies in town until he finds the address a woman suspect visited on a wet evening. So plausible and convincing are the Op's methods that Joe Gores, a private detective before becoming a writer, praised Hammett's stories for providing "a sort of condensed course in the techniques of detection."[15]

When the situation demands it, however, the Op can be as violent as Race Williams. He kills when necessary (he even shoots a woman who ignores his warning to stop), although he doesn't feel compelled to plug his opponents between the eyes to prove his toughness. In his view, "the proper place for guns is after talk has failed." No adherent of Race Williams's shoot-first-and-ask-questions-later philosophy, he believes that "you can't shoot a man just because he refuses to obey an order—even if he is a criminal." Hammett did not "glorify toughness," as William Nolan notes, "he honestly portrayed it."[16] The Op doesn't hesitate to call in the police or some of his fellow ops when the job demands it; the whole idea is to be successful in your operation, not pile up bodies unnecessarily in order to prove your heroism or live up to a reputation as a he-man.

There is also a greater complexity to the character of the Op, a sense of depth beneath the surface that is lacking in the portrayal of Race Williams. Of his private life we know little other than that he is fond of poker. When he says, as he does repeatedly in the stories, "I went home to bed," we do not follow him. His personality is defined almost exclusively in terms of his work, but within these limitations Hammett manages to convey some interesting shadings of character, most notably with respect to the Op's attitude towards violence. In several of his later works, the Op finds himself more and more attracted to brutality. Although he never seems to take the kind of sadistic pleasure in shooting a man that Race Williams does, he nevertheless finds himself in situations in which he begins to experience pleasure in savagery. In this description of a fight from "The Big Knockover"—"Swing right, swing left, kick, swing right, swing left, kick. Don't hesitate, don't look for targets. God will see that there's always a mug there for your gun or blackjack to sock, a belly for your foot"—he even begins to sound like Williams himself.

Such moments of pleasure, however, are offset by a fear that he is enjoying violence too much. He realizes that his many years in the crime business have begun to take their toll. "I've got hard skin all over what's left of my soul, and after twenty years of messing around with crime I can look at any sort of a murder without seeing anything in it but my bread and butter, the day's work."[17] But because he has sensitivity enough to worry about going "blood-simple" like the rest of the citizens of violent "Poisonville," he has not yet become totally inured to brutality. That he is sensitive to his dilemma is a good sign, for it suggests that he has not yet reached the stage of moral numbness represented by his boss, known only as the Old Man, whom he describes as a man with gentle eyes and a mild smile which hide the fact that "fifty years of sleuthing had left him without any feelings at all on any subject."

Hammett portrays the Op as a man capable of actions which reveal that he has not—at least not *yet*—become an unfeeling machine of justice. In "The Scorched Face," for example, he persuades the policeman he has been working with to destroy incriminating photographs of young women who have been lured into a blackmail trap in order to protect their reputations against needless exposure. What he doesn't reveal is that one of the pictures he saw was that of the policeman's wife. In "The Main Death" he refuses to inform a client about his wife's infidelity, arguing that no purpose would be served by it since her actions had nothing to do with the crime he was hired to investigate. He is able to sympathize with the plight of a man whose daughter has been kidnapped in "The Gatewood Caper," even though he has every reason to dislike the man personally. Despite such incidents as these, however, Hammett is careful not to allow feelings to get the better of the Op, who confesses on one occasion that "emotions are nuisances during business hours." In "The Scorched Face," for example, the Op admits to feeling bad about having to question a young man whose wife has just killed herself, but "apart from that, I had work to do. I tightened the screws." And in "The Whosis Kid" he refuses to intervene as two men begin to undress a woman in order to search for jewels they suspect she has hidden on her person: "I'm no Galahad. This woman had picked her playmates, and was largely responsible for this angle of their game. If they played rough, she'd have to make the best of it."

His previous statement notwithstanding, the Op does act as a Galahad figure in *The Dain Curse,* a change in attitude which may have contributed to his termination as a character. In that novel, he devotes his efforts to helping the beautiful young Gabrielle Leggett kick her morphine addiction and overcome her fears that she is suffering from "the Dain curse." He is evasive about his motive, but the clear impression is that he is acting out of affection, perhaps even love, for the young woman. For the first time, a woman has been able to penetrate his hard shell. The conception of

the private eye as a knight figure would be effectively
developed by many later writers (notably Raymond Chandler), but it appears that Hammett wanted no part of it, for
the Op would appear in only three more stories after *The
Dain Curse* before being retired permanently.

Philip Durham suggests that having gone "soft beyond
redemption," the Op was ready for discard.[18] Perhaps it was
simply that Hammett realized that he had taken the Op as far
as he could. Whatever the reason, Hammett soon turned his
attention to a new private eye, Sam Spade, who made his
initial appearance in *Black Mask* in September, 1929, seven
months after *The Dain Curse* appeared in the magazine.
Spade, who has all the toughness but none of the sentimentality that was beginning to leak out of the Op's tough
shell, enabled Hammett to stick to the tough-guy image he
intended for the Op. In the minds of many (thanks in no
small degree to Humphrey Bogart's portrayal of him in the
1941 film version of *The Maltese Falcon*), Sam Spade is *the*
personification of the American private eye. While there can
be no denying the importance of *The Maltese Falcon* and no
overestimating the influence of Sam Spade, without the Op
there would probably have been no Spade. In the three
dozen stories featuring the tough and dedicated Op, Hammett gave shape to the first believable detective hero in
American fiction and led the revolution into realism that had
its rudimentary beginning with Daly.

Hammett's contribution to the development of the new
mystery story involved style and technique as well as character. Whereas Daly's ungainly prose relied upon an uneven
mixture of exaggeration, brash overstatement, and a variety
of crude rhetorical flourishes, Hammett's is a prime example
of what became known as the "hard-boiled" style, a
carefully controlled blend of colorful colloquialisms, terse
understatement, objective descriptions, all narrated in a
detached tone. Even descriptions of the most violent incidents are reported in a matter-of-fact manner. In Hammett's stories there is no need for boasting about one's
toughness or fearlessness; the understated prose effectively

communicates that. Where Race Williams would boast for a page and a half about how tough he is, all the Op has to do to convince the reader of his toughness is shake his head and say "Better get help" to a man who has been ordered to throw him out of a room. Hammett's tight-lipped prose is also effective in conveying a sense that emotions are being held in check. A prime example of this comes in *Red Harvest,* where the Op awakens to find his hand wrapped around an ice pick which is buried in the chest of the woman lying dead next to him. In his narrative the Op concentrates exclusively on his careful and deliberate cleaning up of the scene, thus revealing through action his emotional control. Hammett aimed at accomplishing in the mystery story what Hemingway was attempting to do in his fiction: use a cool, understated style as a vehicle for embodying in a convincing way essential toughness of character.

Hammett is also far more successful than Daly in capturing the sense of confusion and uncertainty that characterized the times. Race Williams largely inhabits a good-guy-versus-bad-guy world. The Op's world is less clearly defined and reflects the kind of cockeyed world Hammett describes in his autobiographical "From the Memoirs of a Private Detective," published in 1923, the same year he introduced the Op. Among other things, Hammett recalls an incident in which, as he describes it, "I was once falsely accused of perjury and had to perjure myself to escape arrest," and another where "a man whom I was shadowing went out into the country for a walk one Sunday and lost his bearings completely. I had to direct him back to the city."[19] Such experiences attest to his own personal encounter with absurdity.

Nowhere is this perception better expressed in Hammett's work than in the famous Flitcraft story Sam Spade tells Brigid O'Shaughnessy in *The Maltese Falcon.* Flitcraft was a Tacoma, Washington, real-estate dealer who led a quiet, orderly, uneventful life until one day a large beam from a building fell and narrowly missed killing him. So shattered is he by his sudden confrontation with the capriciousness of

life—"He felt like somebody had taken the lid off life and let
him look at the works"—that he abandons his wife and
family and moves away. The parable embodies Hammett's
view that life is ruled not by logic but by randomness,
caprice, chance, what the existentialists call "the absurd." It
was this perception of the world that led Hammett and many
of his contemporaries to reject the neatly defined universe
of the classical mystery story in favor of the new realistic
mystery tale.

Despite their differences, Race Williams and the Continental Op both must share credit for precipitating the new
look in the detective story, for here were detectives who
relied on their toughness and their wits instead of their
brains to solve crimes. Instead of puzzling out solutions from
a lofty distance, both were actively, almost aggressively,
engaged in the pursuit of criminals, relying on trial-and-error
methods rather than the strict laws of deductive logic. No
longer portrayed as men of Olympian abilities, both were
capable of mistakes and, especially in the case of the Op,
susceptible to doubts. Both men resorted to violence when
necessary, for both lived in violent worlds; the laws of logic
might have been appropriate tools in a universe of reason,
but in the dangerous streets of New York and San Francisco,
Race Williams and the Op were called upon to dirty and
sometimes bloody their hands if they hoped to succeed. The
cultured mannerisms of the Great Detective and the graceful
style of the formal whodunit gave way to the tough-talking
vernacular of the new hard-boiled mystery. In a significant
departure from the past, these new mystery tales were
narrated by the detective himself, and in his own words. No
longer was there required a Boswell-like intermediary to
record and deify the exploits of the master crime-solver.
There was a new immediacy to these first-person narratives
as the reader shared with the detective his successes and
failures, doubts and determination.

Perhaps most important, both Race Williams and the Op
were portrayed as ordinary men simply going about their

business with courage and dedication. The private eye was no gentleman sleuth solving crimes in his spare time; he was a man whose whole life was dedicated to catching criminals because *that was his job,* which was reason enough for doing it as well as he could. "Liking work," explained the Op, "makes you want to do it as well as you can. Otherwise there'd be no sense to it." In a time of uncertainty and confused values, as the decade after World War I certainly was, there was at least one solid reality one could hang on to, even if one's ideals were in tatters: one could still remain committed to a task, no matter how difficult. Prior to Daly and Hammett, mystery readers were invited to admire from afar the lofty accomplishments of the Great Detective, whose success was always a reminder to the reader of his own intellectual shortcomings. Now, thanks to Race Williams and the Op, readers could *identify* with rather than merely admire the accomplishments of the hero. And although the readers were safe from many of the dangers the private-eye hero faced, they were no strangers to the feeling of being battered and buffeted about by powerful forces, to the sense that violence was everywhere, to the suspicion that there was no longer any logic to the scheme of things. Readers could share in the private eye's successes for they recognized that they represented not the triumph of reason and logic but rather that of courage, self-reliance, and above all a willingness to stick to his guns (both literally and figuratively) in the face of sometimes overwhelming odds. For the first time since his creation by Poe, the detective was portrayed as a hero for the common man, and he has remained so ever since.

2

The Pulpsters

If it weren't for the pulp magazines, the private eye might never have emerged, for it was one such magazine, *Black Mask,* that provided the first forum for the adventures of Race Williams and the Continental Op, the earliest private eyes. A score of other mystery pulps that soon followed its lead made it possible for the fledgling private-eye hero to develop in a number of interesting directions. Unfortunately, as Raymond Chandler noted, a pulp magazine was the "most ephemeral possible kind of publication, one which had a life of thirty days and then was as dead as Caesar,"[1] and as Shakespeare's Mark Antony reminded us on the occasion of Caesar's funeral, although the evil men do lives after them, "the good is oft interred with their bones." Sadly, this has been the fate of most of the pulp output, including a significant amount of first-rate work. With the notable exception of Hammett, Chandler, and a few other lucky ones who were able to achieve a lasting audience thanks to the hardcover publication of their books, most of the pulp writers are relegated to obscurity today. Nevertheless their contribution to the development of the private-eye genre at a crucial stage in its development should not be overlooked. This chapter is an attempt to offer belated recognition to the best of those early pulp writers.

The first pulp (so-called because of the cheap wood-pulp paper used) was launched by Frank Munsey in 1896 when he transformed *Argosy* from a boy's magazine to an adult adventure-story one. Within a decade, circulation of the magazine reached a half million, and other publishers quickly moved to cash in on what Tony Goodstone called Munsey's "rag-paper to pulp-riches form."[2] Soon the pulps supplanted the dime novel as the most popular form of cheap, mass-produced reading entertainment for millions of Americans. Seven by ten inches in size, normally 120 rough-edged pages in length, and selling for anywhere from a dime to a quarter, the pulps were easily recognizable on the newsstands by their colorfully gaudy, and sometimes even lurid, covers, which often featured menacing killers and scantily-clad females in distress. In the case of some pulps, the covers were by far the best thing about them. Growing rapidly in popularity, proliferating from some two dozen titles following World War I to over two hundred separate ones by the beginning of World War II, the pulp magazines featured stories that appealed to every reading taste, from Westerns to love stories, adventure tales to science fiction, aviation dramas to mysteries. Gradually the magazines each began to focus on a single market, with Street and Smith's *Detective Story,* founded in 1915, the first to be devoted exclusively to mystery stories. But it wasn't until the arrival of *Black Mask* magazine a few years later that the private eye would find a home.

Black Mask was founded in 1920 by H. L. Mencken and George Jean Nathan in the hope that it would keep their *Smart Set* magazine afloat financially. Their plan worked; six months later they sold the magazine for a substantial profit. In its first few years there was nothing distinguished about the fare appearing in the magazine, but under the editorial guidance initially of George W. Sutton, Jr. (1922–

24) and his associate Harry North, and later under Phil Cody (1924–26), the mystery stories of Daly and Hammett, as well as those of another popular newcomer, Erle 'Stanley Gardner, began appearing alongside the love stories, Westerns, and aviation tales that were regular features of *Black Mask*. It soon became apparent to the editors, however, that the tough new realistic mystery stories were the most popular items and the magazine responded by offering more and more of them.

This movement toward a magazine that would feature hard-boiled mystery stories almost exclusively was guided by *Black Mask*'s most celebrated editor, Joseph C. ("Cap") Shaw, who took over in November, 1926, and edited the magazine for the next ten years. Shaw cannot be given credit for inventing the private-eye story, having inherited Daly, whose works he didn't much like, and Hammett from previous editors, but he must be credited with attracting the kind of writers to the magazine who were able, under his guidance, to bring the private eye from its infancy to its maturity.

Although Shaw admitted that he had neither seen nor heard of *Black Mask* before taking over the magazine, he proved to be a most worthy editor, for he valued good writing and was a keen judge of talent in writers. He never felt that writing for the pulps (a term he never used, preferring instead to call them "rough-paper" magazines) should be considered an inferior form of work. In his view a popular magazine like *Black Mask* could provide an ideal format for fast-paced, believable action writing, and that's what he set out to achieve.

In an introduction to a collection of *Black Mask* stories he edited in 1946, Shaw stated his guiding principle as editor: "We wanted simplicity for the sake of clarity, plausibility, and belief. We wanted action, but we held that action is meaningless unless it involves recognizable human character in three-dimensional form."[3] Neither Daly nor Hammett may have set out intentionally to create a new type of mystery story, but Shaw did. He deliberately looked for writers who, like Hammett, could tell action-packed stories in a fast tempo employing the new realistic style, with its premium on economy of expression, and who could create believable characters rather than intricate puzzles. Above all, he valued writers who, in his words, did not simply "make their characters act and talk tough" but who "allowed them to."[4] From a group of talented writers, including both those he inherited (Hammett, Frederick Nebel, Raoul Whitfield) and those whom he brought to the magazine (Paul Cain, W. T. Ballard, Roger Torrey, Lester Dent, Norbert Davis, Frank Gruber, George Harmon Coxe, Raymond Chandler), he drew forth tough, realistic stories that exemplified the best qualities of the new hard-boiled fiction.

Erle Stanley Gardner, however, complained that Shaw was trying to "Hammettize" the magazine by forcing writers into the Hammett mold, but an examination of the stories published during Shaw's tenure as editor reveals a remarkable variety of styles, techniques, and characters. With the exception of Gardner, writers were virtually unanimous in their praise of Shaw. From Lester Dent: "In my thirty-five years of free lancing fiction, no one stands out so. . . . Here was an editor who thought his writers were truly great . . . and an editor who didn't pretend his writers were crud-factories was unbelievable. . . . I have never met another like him."[5] From Frank Gruber: " 'Cap' Shaw killed writers with kindness. Yet writers swore by him. I have met and talked to writers all over the country about Shaw and a number of them spoke of him in a tone of awe, as if they were talking about God."[6] From W. T. Ballard: "I loved him. . . . At the risk of sounding euphoric, there was never a relationship between editor and writer to equal my connection with Cap Shaw."[7] From Raymond Chandler: "To some of us I think he was a genuine inspiration in that . . . we wrote better for him than we could have written for anybody else."[8]

What was so significant about Shaw's contribution? With

gentle encouragement, courteous suggestions, infinite patience, and a blue pencil poised to remove any word that
was not absolutely necessary—his advice to writers was
"Prune and cut, don't use a single word that you can do
without."[9] Shaw extracted from his stable of talented
writers stories that explored the possibilities of the new
hard-boiled style and that featured interesting variations on
the new private-eye hero that Daly and Hammett had shown
there to be an audience for. The fruits of Shaw's editorial
tenure were an impressive body of outstanding writing and a
healthy proliferation of private eyes who gave shape and
direction to the revolution begun by Daly and Hammett. Under Shaw the private eye began to mature.

Jo Gar

(Raoul Whitfield)

One of the writers who first benefitted from Shaw's guidance was Raoul Whitfield. Born into a socially prominent
family in New York City in 1897 (he was a relative by
marriage of Andrew Carnegie), Whitfield spent a portion of
his youth in the Philippines, where his father was attached
to the Territorial Government. During World War I he
enlisted in the Air Service and eventually saw combat in
France as a pilot. Following the war he worked at a variety
of jobs, mainly newspaper work. In the early 1920s he embarked on a writing career which would, like Hammett's,
prove to be short but prolific: virtually all his fiction—nearly
one hundred stories, most of which were written for *Black
Mask,* three crime novels, and four aviation novels for
juveniles—appeared between 1926 and 1934. Stricken with
a lingering illness in the mid-1930s, he ceased writing and

died in 1945. His first story was published in *Black Mask* in March 1926, eight months before Shaw became editor. Over the next four years, Whitfield published dozens of stories in *Black Mask,* the majority of which featured aviation in some way, but it wasn't until 1930, doubtless as a result of Shaw's guidance, that he reached his maturity and began producing his best work.

In 1930 alone, Whitfield published two novel-length story sequences in *Black Mask:* "The Crime Breeders," a five-part serialization (which actually began in the December, 1929, issue), published in hardcover later in the year as *Green Ice*; and a three-part sequence featuring Hollywood private eye Ben Jardinn, which appeared in hardcover form the following year as *Death in a Bowl.* In addition, he published two other crime stories under his own name and, using the pseudonym "Ramon Decolta," eight stories featuring Filipino private investigator Jo Gar. The Jo Gar series, which began in the February, 1930, issue of *Black Mask* and ran until July, 1933, eventually numbered twenty-four stories. Whitfield was so prolific during the early 1930s that on at least fifteen occasions, two of his stories appeared in the same issue of *Black Mask,* one under his own name and a Jo Gar story under the Decolta byline.

Whitfield created a succession of hard-boiled characters whose toughness, for the most part, comes not from the barrel of a gun but from an inner strength. Ex-con Mal Ourney, for example, the protagonist of *Green Ice,* is a man whose toughness is demanded by virtue of his crusade to put an end to the "crime breeders," the big crooks who rope in the little ones. In the battle against the forces of the underworld, toughness is an absolute necessity. Private eye Tim Slade ("Inside Job"), on the other hand, needs the kind of emotional toughness that will allow him to put personal feelings aside in order to nail his friend, the man who lent him the money to start his own agency, when he discovers that he is the killer he is looking for. For private eye Ben Jardinn, the hero of *Death in a Bowl,* a hard-boiled attitude is

the best defense against a world in which "so many humans
like to tell lies . . . it's hell finding out what really happens."
When his secretary is murdered, the hard shell softens and
he sheds tears, but only in private; to everyone else he
remains "cold as hell," a mask he wears so no one will
suspect he is anything but the strongest of men.

But it is in the figure of Jo Gar that Whitfield created his
most hard-boiled character, a man whose toughness is no
mask but part and parcel of every muscle and fiber of his
being. Although the setting of the stories is the tropical
climes of the Philippine Islands rather than the violent
streets of New York or San Francisco, and although he is of
Filipino-Spanish descent rather than American, Jo Gar is as
authentic a hard-boiled hero as any detective who appeared
in the pages of *Black Mask*. Despite his Oriental demeanor,
which might at first glance remind readers of Charlie Chan,
it soon becomes apparent that he is much closer in character
to Sam Spade than to Earl Derr Biggers's genial Oriental
sleuth. While there is nothing particularly menacing about
his size nor anything imposing about his physical presence
(usually described as being "diminutive," he has short arms,
narrow shoulders, stubby fingers, and gray hair, which
makes him look much older than he really is), he possesses a
quiet, steely toughness that imparts a convincing sense of
gritty realism to the stories in which he appears.

There are no grandstanding gestures à la Race Williams to
be found anywhere in the Jo Gar stories. As tight-lipped as
Race Williams is verbose, he chooses his words carefully and
speaks in polite, measured phrases. No one should ever
make the mistake of confusing politeness with weakness of
character, however, for when Jo Gar speaks in his quiet way,
he is absolutely convincing. Just as he wastes no words, he
likewise wastes no gestures. Although he often appears to be
dozing, behind the sleepy eyes and expressionless face there
is an active and alert mind at work. As one raised in a
tropical climate, Jo Gar understands the folly of unnecessary
exertion: "I am never aggressive," he explains. "Manila is a

city of heat—heat breeds laziness.'' But what might appear to the casual observer to be laziness is actually intelligent conservation of energy. He can move with catlike quickness when he has to, say to dodge a knife thrown at him, but he prefers to avoid physical activity unless it is absolutely necessary.

Although he seldom speaks openly about his motives for becoming a private detective, we can make several observations about his choice of career. Like Race Williams and the Continental Op, he is a professional who is in the business of catching crooks, although unlike Race Williams he has no taste for heroics, nor is he an organization man like the Op. He works entirely alone, seems to have few private pleasures, and has no apparent interest in women. He inhabits a tiny office above Wong Ling's place just off the Escolta, Manila's main business street. Although he has often thought of moving, in the end he has decided to stay put, mainly because he enjoys the sounds of the nearby Pasig river and the odors of spice and hemp and shell foods that drift up from the shops below. Besides, moving to a more fashionable office would force him to raise his fees, and that might limit his clients to those who could afford to pay. This would make it more difficult for him to take the cases which interest him, a more important consideration, seemingly, than the money involved.

Prior to becoming a private detective, Jo Gar was a member of the Manila police force, and the early stories are marked by a friendly rivalry with Lt. Juan Arragon, whom he likes and respects. After Arragon's death, however, he is succeeded by Sadi Ratan, and Jo Gar's relationship with the police rapidly deteriorates. Ratan actively dislikes him, which only encourages Jo Gar to go out of his way to discomfit Ratan whenever he can. Their rivalry is best illustrated in "The Siamese Cat," where Ratan seeks to embarrass his nemesis by requesting his assistance in a minor matter, locating a missing Siamese cat. When the cat's owner is later found murdered, Ratan peremptorily shoos Jo Gar off the case, arguing that the investigation is now a matter best left to the police. Jo Gar chooses to continue on his own, however; his reward, he tells Ratan, "will be obtained in a way familiar to you, lieutenant. I shall be amused at you." And as usual, he solves the case long before Ratan has any idea what is going on.

There is nothing either mysterious or spectacular about Jo Gar's methods of detection. Like the Continental Op, he is patient and deliberate in his investigations. Much of his success, like that of the Op's, is due to the fact that he knows his world intimately and is able to move freely among all its elements. That he can speak Chinese, Spanish, and Filipino as well as English is also a great help. His favored approach to crime-solving is simply to walk around and ask questions, although as he points out one must know where to walk and whom to question. As he explains to Ratan in "The Man from Shanghai," "In the half hour during which you were talking with people—I have been doing the same thing. But in a different way." Quietly and unobtrusively, he goes about his business solving crimes, bringing criminals to justice, and embarrassing Ratan.

Whitfield is a prime example of the kind of writer Shaw was looking for, one who could, like Hammett, *reveal* toughness of character through action rather than through exposition or description. In the character of Jo Gar, Whitfield illustrates the tight control over emotions that was a trademark of the hard-boiled style. The strongest emotion Jo Gar ever displays is faint impatience; his voice is usually described as toneless, his face expressionless, but by a slight shrug of the shoulders or an almost imperceptible change in his smile, Whitfield reveals the feelings behind the mask. Because the Jo Gar stories are not narrated in first person, we are never privy to the Island Detective's thoughts and reflections; by focusing on his actions, however, Whitfield is able to provide clues that allow the reader to evaluate his innermost feelings. For example, when he discovers the bullet-riddled body of his friend Juan Arragon (which his killers have dumped in his office), he sighs softly, walks slowly to the window, and looks down toward the street "unseeingly." Then he carefully lights a cigarette, draws a deep breath and, thinking of the killers, quietly vows, "I will find them, of course." Jo Gar's deliberate actions and rigidly controlled emotions are similar to those of Sam Spade when he is awakened in the middle of the night by the news that his partner, Miles Archer, has been murdered. In both cases, it isn't that the detective feels no emotion; it's just that Whitfield, like Hammett, endeavors to show emotions held tightly under control.

At its best, Whitfield's lean, hard prose captures a vivid immediacy of experience and a sense of breathless action. Hammett praised *Green Ice* for its "280 pages of naked action pounded into tough compactness by staccato, hammerlike writing."[10] At its worst, as in the following passage from "Red Dawn," the staccato prose degenerates into annoyingly disjointed language: "Women are often—like that. There must be—the first time. And white glass—worth thousands—is a reason—for lies." In addition, many of the stories are marred by endings borrowed from the traditional whodunits, with Jo Gar exposing the Least Likely Suspect in the final scene. Despite such flaws, however, Whitfield's stories are important first of all because of the character of Jo Gar, who represents yet another interesting variation on the evolving new detective hero, and second because of his mastery of the hard-boiled style and his ability to use it as an effective vehicle for embodying essential toughness of character. Whitfield's stories demonstrate that Shaw's dream of developing writers who could follow Hammett's example in employing the tough new realism was bearing fruit.

Tough Dick Donohue

(Frederick Nebel)

Another early *Black Mask* writer who reached his maturity under Shaw's stewardship was Frederick Nebel. Born on Staten Island, New York, in 1903, Nebel reportedly spent only one day in high school before taking off to bum his way around the world. At an early age he began writing and selling stories to the pulps, eventually breaking into *Black Mask* in March, 1926, the same issue that contained Whitfield's first story. In the September, 1928, issue of the magazine he introduced his first important series characters, Captain Steve MacBride of the Richmond City police force and wise-cracking, hard-drinking Kennedy, a reporter for the *Free Press,* who teamed up in thirty-seven *Black Mask* stories over the next eight years.

Nebel also created two series featuring hard-boiled detectives. In the November, 1930, issue of *Black Mask* he introduced Ben Donohue, an operative for the Inter-State Detective Agency in New York, who appeared in a total of fifteen stories between 1930 and 1935. And in November, 1931, he inaugurated a series in *Dime Detective* featuring Steve Cardigan, St. Louis head of the Cosmos Detective Agency, that ran until 1937. Nebel also published three novels in the early 1930s, the most famous of which, *Sleepers East* (1933), was made into a movie three times. In the mid-1930s, Nebel stopped writing for the pulps in order to devote his efforts to the more lucrative slick markets, and his stories soon began to appear in such popular magazines as *Colliers, Cosmopolitan, Good Housekeeping,* and *Saturday Evening Post.* When Joseph Shaw asked him for permission to reprint one of his stories in the anthology of *Black Mask* stories he was preparing in 1945, Nebel declined, arguing that his stories now seemed dated. Five years later, however, Avon brought out *Six Deadly Dames,* a paperback collection of six Donohue tales, the only time any of Nebel's pulp work was ever published in book form.

It is fitting that Donohue's initial appearance came in the same issue of *Black Mask* that saw the final appearance of the Continental Op, for he is in many ways the most authentic successor to Hammett's hard-boiled hero. Billed in *Black Mask* as "Tough Dick" Donohue (although he is usually simply called "Donny"), Donohue is a private detective employed by the Inter-State Agency in New York. Formerly a member of the New York Police Department, he was canned from his job for raiding the wrong gambling joint one night. Described as a "big lanky man with black hair, deep-set dark eyes, a long jaw and a long straight nose," he is ordinarily a genial and easygoing fellow. Once he's riled, however, watch out, for his disposition sours and his face tightens into an angry mask: "Every muscle in his lean brown face was taut, his brows were bent till they met above his nose, and beneath his dark eyes were dead-level, hard with a hard brilliance. He gave the effect of steel drawn."

In many ways Donohue resembles the Continental Op. Both are employed by large detective agencies and both have a decidedly unheroic view of their profession. Donohue describes his job in terms that remind one of the Op:

> I'm just a plain everyday guy trying to make a living—as honestly as possible. There's not a hell of a lot of romance attached to my business. I'm no drawing-room cop. One day I'm here—the next day, somewhere else. That's not romance. It's damned monotonous. When I take on a client, I expect a break. I expect the truth. If it is the truth, I'm just as liable to risk my neck for the guy as not. I'm a nice guy ordinarily. But when a man two-times on me, I'm a louse—the lousiest kind of louse you ever ran across.[11]

On another occasion he confesses he likes his job because "it keeps me in butts and I see the country and I don't have to slave over a desk. . . . No guy ever wrote a poem about it," he admits, "but it's the only hole I fit in."[12] Like the Op, Donohue also enjoys little in the way of a personal life. About all we learn is that he lives in a small apartment-hotel in Greenwich Village near University Place and that he eats four nights a week in the same restaurant near Columbus Park. He displays virtually no interest in women. His whole attitude toward the fair sex is a sour one: "Broads. They trick us, cheat us, and try to murder us."

On the other hand, Donohue doesn't feel as bound by the regulations of his agency as the Op does, reasoning that when "you work against crooks . . . you've got to beat them at their own game." When, for instance, he can't think of a better way to get information out of a pawnshop owner, he suggests to his boss that he take him in the back room and punch him around a little "until the yellow runs." When a lawyer warns him on another occasion that he may be over-stepping his bounds, Donohue shoots back, "Who the hell ever said I cared whether I did or not?" Nor is he motivated primarily by a desire to do his job well simply because it's his job, as the Op is; he often becomes involved in a case for purely personal reasons.

Like most detectives, however, Donohue does adhere to a set of personal guidelines. Money, for example, will not tempt him from his job. In "Save Your Tears" he turns down fifteen thousand dollars for the name of his client and in "He Could Take It" he declines an offer of ten thousand dollars for information about the location of some important evidence. He is also a man of his word, even if he has given it to crooks. In "The Red-Hots," for example, in return for the stolen jewels he is after, he agrees to give a man three hours to get out of town before he goes to the police with the evidence he has linking him to a murder. Finally, he is a man who values friendship very highly. In "Song and Dance" he quits a case when he discovers his client has lied to him, yet he agrees to return when a friend, policeman Kelly McPard, a regular character in the series, asks him to. And in "Pearls Are Tears" he feels obliged to find the killer of a policeman, not because he feels any loyalty to the dead cop who ignored his warning not to enter a house where some gunmen were hiding, but because he wants to protect the reputation of his lawyer-friend who had hired him to make an illegal payoff to the jewel thieves who killed the policeman.

Like most of the other private detectives that were emerging in *Black Mask,* Donohue is a tough guy, but whereas writers like Daly and Hammett focused more on essential toughness of character, Nebel emphasizes the physical indestructibility of his hero. The title of one of the Donohue stories sums it all up—"He Could Take It." In that story, Donohue endures a vicious beating at the hands of a pair of thugs who are trying to get some information from him. Why? Because, as he explains, "I can take it." Throughout the series he is shot several times, beaten frequently, kicked, bitten, and generally manhandled by thugs, but he never allows himself to collapse from the pain until he finishes what he set out to do. Business always comes first for Donohue, who is portrayed as a man who succeeds not because he is smarter or quicker on the draw than his opponents, but simply because he is tough enough to take whatever the bad guys can dish out.

The physical violence Donohue endures is an integral element of Nebel's realism. The Race Williams stories are filled with the sounds of guns firing, yet there is an artificiality to the violence depicted in Daly's fiction. The killings are much more realistically portrayed in Hammett's stories, where the detached, objective tone creates a vivid atmosphere of violence. Nebel, however, is the most convincing of the *Black Mask* writers in conveying the actual reality of violence. Instead of focusing on the man shooting the gun or administering the blow to the guts, he focuses on the man (usually Donohue) who suffers the injury. When Donohue is smashed in the head with a blackjack or kicked in the ribs while lying on the floor, the reader feels the pain. Donohue doesn't win all the fights he is in, and even when he does prevail he suffers as much physical damage as his opponent. There is always a price to be paid for his heroics: one gunshot wound lays him up for a month, another for three weeks. Nebel is not a sensationalist, relying on gratuitous descriptions of graphic violence to add excitement to his tales; rather he uses violence to bring out the physical durability of his hero, a durability paid for by his suffering. Nebel's point is not that Donohue is immune to pain and suffering but that he is tough enough to endure whatever demands his dangerous profession makes on him.

For the most part, Donohue is a tough, no-nonsense fellow, an unsentimental hard-boiled detective whose guiding principle is simple: "I hate like hell to lose. I'm the world's sorest loser." When a policeman, thanking him for his help on a case, remarks, "You must be one of those amateur detectives a guy reads about in books. You go after things for the love of the game," Donohue scoffs at him. "If you think I'm a Good Samaritan, you're off your trolley." Every now and then, however, Donohue confesses that he gets "illusions of grandeur" and thinks he's "St. Patrick driving the snakes out of Ireland." In "Red Web," for instance, he becomes obsessed with the welfare of the eighteen-year-old daughter of a vice queen who has been murdered as a result of helping him gather information. He seeks to protect the girl both from damaging publicity that would ensue if she were revealed in the newspapers as the daughter of Cherry Bliss and from her father, an ex-con who abandoned her at birth. He doesn't rest until he manages to get her safely away in the company of the man who will marry her. Despite his toughness, then, there is in Donohue a gentler quality which Nebel attributes to his heritage: "He was Irish, and that may have accounted in some measure for the sentimental streak beneath the tough hide."

Whether it was because of that streak of Irish sentimentality, or because there were so many Irish policemen in America at the time, or simply because, as D. B. McCandless suggested in a story in *Detective Fiction Weekly* in 1937, the Irish are gifted with an extraordinary "sixth sense," there was an undeniably large preponderance of private detectives with Irish surnames in the pulps in the 1930s and 1940s. A roster of even a small sample of them reads like a County Cork telephone directory. In addition to Nebel's Donohue, Kennedy, MacBride, and Cardigan, there was Pat O'Leary, Pat Mullaney, Joseph McCalley, Mike O'Dell, Pat McCarthy (all Roger Torrey characters); Patrick Fahey (D. B. McCandless); Donovan, Tim Killane (both Robert Leslie Bellem); Terry O'Rourke (George A. McDonald); Jim Doyle (A. Boyd Correll); Big Red Brennan (Steve Fisher); Shamus McGuire (Stanley Day); Ken O'Hara (H. H. Stinson); Jack McGuire (J. J. Ormeaux): and an entire Irish-American fraternity singlehandedly created by Thomas Walsh (Kerrigan, Gavegan, Callahan, Cassidy, O'Mara, O'Neill, Donovan, Flanagan, Mahoney, McCann, etc.).

Nebel was a true master of realistic writing, not simply because of his gritty portrayal of violence but also because he paid careful attention to atmosphere and setting. Whether describing a thunderstorm on a sultry summer night or the slush-filled streets in winter, Nebel gives his readers a vivid sense of the real world in his stories. Most of the Donohue stories take place in New York City, which is depicted with precise detail. As Donohue makes his way through the streets of New York, the reader accompanies him step by step. In this regard Nebel followed the example of both Hammett, who described San Francisco in similar fashion, and Whitfield, who created a familiar Manila for readers who would probably never travel there.

One of the distinguishing characteristics of the newly developing hard-boiled style was a heavy reliance on vernacular speech. Nebel, thanks to his ear for slang, was one of the best of the *Black Mask* writers in capturing the rough eloquence of actual speech. The Donohue stories are filled with colorful expressions: "pipe this, you wiseacres"; "I'll fog your guts"; "primp up, chicken"; "give your legs a walk, sister"; "go roll your hoop, nuisance"; "take the air"; "shovel that bushwa where it hasn't been heard before";

and so on. There is another, less attractive, aspect to Nebel's use of vernacular and that is his use of ethnic slurs. Expressions like "cheap Mick gumshoe," "punk kike," and "poor dumb dago" pepper the stories. Although such phrases are insulting to modern readers, they were very much a part of the common usage of Nebel's day, and anyone who reads the pulps of the 1920s and 1930s must be prepared to encounter a glossary of such disparaging ethnic epithets. The danger of relying on contemporary usage is that as fast as the slang goes out of fashion, what had once been realistic begins to sound archaic. Nevertheless, Nebel manages to capture, thanks to his vivid dialogue, credible characters, detailed descriptions of setting, and unflinching portrayal of violence, a convincing sense of verisimilitude that illustrates the powerful immediacy of effect available to writers who began to experiment with the new realism.

Jack "Flashgun" Casey

(George Harmon Coxe)

In the first decade of his existence, the private eye proliferated rapidly, appearing not just in *Black Mask* but also in a number of other pulps that began to feature the exploits of this new hero. One result of his sudden popularity was that writers were soon faced with a new challenge: how to make their private detectives unique enough to be readily differentiated from the scores of other private detectives who were appearing in the magazines on a regular basis. Many writers solved this problem by creating a character who behaved like a private eye but whose regular occupation was not actually that of private detective. One of the most popular of such figures was the newspaperman, who could be as tough and fearless as the private eye and whose job allowed him to act like a private investigator. Frederick Nebel's *Free Press* reporter Kennedy and Richard Sale's Daffy Dill (featured in a series in *Detective Fiction Weekly*) are two such examples. One of the most popular of all the newspaper heroes who came to prominence in the pulps, however, wasn't a reporter at all but a newspaper photographer by the name of Flash Casey, introduced by George Harmon Coxe in a story entitled "Return Engagement" in the March, 1934, issue of *Black Mask.*

Jack "Flashgun" Casey, formerly number one camera for the *Boston Globe,* later for the *Express* following his departure from the *Globe* as a result of a dispute over a photograph of his, is a tough, aggressive photographer whose greatest thrill is getting an exclusive picture even if he has to risk his neck to do so, for he knows that "he didn't get his reputation snapping pictures of the obvious. Anybody could do that. Trouble and exclusive pictures went hand in hand. If you wanted one you had to take the other, and you couldn't score any runs asking people to pose for you."[13] Because of his job, he often finds himself in the center of the action; in fact, he has such a habit of discovering dead bodies that his friend, Lieutenant Logan of the Boston police, complains, "Can't we have just one little murder without you horsing around and getting in the way?" But thanks to his natural curiosity, fearless nature, and omnipresent camera (itself often a useful instrument of detection), it is entirely credible that a photographer like Casey would often find himself in situations usually associated with the professional private eye.

Physically, Casey fits the tough-guy mold. Six foot one, 215 pounds ("all of it bone and muscle"), he is a large rumpled man with a rugged face and unkempt shaggy hair streaked with gray at the sides. Generally a genial and easygoing fellow, Casey has a quick temper and when angered gets "pig-headed" and mean as a hungry bear. Even though he is usually armed with a camera rather than a gun, he keeps a .38 revolver in his office desk (along with a trusty bottle of whiskey) and is capable of putting "a slug where he aimed." His reputation as the city's top photographer is a result of the same qualities demanded of the successful private eye: "nerve, aggressiveness and two big fists that he knew how to use."

When it comes right down to it, though, Casey is a softy. An easy touch, he slips money to friends on the skids. A Good Samaritan, he puts drunken acquaintances to bed and looks out for the welfare of those who he thinks need it. In *Silent Are the Dead,* for example, he talks a friend into lending him $150 of his gambling winnings because he knows that that is the only way he can keep him from losing it all back to the house, and at the end of *Murder for Two* he insists that the five-thousand-dollar reward coming to him be given to the USO. As Tom Wade, the young associate whom Casey has taken under his wing and whose job he has saved on more than one occasion, says of his friend: "He's got a heart that big and he doesn't want anybody to know that 'way down deep he's a sentimentalist or that he'd break a leg for a guy he liked."

Casey's soft heart is what usually gets him personally involved in a case in the first place. In "Once Around the Clock" he seeks to prove a man's innocence because a girl he likes is in love with the man and he doesn't want anything to spoil her happiness. In *Murder for Two,* upset at the cowardly way a reporter on the *Express* is murdered—shot in the back of the head—he vows to find the killer. In *Silent Are the Dead,* because he feels personally responsible for the death of a fellow photographer who was killed by someone looking for a picture Casey had given him, he sets out to get the murderer. Casey isn't interested in detection for its own sake. He's simply the sort of big-hearted guy whose job provides him with ample opportunity to act like a private eye. Furthermore, as his editor reminds him, "if you didn't have some excitement and get slapped around a bit you'd go nuts."

Casey is tough when he has to be, especially when someone causes his temper to flare, but he is nowhere near as hard-boiled as the typical *Black Mask* detective of his day. He has a underlying sense of humor, a big heart, and, like his friend Lieutenant Logan, "the faculty of being as tough and hard as the occasion demanded," although his "acquired hardness was not a quality that he flaunted indiscriminately." In other words, for Casey toughness is a quality to be used sparingly, summoned only when needed and not paraded about or employed as the sole currency of his life. This is in keeping with the overall tone of the Casey stories, which are distinguished by a kind of benevolent humaneness missing from many of the hard-boiled tales of the day. Coxe's characters generally have respect and affection for each other. Loyalty, honesty, and hard work are celebrated; even the police are shown to be honest and efficient. In fact, the only character who comes close to being a villain in the Casey series is Blaine, Casey's city editor, and his nastiness is tempered by the fact that he is the best desk man in the city.

George Harmon Coxe was born in Olean, New York, in 1901. After attending both Purdue and Cornell, he became a newspaperman, first in California, later in New York. He began writing for the pulps in the 1920s, eventually selling his first story, a Flash Casey adventure, to *Black Mask,* in 1934. When he accepted the story, Joseph Shaw told Coxe he wasn't interested in another series character, but when Coxe sent him a second Casey story anyway, Shaw liked it even better than the first one and asked for more. Between 1934 and 1936, a total of eighteen Casey stories appeared in *Black Mask.* Casey's popularity in the 1930s also led to two Hollywood films based on the stories: *Women Are Trouble* (1936), with Stuart Erwin as Casey, and *Here's Flash Casey* (1937), this time with Eric Linden as Casey. After a four-year absence, Casey returned to *Black Mask* in 1940 and was soon featured in two novel-length story sequences: "Killers Are Camera Shy" in 1941 (reprinted in 1942 as *Silent Are the*

Dead) and "Blood on the Lens" in 1943 (reprinted later that year as *Murder for Two*). This marked his final appearance in *Black Mask,* although four of Casey's *Black Mask* novelettes were reprinted by Avon in 1946 as *Flash Casey, Detective.* In 1935 Coxe also introduced another popular photographer hero by the name of Kent Murdock; more sophisticated and less rugged than Casey, he never appeared in the pulps, although he was featured in twenty-one novels.

In the early 1940s, a radio serial with Staats Cotsworth as Casey began a run that was to last for eleven years, and in 1951 Casey even made it to television in a series entitled *Crime Photographer,* with Darren McGavin as Casey. Then, after an absence of almost two decades, Casey returned to print in three novels published in the early 1960s: *Error of Judgment* (1961), *The Man Who Died Too Soon* (1962), and *Deadly Image* (1964). Although he was never as tough as many of his contemporaries, nor did Coxe make a significant contribution to the development of the hard-boiled genre, Flash Casey proved to be one of the most durable and most popular of all the early *Black Mask* heroes. Coxe's success with his likable photographer demonstrated that despite his relative youth the private-eye hero was already flexible enough to assume a shape that was not rigidly patterned after either Race Williams or the Continental Op.

Steve Midnight

(John K. Butler)

In addition to newspaper reporters and photographers, private eyes assumed a wide variety of other shapes and sizes in the pulps: encyclopedia salesmen (Frank Gruber's Oliver Quade); race-course detectives (W. T. Ballard's Red Drake);

movie studio trouble-shooters (W. T. Ballard's Bill Lennox); hotel dicks (Stanley Day's Shamus Maguire); bail-bondsmen (Norbert Davis's William Dodd); telephone-company investigators (John K. Butler's Rod Case); to name but a few. To accommodate the rapid proliferation of the private eye, and to capitalize on the growing popularity of the new detective hero, new pulps appeared and established ones changed in order to feature private-eye tales more prominently.

Among the many imitators of *Black Mask* the most successful was *Dime Detective*; in fact, after Joseph Shaw was dismissed from *Black Mask* in 1936, many of the writers who had written for him, including Raymond Chandler, moved to *Dime Detective*. In the early 1940s, *Black Mask* was sold to Popular Publications, publishers of *Dime Detective,* and both pulps came under the direction of the same editor, Kenneth S. White. One of the most popular of the *Dime Detective* writers was John K. Butler, who created a series featuring the adventures of a cab driver/private investigator who had an uncanny knack for getting himself involved in one crime after another.

Steven Middleton Knight, formerly a "playboy, matinee dancer [and] tea-cup balancer," has been the hard-working sole support of his mother and sickly sister ever since his father killed himself after losing everything in the Depression. Although by profession a taxi driver for the Red Owl Cab Company in Los Angeles, his real business more often than not turns out to be crime-solving. As a moneyed youth he rode in the back seat of cabs and was nicknamed Steve Midnight because he had the reputation of being a "midnight playboy on a nation-wide scale." Now, however, he sits up front where he drives the cab and has such a pronounced knack for finding trouble that his nickname refers to the fact that he's always in a jam "when the cuckoo chirps twelve."

For those writers who desired to create a series character who would be a private eye by circumstance rather than by

profession, the challenge was to make the hero's involvement in crime credible. In the case of Flash Casey, as
we have already seen, the nature of his newspaper assignments made his crime-solving activities believable. Butler
achieves a similar credibility in the case of Midnight thanks
to the nature of his job. When you drive a cab in Los Angeles
after midnight you can expect to meet, as Steve Midnight
notes, "such screwy people," and many of them live on the
wrong side of the law.

Also helping to establish Midnight's credibility is that,
again like Casey, his involvement in most cases is prompted
by personal motives. He has no professional interest in a
case, either as a defender of justice or as someone hired by a
client, nor does he meddle in police affairs as a whim. In
"The Saint in Silver," for example, his involvement begins as
a simple desire to recover the fare money that was stolen
from him. In "The Hearse from Red Owl," he aims to clear
up the suspicion that he chiseled his employers out of ninety
cents. In "The Corpse That Couldn't Keep Cool," a fare slits
his wrists in his cab, and when he comes under suspicion in
the man's death he sets out to clear his name. In "The Killer
Was a Gentleman," he offers his assistance to a fare who is
suffering from amnesia. In each case, his involvement soon
leads him into deeper water. Usually his investigations are
carried out during his off hours and are successful thanks to
his dogged and persistent efforts. Ironically, he does not
own a car and is forced to get around town by trolley,
borrowed motorcycle, or rented cab. When Captain
Hollister of the Los Angeles police asks half-jokingly after
Midnight has beaten him to the punch again if he found his
solution in a crystal ball, Midnight replies somewhat in-
dignantly, "I worked like hell for it." His tenacity results in
such a record of success that Hollister finally admits, "I'm
glad you're not a cop. You'd be taking over my job."

Unlike some of his private-eye colleagues (and despite his
reduced financial state), Midnight is not motivated by
money. In "The Saint in Silver," for example, a religious
charlatan, mistakenly assuming he has come for the purpose

of blackmail, offers him five thousand dollars. Interested only in the thirty dollars the man's wife owes him for a fare, Midnight declines the easy cash. His indifference to money prompts a fellow worker to grumble that Midnight is "the kind of screwball who don't have proper respect for money." Perhaps having so much money when he was younger satisfied his desire for it. Now that the ex-playboy has grown up, he is interested in other things, and this often results in his acting, in his own words, like a "goddam sucker" by sticking his neck out for others. His penchant for getting involved on behalf of those in need prompts Captain Hollister to dub him "Sir Galahad. Santy Claus. The Robin Hood of the Red Owl Cab Company."

Butler was no innovator as far as the new private-eye genre was concerned, but he did contribute a credible example of a hero whose toughness was tempered by a strong sense of decency and fair play. In fact, Butler's stories are populated by characters who share Midnight's simple decency and who often act, as Midnight does, like "goddam suckers" on someone else's behalf. In "Dead Man's Alibi," Midnight is touched by a man who was crippled in an incident in which he saved the life of his young wife and now sits confined to his wheel chair, bravely making excuses for her while she is out carousing with other men. The same story also features Wild Bill Durand, a test pilot who commits a murder for the woman he loves. When he is found out, he escapes in a plane. His final act, a suicidal one, is aimed at proving to the manufacturers of the new plane he is flying that there is a faulty design in its construction. He gives his life to prove his point. There are also several other examples of men who chivalrously take the rap for crimes committed by the women they love. Thus even though the stories are punctuated by murder, it is the decency of Butler's characters, some of whom are even killers, that comes through.

As a writer, Butler possessed two notable qualities: first, he was adept at developing a plot well, unfolding his mystery with sure pacing while also allowing for excellent character development; second, he paid careful attention to details, both in the creation of his characters and in the description of his settings. Like Raymond Chandler, he wrote about Los Angeles in the early 1940s, and his stories provide a vivid sense of place. Many of his capsule descriptions—such as this portrait of a ritzy section of Beverly Hills: "It was a district where even the trees seemed to be shaped like dollar signs and the raindrops clinging to their branches were fourteen carat diamonds"—rival Chandler's in their effect.

In addition to Steve Midnight, Butler created two other series characters of some note: Rod Case, an investigator for the General Pacific Telephone Company, who was featured in a series in *Black Mask* in the early 1940s; and Rex Lonergan, a San Francisco police detective who, like Midnight, appeared in *Dime Detective*. The Midnight series numbered only eight stories between July, 1940, and March 1942, when Butler, like many other writers at the time, turned his attention to film writing. Because his stories never enjoyed hardcover publication, Butler has been relegated to obscurity, another of those writers who turned out consistently high quality work yet who, thanks to the vagaries of the publication market, is known today only to devoted pulp collectors. Nevertheless, in the character of Steve Midnight he created a believable and popular hero who revealed yet another dimension of the new private-eye hero.

Max Latin

(Norbert Davis)

One of the most original of the pulp writers was Norbert Davis, who demonstrated that crime did not always have to be taken seriously to be popular with readers. Typical of his offbeat brand of humor are the short stories and novels he wrote about the exploits of Doan and Carstairs, one of the most improbable detective teams in the history of the genre. Doan, described as being "small and plump and pleasant looking," with a "naively appealing smile and a smooth, roundly pink face," is a top-notch investigator for the Severn International Detectives. Although his round face, dimpled cheeks, and corn-yellow hair give him the appearance of being "the epitome of all the suckers that had ever come down the pike," the truth is that "he was innocent and nice only when it paid him, and he was as harmless as a rattlesnake." His companion, Carstairs, is an enormous Great Dane he claims to have won in a crap game. Snooty in manner, Carstairs seldom even condescends to walk beside Doan because "he had never been able to reconcile himself to having such a low person for a master." Carstairs is especially disapproving of Doan's predilection for drinking, so much so that Doan feels compelled to limit himself to a single drink a day—a beer glass filled to the brim with bourbon.

Despite their appearance, and despite the flippant tone of the narrative, one shouldn't rush to any conclusions, for behind Doan's wisecracks (and his irreverence rivals that of Groucho Marx) is a tough and sometimes ruthless man who isn't afraid to use his fists or his gun to get his man. And despite the humorous nature of their relationship, Doan and Carstairs are, surprisingly, a convincing detective duo, with Carstairs, for example, awakening his friend at the first sound of suspicious noises, guiding him through the dark like a Seeing Eye dog, and helping him keep on the trail of a fleeing suspect. But because Doan refuses to take himself seriously (nor does Davis take him all that seriously himself), there is a light touch, a whimsical tone that makes these works excellent examples of the screwball side of detective fiction.

Another Davis character, Max Latin, a private detective created for a series in *Dime Detective* in the early 1940s, is the exact opposite of Doan in that while he gives the appearance of being ruthless and totally unscrupulous, he is ac-

tually an effective and principled investigator. Billed as "the
shamus with a shady rep," Latin always seems to be in
trouble with the law, having in the course of his career been
charged with murder, blackmail, perjury, intimidation of
witnesses, bribery, and conspiracy to defraud, among other
crimes. Whenever it is to his advantage, he will casually sup-
press or destroy evidence, impersonate a police officer, or
even relocate a dead body. To a woman who questions
whether he is really as shady as he claims, he replies
proudly, "Not shady. . . . Black as night."

But as usual with Davis's characters, what one sees isn't
necessarily what one gets. Despite the many charges the
police have leveled at him, they have been forced to give
him a clean bill of health each time, which prompts In-
spector Walters, a regular character in the series, to conclude: "You bend the law around like a pretzel, but you
never quite break it." When he accuses Latin of even being
fundamentally honest, Latin threatens to sue for libel,
stoutly maintaining, "I'm as crooked as a swastika." But if
one pays close attention to his actions rather than his words,
one is forced to agree with Walters that Latin's shady
reputation is ill deserved.

The enigmatic nature of Latin's character makes him a
most intriguing hero. If there is a private eye on whom he
can be said to have been modeled, it is likely Sam Spade, not
just because of his hard-boiled posture but also because of
the ambiguous way he is presented to the reader. Spade's
confession to Brigid O'Shaughnessy in *The Maltese
Falcon*—"Don't be too sure I'm as crooked as I'm supposed
to be. That kind of reputation might be good business—bringing in high-priced jobs and making it easier to
deal with the enemy"[14]—applies equally well to Latin, who
manages to keep everyone, including the police and his prospective clients, offbalance by his apparent amorality.

In his assertion that his primary passion is money—"If
people get between me and a nice juicy fee, is it my fault if
they get trampled in the rush?"—he sounds a lot like Race

Williams, but his actions reveal that his true motives are far
less pecuniary. In "Watch Me Kill You," for example, he
tricks a client into confessing to a murder even though he
knows it will cost him the five thousand dollars he was to
have been paid by the man for taking his case. In "You Can
Die Any Day," he patriotically cooperates with the FBI in
nailing an unscrupulous individual who promises to deliver
war-rationed materials to manufacturers for a stiff price. In
"Charity Begins at Homicide," he charges no fee to investigate whether a British fund-raiser is actually conning his
American contributors. Although his methods may be unorthodox, and at times even downright illegal, his goal is
usually justice, and his motivation in such cases is a simple
desire to satisfy his own curiosity as to the identity of the
culprit. A widely publicized reputation for shady behavior
provides a very effective cover and in addition is good for
business, but behind the mask Latin is a responsible member
of the private-eye fraternity.

No Davis story is far removed from comedy, which in the
Latin series is provided largely by the cast of characters with
whom Latin associates. Preferring the noise and confusion
of a crowded restaurant to the privacy of a lonely apartment
or an out-of-the-way office, Latin works out of the last booth
next to the kitchen in a dingy restaurant managed by a foul-
tempered chef by the name of Guiterrez. Latin, however, is
secretly the owner of the place. The restaurant is usually
crowded and "noisier than a street fair on Saturday night,"
with a mangy horde of waiters banging dishes and swearing
at each other and at the customers, a cash register clanging
constantly, and a juke box shrieking in the corner. But like
so many things in the Latin stories, appearances are
deceiving, for the noisy restaurant is renowned for the excellence of the food prepared by Guiterrez. The popularity
of the restaurant displeases him, however, for like the artist
who feels misunderstood and unappreciated, he stands
around cursing his customers for their table manners and
lack of proper respect for his culinary effects. He saves his

best dishes for the kitchen help. Also contributing to the
unruly atmosphere in the restaurant are such characters as
Pete, the dishwasher, and Dick, a sour, wizened little waiter
whose main job is to keep Latin's glass filled from the bottle
of brandy he hides beneath an apron the size of a parachute.
One of the most important responsibilities of the restaurant
help is to provide an alibi for Latin whenever he needs one.
To this end Dick keeps a filled ashtray handy, ready to place
it on Latin's table as "proof" that he has been sitting there all
night.

Latin combines the wise-cracking manner of the private
eye with the toughness of character typical of most of his
fellow pulp detectives, although in his case much of that
toughness is a mask, a feature of his carefully cultivated
reputation as a shady operator. Not that he can't be tough
when he has to be. He carries a .38 automatic in the waist-
band of his trousers and is ready to mix it up with the
toughest opponents when he has to. Nor does he have any
hesitation about striking a woman, as he does when one attempts to blackmail him by producing a photograph she
took of him standing over a dead body in an alley. After
smacking her in the face, he warns, "You're not dealing
with Charlie Chan now." But the toughness in his character
and the violence in the stories are generally tempered by a
dash of whimsy, a lightness of touch that makes Davis's
work unique among the pulp productions of his day.

Davis was born in Illinois in 1909 and began writing and
selling stories to the pulps while still a student at Stanford
University Law School. By the time he received his degree in
1934, he was already a regular contributor to several pulps,
and so instead of taking the bar exam he devoted his efforts
to writing full time. He moved to Los Angeles and became
friendly with several of the pulp writers living in the area,
among them W. T. Ballard, Cleve Adams, and Raymond
Chandler, who in 1940 lived only two doors away from
Davis in Santa Monica.

Davis could create credible tough characters and convincing scenes of violence, but he also had a knack for seeing
humor that other writers lacked. It was Raymond Chandler's
opinion that because Davis "took his murders rather lightly
when allowed,"[15] he never became a regular *Black Mask*
contributor since Shaw preferred his fiction less whimsical.
Despite his reservations about his work, Shaw spoke highly
of Davis the man, noting that "if we were to pick anyone
who, in spite of all human trials and tribulations, looks upon
life resignedly and mostly all in fun, our nominee would be
Bert. His sense of humor is prodigious."[16] Davis had a way of
viewing the world that, by emphasizing the incongruous and
the absurd, lent a refreshing air of originality to his stories:
for the incongruous, for example, René and Raymond, two
torch murderers Latin hires in "You Can Die Any Day," are
portrayed as gentlemen of unfailing politeness and gentility;
for the absurd, a local policeman in *Sally's in the Alley,* a
Doan and Carstairs novel, encourages young boys to toss
rocks through windows, aiming to create future criminals
because, as he explains it, if the supply of criminals should
ever dry up he would be forced out of business.

In addition to Max Latin, Davis created another successful
Dime Detective series featuring "Bail-Bond" Dodd, as well
as the three Doan and Carstairs novels, *Sally's in the Alley,
Dead Little Rich Girl* (both 1943), and *Oh, Murderer Mine*
(1946). Yet he, like so many of his fellow pulp writers, failed
to reach a lasting audience, and in 1949, at the age of forty,
he committed suicide. One indication of his sad plight at the
time was a desperate appeal he made to Raymond Chandler
shortly before his death for a loan of two hundred dollars,
which Chandler sent him. While purists might complain (as
apparently Joseph Shaw did) that his comic flourishes only
detracted from the seriousness one came to expect from the
pulp private-eye stories, Davis's works successfully combine
fast action and effective characterization with the kind of

amusement seldom found in the hard-boiled genre. Like the
best of his fellow pulp writers, he managed the tricky task of
adopting a fresh and original approach while remaining
faithful to the basic conventions of the genre.

Dan Turner

(Robert Leslie Bellem)

No history of the private eye would be complete without
mention of Robert Leslie Bellem's Dan Turner who, with the
possible exception of Race Williams, enjoyed the longest run
of any of the pulp detectives. Norbert Davis in his private-
eye fiction demonstrated the effectiveness of tempering
believable toughness with a sense of humor. Bellem, far
more interested in laughter than toughness, used humor as
an end in itself to create in the Dan Turner stories one of the
most amusing series in the history of the genre.

Dan Turner isn't a very complicated figure. His interests
are simple and few: Scotch (always Vat 69), money ("I'm
trying to save up a retirement fund before some sharp
disciple whittles my name on a bullet"), and women,
although he is usually more than willing to forego the former
in favor of the latter ("I'm a sucker for dames in distress—especially when they're young and lovely"). There
haven't been many private eyes with a larger libido or a
more salacious eye than Dan Turner. Unlike such
predecessors as the Continental Op and Jo Gar, who had little time for women, Turner is always ready and willing to
pause for an amorous interlude with a beautiful woman, and
even amenable to bargaining for her favors. In "Skyrocket's
Husband," for example, he accepts a woman's offer of her
body in exchange for his promise to keep the heat off her
boyfriend. "I never could see any reason why a guy

shouldn't mingle business with pleasure," Turner reasons. "After all, what the hell?"

Between his first appearance in *Spicy Detective* in April, 1934, and his final one in *Hollywood Detective* in 1950, Dan Turner appeared in hundreds of stories. He was featured in every issue of *Spicy Detective* (whose name was later changed under pressure to the tamer *Speed Detective*) between 1934 and 1947, and also had his own magazine, *Dan Turner, Hollywood Detective* (later just *Hollywood Detective*), which ran from 1942 to 1950. The same complaint, however, can be made against Bellem that a music critic once made against Vivaldi—that instead of composing hundreds of concertos, he actually composed the same concerto hundreds of times. Each Dan Turner story follows a predictable pattern: Dan Turner, "Hollywood's hottest hawkshaw," is hired or otherwise persuaded to solve the murder of some glamorous movie figure (starlet, actor, agent, producer, director, etc.). After running around a bit, during which he has at least one romantic encounter with a beautiful woman, he miraculously comes up with the solution which fingers the least likely suspect. More often than not, the story ends with him returning to the waiting arms of one of the women he has encountered along the way. What distinguishes Bellem's stories is certainly not originality of plot or depth of characterization but rather the incredibly inventive variations he is able to play on his standard situations, the secret of his success in this regard being one of the most colorful narrative styles in the history of the mystery novel.

There are, for instance, only just so many ways to describe a dead body, and Bellem seems to have used them all: "dead as a mackerel," "dead as an iced catfish," "deader than slapstick comedies," "dead as vaudeville," "dead as a Hitler promise," "deader than George Washington's cherry tree," "dead as a skull on a sinus doctor's desk," and so on. More challenging to his creative imagination are the spicy description of female pulchritude that are the centerpiece of each

Turner story. Because virtually every woman he meets is either garbed in a negligee "that flowed around her delishful shape like poured mist" or covered by gossamer pajamas "that must have been spun when half the silkworms were on a sit-down strike" or upended in such a way to give him a good look up her skirts, Turner is presented with countless opportunities to describe in salacious detail exactly what he sees, from the woman's "cuddly contours" and "resilient curves" to her "lyric hips" and "dulcet thighs." Each leering chronicle usually concludes with his favorite anatomical item, the female breast, descriptions of which tax his imagination to its limits as he ogles the woman's "taut little hillocks of girl-flesh," her "thems and thoses," "mounded yumphs," "creamy bon-bons," "perky pretty-pretties," "tiddlywinks," or "whatchacallems."

Style is virtually everything in a Dan Turner story, for while there is nothing unusual about the character of Turner (like the typical private eye, he stood over six feet two, weighed about two hundred pounds, and possessed the two things absolutely essential for a tough detective: a .32 automatic and a concrete skull), there is nothing ordinary about his manner of narration. Any private eye could talk tough, but few could do it with quite the flair that Turner could. For example, he quiets one woman by warning her to "cork it before I lump you up, sister," and threatens another by admonishing her to "quit stalling before I start shooting dice with your front teeth." "One yeep out of you," he cautions a character, "and I'll spatter your brains from here to San Pedro," and although the literal meaning may be a bit obscure, there can be no mistaking his message when he tells another to "lay off . . . before I bunt the living bejiminies out of you."

In many ways a Dan Turner story can be enjoyed simply as an exercise in linguistic ingenuity, as Bellem never employs a merely serviceable word where a more colorful or inventive one will do. Thus guns never just fire, they bark "Chow-chow" and sneeze "Ka-Chowp! Chowp! Chowp!" Turner never just lights a cigarette, he "sets fire to a gasper." Nor does he just drive his car away, he "gooses the kidneys out of my carburetor" or "bores a hole through the night with my radiator ornament." Bellem employs such a rich array of creative terms that one could from his stories compile a complete glossary of colorful colloquialisms: women are "frails," "wrens," "cupcakes"; movies are "shrieking tintypes," "audible tintypes," "galloping snapshots"; guns are "rodneys," "rodericks," and "roscoes"; even crime is given its distinctive terminology—"killery," "shootery," "stabbery," "bumpery," and "croakery."

Bellem knew how to spice up a story by using leering language. An early admirer, humorist S. J. Perelman, described the stories in *Spicy Detective* as "the sauciest blend of libido and murder," achieved by juxtaposing "the steely automatic and the frilly pantie."[17] He knew how to enliven a narrative by employing alliterative phrases—"as haywire as hailstones in Havana"—and action verbs. The following passage provides a typical example of how Bellem was able to generate a headlong rush in his stories by relying almost exclusively on concrete verbs:

> I peeled off my pajamas, zipped into a set of threads, and walloped out into the corridor; propelled my hundred and ninety pounds of heft up the stairs. I gained the door of the flat over mine; thumped it.

Words like "zipped," "walloped," and "propelled" help to create a breathless, frenetic pace that seldom slackens in the Turner tales.

Bellem was born in Philadelphia in 1902, the son of a railroad detective whose bravery in apprehending a freight-thief who had wounded him provided the young Bellem with one of his most meaningful memories:

> To me from then on, cops were heroes; guys who fought through to victory with their brains backed up by knuckles

were supermen; they still are. Sometimes I wish I'd followed
in the old man's footsteps instead of becoming a newspaperman.[18]

Bellem did the next best thing, eventually abandoning his
journalistic career to become one of those million-words-a-
year writers who kept the pulps filled with tales about tough
private-eye heroes. In a career that eventually spanned more
than twenty-five years, he cranked out some three thousand
stories in every conceivable genre, under both his own name
and an assortment of pseudonyms (Jerome Severs Perry,
Harley L. Court, Harcourt Weems, Justin Case, Ellery Watson Calder). He also wrote several novels, among them two
under his own name (*Blue Murder* [1938] and *The Window
with the Sleeping Nude* [1950]) and two in collaboration
with Cleve F. Adams (*The Vice Czar Murders,* as by Franklin
Charles [1941] and *No Wings on a Cop,* under Adams's
name, in 1950). When the pulps died out in the early 1950s,
Bellem turned to television writing and produced scripts for
such shows as *Dick Tracy, Superman, Captain Midnight,*
and *The Lone Ranger* as well as for *The FBI, 77 Sunset Strip,
Perry Mason,* and even several episodes for Ronald Reagan's
Death Valley Days. He died in Los Angeles in 1968.

While Dan Turner may not be a very crucial figure as far as
the development of the private-eye hero goes, his stories
nonetheless deserve serious consideration. For one thing, as
parodies they clearly demonstrate that a scant decade after
its initial appearance, the private-eye tale had already
established conventions—the tough-talking detective, the
fast-paced narrative, the use of colloquial style, the beautiful
women, the handy bottle of whiskey—familiar enough to
readers to be made fun of. S. J. Perelman in a nice twist once
parodied Bellem's parodies with one of his own entitled
"Farewell, My Lovely Appetizer." Although Perelman tab-
bed Dan Turner the "apotheosis of all private detectives.
Out of Ma Barker by Dashiell Hammett's Sam Spade,"[19] it
was largely Race Williams's outrageous posturing and the

colorful slang of private eyes like Frederick Nebel's Tough Dick Donohue that were the inspiration for Bellem's burlesques.

Moreover, the Dan Turner tales can be enjoyed simply for the comic variations Bellem played on the first-person narrative style that other mystery writers, notably Raymond Chandler, were exploring on a more serious level. For although Bellem's plots are shopworn and his characters paper-thin, his stories are redeemed by the sheer narrative energy and comic exuberance that characterizes Dan Turner's wacky style and character. Whether read as pastiche, parody, or simply for pleasure, the Dan Turner stories will appeal to anyone, contends mystery writer Bill Pronzini, "whose sense of humor leans toward the ribald, the outrageous, the utterly absurd."[20] Dan Turner's "tongue-in-cheek-toughness"[21] provided a welcome relief from the chest-thumping toughness of characters like Race Williams. By treating crime as a laughing matter, Bellem made a unique and colorful contribution to the history of the American private eye.

In the late 1940s, caught up in a squeeze between rising production costs on the one hand and declining circulation, largely due to the increased competition from comic books, the new paperback book boom, and the introduction of television into the American home on the other, the pulps began to fade. By the early 1950s, they were virtually gone, but although the magazines died out, the private eye did not. Having been given his birth in the pulps in the 1920s and then nurtured through his development in the 1930s and 1940s, the private eye was assured continued life in movies, radio and television series, and in hardcover and paperback book form. One unfortunate result of the demise of the pulps, however, was that many writers were left without an audience for their works, and their names are remembered today only by collectors of pulp magazines. Their con-siderable contributions to the development of the private-eye genre, however, deserve recognition. The writers included in this chapter—and to the list could also be added such names as Frank Gruber, Paul Cain, Roger Torrey, W. T. Ballard, and Erle Stanley Gardner, among others—produced some of the best of the pulp writing, their works exemplifying the wide range of achievement, the varieties in style, and the adaptability of the new detective hero that have become hallmarks of private-eye fiction. The pulps may be gone forever, but the private eye remains as a notable testament to their importance in the history of American popular entertainment.

3

Life beyond the Pulps

Within just a few short years after his birth in the pulps, the private eye began making his first appearances in hardcover form, although his earliest ones were simply reprintings of previously published pulp tales. Daly's *Snarl of the Beast* (1927) and *The Hidden Hand* (1929), Hammett's *Red Harvest* (1929), *The Dain Curse* (1929), and *The Maltese Falcon* (1930), and Whitfield's *Death in a Bowl* (1931), the earliest hardcover private-eye novels, all appeared in *Black Mask* before publication. The revolution in the mystery story that began with Daly and Hammett in the 1920s, however, soon began to have an effect on writing outside the pulps. For example, two of the most popular mystery series of all time, both originating in the early 1930s, show the influence of the new hard-boiled school of writing. Erle Stanley Gardner, a veteran of the pulps, introduced Perry Mason in *The Case of the Velvet Claws* in 1933. A lawyer rather than a private detective, Mason in his early cases exhibits many of the character traits—toughness, courage, tenaciousness—that were hallmarks of the *Black Mask* heroes. In 1934 Rex Stout inaugurated the Nero Wolfe series with *Fer-de-Lance*. While

Wolfe himself belongs to the tradition of the Great Detective, Archie Goodwin, his associate and narrator of the books, is a resourceful, wise-cracking investigator whose character in many ways resembles the private eye.

William Crane

(Jonathan Latimer)

But the distinction of creating the first hardcover series to feature as the central character a private eye who was not a veteran of the pulps but an original creation belongs to Jonathan Latimer who in 1934 published *Murder in the Madhouse,* the first of five novels about a tough detective named William Crane. The others were *Headed for a Hearse* (1935), *The Lady in the Morgue* (1936), *The Dead Don't Care* (1938), and *Red Gardenias* (1939). By employing a character who displayed several of the basic traits of the hard-boiled detective hero in novels whose plot structures (especially the locked-room puzzle) were borrowed from the classic whodunit, Latimer helped introduce the private eye to a readership beyond the pulps.

A handsome man in his early thirties, William Crane is an operative for a New York-based detective agency headed by a man named Colonel Black. Like the traditional sleuth, Crane relies on logic and deductive reasoning for many of his solutions. In *Murder in the Madhouse,* which takes place in a mental institution, he even tries to pass himself off as the famous C. Auguste Dupin. But like his hard-boiled counterparts, Crane (who admits to being a reader of *Black Mask*) is willing to risk his neck for his clients. In *Murder in the Madhouse,* for example, he has himself committed to the mental institution in order to investigate first-hand the theft of valuables from a patient. And in *The Dead Don't Care* he risks his life in a desperate attempt to rescue a woman from her kidnappers, who are about to rape her. At times he also resorts to the kind of physical actions repugnant to most of the intellectual sleuths. In *Murder in the Madhouse,* for example, he grinds his heel into a man's nose, then casually wipes his shoe off on the grass. And although he ordinarily doesn't carry a gun, he kills a man in *The Dead Don't Care* by splitting his head open with a wrench.

It isn't his methods, however, that command our attention in the books, it's his character. Latimer has admitted that his intention was to kid the hard-boiled school of writing that was rapidly becoming so popular. For one thing, he felt that Sam Spade was, in his words, "a pretty deadly serious guy. Hammett's characters never had much fun."[1] And so he created a private eye with a highly developed sense of fun. Unlike the Continental Op or Sam Spade, who were all business, Crane "belonged to the pleasure school of crime detection. . . . His best ideas came while he was relaxed," and in order to get himself relaxed he often gets himself intoxicated. His predilection for drinking on the job might tempt one to conclude that the only proof he is ever really interested in is the alcoholic variety.

Crane is a whiskey gourmet whose taste in spirits includes just about everything, from martinis, old fashioneds, and bacardis to such exotic concoctions as champagne mixed with stout, bourbon blended with absinthe, and whiskey laced with laudanum. His eagerness to gulp almost anything he can get his hands on causes him acute discomfort on at least one occasion, for when he takes a healthy swig from a bottle of Dewar's White Label he finds hidden in the drawer of a filing cabinet in a mortuary, he discovers to his chagrin that it is filled with embalming fluid instead of scotch.

Had Latimer been content to portray Crane as just another hard-drinking private eye, there would have been nothing special about him. Instead he portrays him as a hard-drinking private eye *who gets drunk,* and that makes all the difference, for he thus makes his hero the butt of much of the humor in the books. Like the typical private eye of his day, Crane experiences an undue amount of physical pain and suffering, but in his case most of it comes in the form of hangovers. When tipsy, Crane bumps into furniture, spills drinks on his trousers, and stumbles over words when he speaks, all the while stoutly proclaiming his sobriety. Latimer's humor arises from the contrast between Crane's attempts at maintaining his dignity while drinking and his laughable inability at times to stand up straight or even to stay awake. In such passages as these—"He started down the hall, using his left hand as an additional means of locomotion by shoving himself away from the wall every time he veered into it" and "He felt very pleased he had fooled them into thinking he was drunk. . . . He carried out his role so thoroughly he had to be helped into the phone booth"—Latimer creates humor by describing in deadpan fashion the gap between Crane's sober self-image and his sodden state.

Despite his love for the bottle, Crane is not an ineffectual detective; Latimer's intention is not to debunk the private eye totally but to deflate his image slightly. In fact, Crane is usually the only one smart enough to solve the case, again and again demonstrating the truth of his motto, "I solve 'em, drunk or sober." And when the occasion demands it, as in *Headed for a Hearse,* where he is in a race with the clock to establish a condemned man's innocence before he is sent to the electric chair, he even swears off whiskey entirely, limiting himself to milk until the case is over. However, you can be sure he will never go so far as his contemporary Humphrey Campbell, a private eye created in 1938 by Geoffrey Homes, who refuses ever to drink anything stronger than milk.

It would be an overstatement to claim, as Geoffrey O'Brien does in *Hardboiled America,* that in the Crane books "whiskey drinking is the central activity, occasionally interrupted by the plot,"[2] for Latimer proved to be more skilled than many of his fellow private-eye writers in devising puzzling, well-constructed plots. He was particularly adept at coming up with dramatic openings for his books—Crane, handcuffed in the back of an ambulance driven by a drunken man, hurtling along a winding road toward a mysterious destination that turns out to be a mental institution, where he is admitted as a patient (*Murder in the Madhouse*); a grim scene along Death Row as the condemned men spend their last anxious hours awaiting their appointments with the executioner (*Headed for a Hearse*); a beautiful blonde woman, an apparent suicide, snatched from under Crane's nose while he is in attendance at the morgue (*Lady in the Morgue*). From such promising beginnings, Latimer constructs convincing mysteries which require all of Crane's intelligence to solve. With the help of fellow operatives (and drinking buddies) Doc Williams and Tom O'Malley, Crane manages to clear up each mystery, although his reliance on a final confrontation scene in which he fingers the guilty party from among the assembled suspects reveals the strong influence of the classical whodunit on Latimer. Each of the Crane novels is distinguished by convincing mystery elements, good deduction, and a lively narrative which is tightly plotted yet loose enough to allow for Crane's frequent intoxicated interludes.

Crane's misadventures with the bottle, however, aren't the only source of humor in these novels. For one thing, there is a goodly amount of bawdy humor. Also, even when sober, Crane seems to get himself involved in situations that border on the farcical. In *Lady in the Morgue*, for example, he climbs through the window of a hotel room to avoid the police, discovers a sleeping couple, drags the man out of bed, slips under the covers beside his astonished and very naked partner, and poses as her companion when the police knock on the door looking for him. And in another encounter with the police in that novel, he does some fast talking to keep the officer who has stopped the car he is riding in from discovering that the woman he is cradling so

tenderly in his arms is actually a dead woman whose body
was stolen from the morgue. Crane handles such ticklish
situations with his usual aplomb and wit: bidding farewell to
the naked woman in bed, he bows gallantly and says, "I
hope I'll see less of you sometime, madam," and to the
policeman who thinks the dead woman in his arms is simply
drunk, Crane remarks wryly, "She's stiff practically all the
time." He is also quick-witted in fending off insults with
barbs of his own. When a character confesses to Crane that
he doesn't much like him, Crane replies loftily, "Kraft-
Ebbing will never have to write a case history of my passion
for you either." Nowhere is his penchant for wisecracks
more pronounced, however, than in *Red Gardenias,* in
which he is paired with Ann Fortune, his boss's niece, who is
posing as his wife during an investigation. Their witty ex-
changes are reminiscent of those between Nick and Nora
Charles, Hammett's bantering husband-and-wife team
whose adventure, *The Thin Man,* appeared only five years
before *Red Gardenias.* All in all, Latimer's handling of the
comic elements enabled him to achieve humor without un-
dermining the mystery elements of his fiction. Drawing
upon an analogy that Crane himself would appreciate, Jim
McCahery described Latimer's deft blending of humor with
suspense as "masterful—the proper proportion of dry ver-
mouth to produce a fine martini, all without bruising the
gin."[3]

Latimer was far more than just a comedian, however. He
was a talented writer who could create believable scenes of
chilling intensity (Crane awakening in *The Dead Don't Care*
to find the woman he went to bed with the night before now
lying dead beside him) and vividly evoked atmosphere (the
grim setting along Death Row in *Headed for a Hearse* or the
creepy backdrop for the bizarre nocturnal activities in the
sanitarium in *Murder in the Madhouse*). And although in
style he was basically an adherent of Hammett's detached
matter-of-fact approach, he often employed images that
reveal a poetic touch, as in descriptions of sunlight as

"the color of overripe Camembert cheese" or "like butter
on a hot frying pan" and of the hair of a beautiful woman as
"the color of sun-dried bamboo" or "the straw that champagne bottles come in."

Jonathan Wyatt Latimer, named for an ancestor who
served on George Washington's staff during the Revo-
lutionary War, was born in Chicago in 1906 and educated at
Knox College in Galesburg, Illinois, where he was elected to
Phi Beta Kappa. Like many of his fiction-writing contemporaries, Latimer began as a newspaperman. In fact, the
first two Crane books were written while he was still
working as a reporter in Chicago. Although the Crane series
proved to be very popular (three of the books were made into films in the late 1930s with Preston Foster as Crane),
Latimer abandoned his bibulous hero after only five books.
His reasons for doing so are not entirely clear. In one interview he admitted, "I don't know exactly why I abandoned Crane. Perhaps because I felt I was repeating
myself,"[4] although in another he confesses, "I just got kind
of bored with him."[5] At any rate, following a stint in the
Navy during World War II, he settled down in La Jolla,
California, where he would later become friends with
Raymond Chandler, and devoted himself to the more
lucrative job of writing film scripts.

Among the twenty films he wrote were *Topper Returns*
(1941), *The Glass Key* (1942), *The Big Clock* (1947) and *The
Night Has a Thousand Eyes* (1948). Later he became a successful television writer and, among other things, turned out
over fifty *Perry Mason* episodes. During his writing career
he also published four other novels, the last one, *Black Is the
Fashion for Dying* (1959), a murder mystery set in
Hollywood.

Latimer lacked the serious commitment of writers like
Hammett and several of his *Black Mask* contemporaries who
were striving to forge a new mystery genre. He was content
simply to have fun with his writing and with his hero.
Without either the pugnacious toughness of Race Williams

or the single-minded devotion to duty of the Continental Op, Crane is a hero whose toughness can perhaps best be described as well-distilled rather than hard-boiled. But by combining effective writing with a keen sense of humor, Latimer produced five splendid mystery novels which today still provide fresh and lively reading, and which stand as classic examples of what mystery critic James Sandoe once described as the "rye-soaked, zany-cum-sex school" of mystery fiction.[6]

Philip Marlowe

(Raymond Chandler)

The goal of every pulp writer was to break into the hardcover market, but few managed to do so as successfully as Raymond Chandler. His novels, unlike those of Daly and Hammett, were more than simple reprintings of previously published pulp stories. Although frequently based on his pulp tales, they were reshaped into fully developed works of fiction that introduced to readers beyond the pulp audience a private eye who was to become the most important and influential of them all, Philip Marlowe.

Raymond Chandler was something of an anomaly among pulp writers. An American by birth, at the age of eight he moved with his mother to England, where he received a classical education at Dulwich, a British public school. He returned to the United States as a young man and eventually became a successful businessman in Los Angeles, acting as director of several independent oil companies. At the age of forty-five, however, having lost his job, he embarked on a new career as a pulp writer.

Unlike most of his pulp-writing colleagues who were able

to earn a living by cranking out immense amounts of words (including several in the million-words-a-year category), Chandler was a painfully slow and deliberate writer. His first pulp story, an eighteen-thousand-word effort entitled "Blackmailers Don't Shoot" (published in the December, 1933, issue of *Black Mask*), took him five months to write. Chandler's deliberate methods of composition prevented him from ever becoming prolific. Between 1933 and 1939, the year his first novel, *The Big Sleep,* appeared, he published a total of only nineteen pulp stories, eleven in *Black Mask,* seven in *Dime Detective,* one in *Detective Fiction Weekly.* While most of his contemporaries were simply trying to survive by turning out as many stories as they could, Chandler was systematically and deliberately learning and perfecting his craft, in the process of which he was gradually bringing into existence the private-eye hero who, in *The Big Sleep,* would be given the name Philip Marlowe.

Whether named Mallory, John Dalmas, Ted Carmady (or left nameless, as he was in some of the stories), Chandler's pulp detectives were on the surface indistinguishable from the standard fare. All were basically tough, wise-cracking, hard-drinking, courageous men who were ready to meet violence with violence, to use their fists, their guns, and if necessary their rock-hard heads to get the job done. However, beginning with Mallory, the private investigator in his very first story (whose name in its close resemblance to Malory, author of *Le Morte d'Arthur,* first established the link between Chandler's private eye and the Arthurian Knights of the Round Table), Chandler revealed an interest in qualities other than simple physical toughness, an interest which eventually led to the identification made in the opening pages of *The Big Sleep* between his private eye, now named Philip Marlowe, and an Arthurian knight. In that novel, Marlowe, noticing a stained-glass panel over the entrance doors to General Sternwood's mansion which depicted a knight in armor rescuing a lady tied to a tree, observed that the knight "was fiddling with the knots on the

ropes that tied the lady to the tree," but wasn't getting
anywhere, which prompted him to conclude, "if I lived in
the house, I would sooner or later have to climb up there
and help him." Thus was born the private eye as knight
figure, as rescuer of the weak and defenseless.

One of Chandler's many contributions to the development of the private eye was to take a quality that had been
implicit in the stories of some of his predecessors—the
detective's capacity for compassion—and make it explicit,
make it in fact Philip Marlowe's guiding principle. In *The
Dain Curse,* for example, the Continental Op fell victim to a
desire to rescue the beautiful young Gabrielle Leggett from
her distress, and Tough Dick Donohue became obsessed in
"Red Web" with concern for the welfare of the vulnerable
young daughter of the vice queen who was murdered for her
efforts in helping him. Beneath the bluster even Race
Williams at times revealed a compassionate streak, particularly when very young girls were concerned. But in each
instance, such impulses were shown to be exceptions to the
detectives' generally hard-boiled attitudes. In the case of
Marlowe, however, Chandler placed his hero's compassion
in the forefront, and although Marlowe could be hard-boiled
when necessary, it was his concern for others rather than the
demonstration of his toughness that was emphasized.

As early as "Killer in the Rain," Chandler's fourth
published story (which like many of his pulp tales was, in his
word, "cannibalized" to form a novel, in this case, *The Big
Sleep*), the nameless private eye endeavors to spare a sickly
old man from heartbreak by rescuing his daughter from a
potentially embarrassing blackmail scheme. It isn't money or
a desire to find the person responsible for a murder committed during his investigation that motivates him; it's simply a humane wish to prevent any further suffering on the
part of a man he feels sorry for. Ted Carmady, the hero in a
number of Chandler's pulp tales, is a self-styled "All-
American sucker" who slips money to an elevator operator
whose child is ill and who risks his neck for a woman in a
jam in "Guns at Cyrano's." When in "The Curtain" Car-

mady discovers that the killer he is looking for is actually an emotionally disturbed young boy, he chooses not to inform the police about him because he knows that it would kill his aged grandfather to learn the truth about his grandson. The unnamed detective in "Red Wind," usually given the name Marlowe in later reprints of the story, becomes interested in a case that involves blackmail and murder simply because he takes a liking to a blonde involved in the middle of it. At the end of the story he even goes to the trouble of having a phony set of pearls constructed in order to convince the girl that the "real" pearls—which he knows to be fake—have been lost, thus chivalrously protecting the reputation of the dead lover who gave them to her from the damaging truth. He also generously donates the five-hundred-dollar fee he receives for the case to the Police Relief Fund.

Rather than settling for a two-fisted but two-dimensional character who could simply be put through his paces on demand (as Daly did with Race Williams), Chandler strove to create a complex hero with as much credibility as he could manage. Initially his intention was simply to see how far he could extend beyond the limits of the pulp formulas he inherited. His aim was modest: "I thought that perhaps I could go a bit farther, be a bit more humane, get a bit more interested in people than in violent death."[7] Later, after having written several Marlowe novels, his attitude toward Marlowe became considerably more ambitious, bordering on the idolatrous when he came to make his now-famous pronouncement that

> down these mean streets a man must go who is not himself mean, who is neither tarnished nor afraid. The detective in this kind of story must be such a man. He is the hero; he is everything. He must be a complete man and a common man and yet an unusual man. He must be, to use a rather weathered phrase, a man of honor—by instinct, by inevitability, without thought of it, and certainly without saying it. He must be the best man in his world and a good enough man for any world.[8]

It is because he took his hero so seriously that Chandler managed to create a private eye with greater depth and complexity than any writer before him. Perhaps because Philip Marlowe was one of the first private eyes to have been created specifically for the novel rather than the short story (although, as we have seen, his genesis was unquestionably in the pulp tales), Chandler enjoyed the luxury of being able to develop his character in a way denied his predecessors. Sam Spade was, of course, also introduced in the novel-length format in *The Maltese Falcon,* which ran as a series in *Black Mask,* but Hammett, for reasons of his own, chose to develop him in only three additional stories. By taking full advantage of the first-person narrative technique, Chandler created a controlling voice and mind in each of the novels. Marlowe developed into such a fleshed-out character that Chandler was able to write a lengthy letter to a correspondent in which he provided an exhaustive analysis of his hero's background, physical appearance, interests, hobbies, smoking and drinking habits, likes, and dislikes. That Chandler could detail so much about his character gives ample evidence of the care he took in creating a hero who was designed to be seen as a real person.

Far more important than the many details about Marlowe's personal life, however, is the deliberate shift Chandler made away from the hard-boiled dick to the detective as knight hero. For Marlowe, it isn't the money or the thrill of the chase or even the desire to do a job well that motivates him; it is rather a curiosity about and interest in other people coupled with a wish to alleviate their suffering that directs his actions. For Marlowe, a case often becomes a crusade, his goal defined not as solving the mystery but rather as protecting the innocent and ministering to the helpless. Thus in *The Big Sleep* he concerns himself with General Sternwood's two wild daughters because of his compassion for the dying man and his desire to "protect what little pride a broken and sick old man has left in his blood." In *Farewell, My Lovely,* simple curiosity combines with admiration for Moose Malloy's Gatsby-like obsession with Velma Valento to prompt his involvement. In *The Long Goodbye,* his entanglement in a long and complicated investigation begins innocently enough with his desire to help a friend. Like the typical private eye of his day, Marlowe endures being shot at, drugged, sapped, lied to, and so on (all at the modest rate of twenty-five dollars a day plus expenses). The difference between him and his colleagues is his willingness to suffer on behalf of others, including some who aren't even his clients.

Marlowe is a man burdened with a sense of mission. "I'm a romantic," he confesses in *The Long Goodbye.* "I hear voices crying in the night and I go see what's the matter. You don't make a dime that way. You got sense, you shut your windows and turn up more sound on the TV set. . . . Stay out of other people's troubles. All it can get you is the smear."[9] It is a measure of Marlowe's noble character that he doesn't turn his back on those in distress but rather, like the knight in shining armor he really is, remains at the ready to risk his life for damsels in distress and, if need be, to remove the dragons that lie in the way of their happiness.

An important aspect of Marlowe's role as knight errant is the fact that he is shown to be a man of conscience, not a social conscience (Chandler said Marlowe "has as much social conscience as a horse")[10] but a personal conscience that, his creator maintained, is an entirely different matter. Marlowe is the sort of man who is tough enough to knock a man out but then, after tying him up and gagging him with a sheet, is considerate enough to satisfy himself that the man can breathe adequately through his smashed nose before he'll leave. In order to function effectively in his knightly role, Marlowe must also be on the alert against temptations, especially those involving sex and money. Celibacy, therefore, becomes an important measure of his purity of character. When Carmen Sternwood shows up naked in his bed in *The Big Sleep,* for example, he has no choice but to boot her out if he is to live up to the rigid demands of his self-imposed code. He must not succumb to any temptations that might distract him from his goal nor do anything that would sully his self-image. As for money, he keeps a five-thousand-dollar bill in his safe and takes it out and examines it from time to time, but he knows he cannot spend it "because there was something wrong with the way I got it." A man of Marlowe's unshakable honesty may be doomed to a life of poverty, but this is one of the assurances we have that he will never be dissuaded from the noble tasks he undertakes.

Chandler once described Marlowe as the sort of man who "will always be awakened at some inconvenient hour by some inconvenient person to do some inconvenient job,"[11] but he also maintained that if there were enough men like him, "the world would be a very safe place to live in, without being too dull to be worth living in."[12] Like Hammett and the other *Black Mask* writers whose mystery tales rejected the tidy reassuring conclusions of the traditional whodunits, Chandler knew that one could not assume that justice will prevail "unless some very determined individual makes it his business to see that justice is done."[13] Marlowe was Chandler's arbiter of earthly ills and even though he proved to be less efficient than Sherlock Holmes in clearing up mysteries and, judged by one common measurement of his society, he may even be deemed a failure (because he will always be poor), it is he who sets the standard for ethical behavior in his corrupt world. Marlowe's triumph is not that he always succeeds but that, as Robert B. Parker, a longtime Chandler admirer, puts it, in a world of "corruption and schlock" he is "tough enough and brave enough to maintain a system of values that is humanistic, romantic, sentimental, and chivalric"[14] without either compromising or forsaking it.

Raymond Chandler's contributions to the development of the mystery genre in America are many—among them, as the first mystery writer to explore the colorful Southern California setting in his fiction, he virtually identified the private eye with L.A. He extracted the poetry that exists in American vernacular speech. And he elevated the apt simile to an art form—but none is more important than his refashioning of the private detective. He conceived Philip Marlowe as both a more humanly believable figure than Race Williams and a more literary one than the Continental Op. Hammett achieved verisimilitude in his stories by basing his private detective on his own life and experiences as a Pinkerton detective and by modeling him on operatives with whom he actually worked. Chandler, on the other hand, considered the real-life private eye to be "a sleazy little drudge from the Burns agency" who possesses "about as much moral stature as a stop and go sign,"[15] and consequently turned to such literary models as the nineteenth-century frontier prototypes of Daniel Boone and Natty Bumppo and the archetypal heroic figures from the distant Arthurian past as models for his detective. In the process he romanticized the private eye and softened his hard-boiled attitudes in order to create the kind of hero, as Philip Durham described him, "that men in their feckless souls imagine themselves being" and that "women in their optimistic hearts hope they have married."[16]

Philip Marlowe has been described in many ways: "an odd combination of Don Quixote, Huck Finn, and Captain Ahab";[17] "Spade with a capacity for empathy, Huck Finn wised up";[18] a "shop-soiled Galahad";[19] "a thinking man's warrior at once saintly and dangerous, raging and mild";[20] "an eagle scout among the tough guys."[21] However one chooses to characterize him, his enduring appeal rests upon the fact that he is a figure of unquestionable honesty and integrity trying his best to function in a corrupt and venal world, a man of toughness as well as compassion, of courage as well as decency. By elevating the pulp detective from a mere tough guy with a concrete head and a ready gun to a figure of almost mythic proportions, Raymond Chandler transformed the private eye into an authentic American hero.

Rex McBride

(Cleve F. Adams)

Another of those writers who, like Chandler, were fortunate enough to make the successful transition from the pulps to hardcover publication of his private-eye tales was Cleve F. Adams. Like Chandler, who was a friend and fellow member of "The Fictioneers," a group of local Los Angeles writers founded by Adams and W. T. Ballard, he came to writing rather late in life, with his first novel published when he was forty-five. He followed a checkered career as, among other things, a soda jerk, copper miner, window trimmer, motion-picture art director, interior decorator, life-insurance executive, candy-store operator, and even detective. He too, like Chandler, created a number of pulp detective heroes in the 1930s. These heroes can be viewed as early versions of the private eye who was given the name Rex McBride in *Sabotage,* Adam's first novel, published in 1940, one year after the initial appearance of Philip Marlowe.

Despite the similarities to Chandler, Adams wasn't the writer Chandler was nor was McBride the character Marlowe was, for while Chandler's hero grew in depth and complexity far beyond his pulp origins, McBride remained in many ways the typical hard-boiled figure from the pulps. Adams was a far better writer than Daly and was consequently able to create a hero with considerably more complexity of character than Daly was. By turns, McBride is moody, arrogant, generous, profane, sentimental, cold-hearted, rude, and thoughtful. But in the end he lacked the spark of originality that transformed Marlowe from a type into an archetype.

Just under six feet tall, McBride has a compact, well-tailored body and a face that with its dark features has the sculpted appearance of a Sioux warrior, evidence that perhaps "some of his Black Irish ancestors who had helped drive the Union Pacific through Sioux territory might have been on more than amicable terms with the female of the species." More than any other item, it is his eyes that hold the key to his character:

> They reflected his capacity for deep, brooding silences, for sudden ribald laughter, for tremendous rages and an aloof arrogance bequeathed him by his Black Irish ancestors.

A specialist in insurance cases, McBride isn't afraid to bloody his hands in pursuit of the solution to a case, eschewing the "Induction-Deduction Twins" in favor of what he calls "dynamiting": "When you don't know what you're doing you light a fire under everybody and sort of hope something boils to the surface." One consequence of such a method, however, is that he must often pay a stiff penalty for his efforts in the form of physical pain. In addition to a fair number of beatings, he is tortured by having the bottoms of his feet burned off, his apartment is bombed, and he narrowly cheats death when a fisherman happens to see him, arms bound, tossed from a cliff into a lake. Despite such close calls, McBride never gives up, relying upon a singleness of purpose which, according to his creator, is his most admirable quality: "He has been hired to do a job," boasts Adams, "and he's going to do it. Come hell or high water, he's going to do it."[22]

There are two important elements in McBride's life that help to explain his character. The first is his upbringing. A "gutter-bred news kid," McBride never got beyond the eighth grade, his education coming instead from the streets of Los Angeles, where he survived by peddling papers and rolling drunks. Now in his early thirties, he is still a tough kid with a chip on his shoulder who harbors an innate distrust of all establishment types—politicians, bankers, company presidents, reformers who liked the sound of their own voices. Proud of his rough background, he takes pleasure in displaying his chest, which is criss-crossed with scars from

old wounds, as a badge of honor. As for his attitudes, they
can best be described as cynical. A typical example: "A guy
can take care of his enemies. Friends are just a plain damned
nuisance." His self-reliance extends to everything he does,
including the way he prays:

> McBride didn't pray much, being the kind of guy he was, and
> on those rare occasions when he did it was never for himself.
> You got yourself in jams; you got yourself out; or you took
> the consequences. You didn't lead the kind of a life you damn
> well pleased and then ask God to help you if your foot
> slipped. [23]

The other element essential to an understanding of his
character involves his experience with a woman named
Sheila Mason. In his first case, McBride is hired by a group of
insurance companies to find out who is behind the repeated
attempts at sabotaging a major dam project in Nevada. At the
end of *Sabotage* he is pained to discover that his fiancée,
Sheila Mason, an attorney for one of the insurance companies, has been conspiring with the president of the company in the various sabotage efforts. Thanks to McBride's
testimony against her, she is sent to the gas chamber because
one of the accidents the duo ordered caused the deaths of
fourteen workers. As a result of his betrayal by Sheila, Mc-
Bride is wary of any further emotional attachments, which
consequently colors his relationship with Kay Ford, a
woman he meets in *Sabotage* who will become a recurring
character in the series. Although he clearly feels a deep affection for her, he cannot admit it openly and honestly. To
protect himself from further emotional pain, he keeps her at
arm's length by treating her in an often reprehensible manner, although his less than gallant behavior and his
emotional gaucheries are at least partly explained by the
emotional wounds left by his experience with Sheila Mason.

Thus unlike Raymond Chandler, who was turning Philip
Marlowe into Sir Galahad, Adams was content to portray

McBride as something of a heel. In addition to his often shabby treatment of Kay Ford, he is an inveterate gambler, a man who compulsively makes passes at most women he meets, who drinks to excess, trusts no one, and lies to even his closest friends. However, as was true of a character like Norbert Davis's Max Latin, appearances can sometimes be deceiving, for McBride's image as a heel is at least partly cultivated as a defensive posture, as a way of dealing with his inability to follow through on the decent impulses he often has. The truth of the matter is that McBride is nowhere near the unfeeling heel he thinks he is or would have us believe he is.

Even Kay Ford, who in a fit of pique accuses him of being "an egoist of the first water, a preyer upon women, a selfish creature with no morals and little or no heart," acknowledges that there is more to McBride than his sometimes awful behavior. "He is a heel," she admits, then adds, "but I'm afraid he's the kind of heel that if you lose it you go back and pick it up." Even McBride himself at times tires of trying to live up to his swinish reputation, on more than one occasion expressing a desire to become a truck driver or a plumber, some occupation that wouldn't require him to be as much of a heel as being a private detective does.

Although he isn't then a complete scoundrel, McBride does have more of the anti-hero than the hero in his character. It is true that he often regrets his behavior. Angry with himself for roughly grabbing his suitcase from a redcap, he tips the man an excessive amount, and in *Sabotage* he almost goes broke sending flowers to women he treats badly. His cold-hearted attitudes notwithstanding, he is capable of tears, as for instance when he hears of the death of a ship's steward he hardly knew but who was helping him on a case in *And Sudden Death*. But he is also guilty of actions to which a man with Marlowe's high-minded ethics would never stoop. In *Decoy,* for example, McBride causes the death of a character by maneuvering him into grabbing for a gun, from which he had removed all the bullets beforehand; this forces the police to shoot the man. In *Murder All Over,* he ignobly kicks a man in the teeth while he is lying semi-conscious on the ground. Later in that same novel, he orders the brutal torture of a suspect in order to make him talk, defending his storm-trooper tactics against the man, a Nazi agent, by arguing that maybe "an American Gestapo is goddam well what we need. . . . The only way you can lick these guys is to fight as dirty as they do; forget the Marquis of Queensbury [*sic*] rules and bite and gouge and use a knee where it will do most good."[24] Unlike Marlowe, who chose to rise above the evil in his world by adhering to his ethical principles, McBride all too often sinks to the level of the evil in his.

Adams wasn't a very gifted or original writer. For one thing, he lacked Chandler's facility with language. While notably effective in capturing the rough-and-tumble quality of McBride's character and the violent nature of his world, he does not have Chandler's stylistic delicacy. What few striking images there are in Adams's novels are usually stolen from someone else. For example, the following line from *Murder All Over*—"Loeb's laugh ran around the room like mice in the wainscoting"—is nothing more than a blatant theft of Philip Marlowe's description from *The Big Sleep,* published four years earlier, of Carmen Sternwood's laugh—"The giggles got louder and ran around the corners of the room like rats behind the wainscoting." Adams was even cheeky enough to borrow Chandler's name for one of the characters in this novel.

Adams himself acknowledged that he wasn't much of a plotter. "In the generally accepted sense I myself do not plot," he conceded.[25] He preferred simply to allow the various story elements to pile up around McBride, causing him to be in "one terrific jam" and then tried "to figure out why everybody did what he did." His inability to create an effective plot on his own led him to borrowing again, this time from Hammett's *Red Harvest,* the plot of which he used in both *Sabotage* and *The Crooking Finger.* Unfortunately, he lacked Hammett's ability to resolve plot complications and thus left McBride at the end of each book to solve the muddle he finds himself in by a combination of lucky breaks and sheer guesswork. Even when Adams attempts something different, as in *Up Jumped the Devil,* which opens with McBride discovering a dead man sitting in a chair in his hotel room, the plot becomes a muddle. When Adams found something to his liking—a line, a scene, a character type, a plot situation, even a character's name—he used it over and over again. About the only thing that changes from novel to novel is the setting, as McBride, rather than being restricted to a single locale as most detectives are, travels to Nevada and ranges up and down the California coast.

All told, McBride appeared in six novels, the first three of which—*Sabotage* (1940), *And Sudden Death* (also 1940), and *Decoy* (1941)—appeared initially as serials in *Detective Fiction Weekly.* These were followed by *Up Jumped the Devil* (1943) (also published as *Murder All Over*) and *The Crooking Finger* (1944). *Shady Lady* (1955) was left unfinished at Adams's death and completed by another writer, probably Robert Leslie Bellem, with whom Adams had co-authored two other novels: *The Vice Czar Murders* (1941) by "Franklin Charles" and *No Wings on a Cop* (1950), published under Adams's name. He also published three mystery novels in the early 1940s under the name of John Spain.

If it weren't for Chandler, Adams might have been given more credit for contributing to the successful transition of the private eye from the pulps to hardcover publication. His novels, for all their faults, are distinguished by a wry humor and an energetic narrative pace, and despite his protestation that he is a "sow's ear," McBride is an oddly likable character, his vacillations between decent and ill-mannered behavior showing him to be a very human and believable figure. By the standards of his day, McBride was a convincing and well-drawn character; unfortunately for him, Chandler's success with the character of Philip Marlowe only exposed Adams's limitations as a writer. McBride was quickly overshadowed by the imposing figure of Philip Marlowe, who raised the standards by which all future private eyes were henceforth to be judged.

Mike Shayne

(Brett Halliday)

To speak of Michael Shayne is to speak of a phenomenon as well as a private eye, for no fictional detective has had a wider exposure than Brett Halliday's redheaded hero. Like Philip Marlowe, Shayne made his debut in 1939 (in *Dividend on Death*), but there the similarities end. Published at the rate of two, and sometimes three, books a year, the Shayne series eventually numbered some sixty-nine volumes. In addition, Shayne has been prominently featured in films. Twelve appeared between 1940 and 1947, with Lloyd Nolan and later Hugh Beaumont in the title role. Interestingly enough, only the first and last were actually based on Halliday's novels. Among the other sources for the Shayne movies were Frederick Nebel's *Sleepers East* (released as *Sleepers West*) and Chandler's *The High Window* (released as *Time to Kill*). On radio, Shayne appeared in a CBS series in 1949, with Jeff Chandler as Shayne. On television, Shayne appeared in 1960, with Richard Denning as Shayne. Since 1956, Shayne has been featured each month in the magazine, *Mike Shayne Mystery Magazine*. He has become such a well-established figure that even the death of his creator in 1977 failed to bring a halt to his career as Miami's best-known private eye, and he continues to make regular monthly appearances in the magazine.

Yet despite his enormous popularity, there is nothing either unique or original about Shayne. In many ways he is simply another version of the two-fisted, tough-talking private eye who, beginning with Race Williams, became a staple of the pulps. A typical Williams-like boast from his first novel: "Men don't beat me up . . . without paying for it." In the character of Philip Marlowe, Chandler demonstrated that a talented writer could push beyond the limitations of the pulp formula to create a figure of complexity and depth. Halliday, on the other hand, proved that there was still an audience for the pulp hero, and he has continued, with the assistance of those who also had a hand in writing the stories, to keep that audience satisfied for well over four decades.

This is how Halliday describes Shayne in his first case:

> He had a tall angular body that concealed a lot of solid weight, and his freckled cheeks were thin to gauntness. His rumpled hair was violently red, giving him a little-boy look curiously in contrast with the harshness of his features. When he smiled, the harshness went out of his face and he didn't look at all like a hard-boiled private detective who had come to the top the tough way. [26]

Prior to going into business for himself, Shayne was an employee of a large detective agency in New York, but since moving to Miami he has established a reputation as the city's ace private eye, his daring exploits often front-page news. In fact, his reputation becomes so widespread that people in distant cities recognize his name. Nor is Shayne himself, it must be admitted, modest about his abilities, once boasting, "I'm the best in the business." He lives in a small apartment hotel in downtown Miami, which at one time also served as his office, but under the guiding hand of secretary Lucy Hamilton he now maintains a separate office and keeps regular office hours. Although at one time he had a reputation as a womanizer, after his marriage to Phyllis Brighton he settles down. Even after her death, he remains, if not celibate, at least measured in his relationships with women.

Shayne has a few distinctive habits, the most prominent of which involves drinking. He consumes ungodly amounts of cognac (Martell is his favorite), usually poured into a wineglass with a glass of ice water beside it for a chaser. Unlike William Crane, however, he seldom shows the effects of all the drinking he does. Whenever deep in thought, he customarily tugs at his left ear lobe, a sure sign that he is puzzling over one element or another. And although he is not in the habit of carrying a gun (he is more apt to grab a bottle of brandy than a gun when going off on an investigation), preferring to use his wits and if necessary his fists to do his work for him, he is not reluctant to kill when necessary.

Especially in his early cases, Shayne is anything but a knight errant, motivated as he is less by a concern for justice or a desire to assist those in distress than by the same drives that spurred Race Williams into action: love of money and love of danger. Ordinarily he won't work on a case "until I see the glint of a stray dime that may be in it for a guy named Mike Shayne." When dollars are involved, he admits, "no one can say Michael Shayne is modest about stepping to the front and getting his." He also confesses to being attracted to the excitement that accompanies a dangerous case when everything depends upon "split-second timing with lives hanging in the balance while he sat back and pulled the strings." Shayne especially savors the feeling of "sitting atop a powder keg. Moments like this were what made life worth while."

Shayne didn't earn his reputation as an ace private eye by playing by the rules or by adhering to a noble code of knightly behavior. His cavalier attitude toward the law allows him to destroy evidence when it suits his purposes or to plant it when he can't come up with a better way to thwart a criminal. In *The Uncomplaining Corpses* (1940), for example, he forges a letter to mislead the police long enough to give him an opportunity to "jimmy some dough" out of the man he knows is the guilty party. In *Dividend on Death,* he even goes so far as to set a trap in which he knows men will be killed, although he assures the police that everything will be all right because the killings will be "justifiable homicide" since the participants, all criminals, will only kill one another.

His morality is as loose as his legal ethics. "Thank God my morals are elastic enough to meet an emergency," he proudly proclaims. Shayne seldom questions his behavior or worries that what he is doing might not be the right thing to do. In his view, results are what count. Halliday ballyhoos his hero in the early books as "The hard-boiled dick who had fought his way savagely to the top with a ruthless disregard for everything that stood in his path,"[27] including apparently such things as law and morality, extolling him as the sort of determined hero who gets a "savage thrill in playing fast and loose against every conventional morality and coming out on top against tremendous odds."[28]

As the series progresses, however, Shayne's character undergoes an interesting transformation, and he begins to act less like Race Williams and more like Philip Marlowe. He loses interest in money as a motivating principle and starts to display a greater concern for others. In *Murder Is My Business* (1945), for example, he agrees to investigate the death of a young soldier whose mother comes to him for help, even though she has no money to pay him. Shayne tells her not to worry, lying to her that the government will take care of his expenses. In *When Dorinda Dances* (1951), he becomes interested in a case because he sees an opportunity to help a liberal Washington judge who is being hounded by what he calls "hysterical right-wingers." By contrast, ten years earlier, in *Bodies Are Where You Find Them,* the only way he could work up any interest in the mayoral election in Miami Beach was by placing a large bet on one of the candidates—and the only reason he picked that candidate was because Peter Painter, ambitious chief of detectives in Miami Beach, was supporting his opponent.

The most dramatic instance of his transformation from investigator-for-profit-only to a kind of crusader for justice comes in *A Taste for Violence* (1949). Summoned to the mining town of Centerville, Kentucky, by a man fearful for his life, Shayne arrives in town too late to save his client, who has already been murdered. He does not simply leave town with his fee, which has been paid in advance, but, disturbed by the political corruption he sees everywhere in Centerville, he decides to stick around to clean things up. Unlike the Continental Op, who resolved a similar situation in *Red Harvest* by pitting the feuding factions against one another in a bloody shootout, Shayne cleans up Centerville by getting himself named chief of police and taking over the operation of the town for six months. One measure of his commitment is his decision to stop drinking cognac until the job is finished. As far as stubbornness, cockiness, and rugged independence are concerned, Shayne's basic character remains unchanged, but his motives and attitudes toward his work become modified to the extent that his friend Will Gentry, who has known him for years, is now prompted to refer to him as "Michael Galahad Shayne."

One reason for the success of the Shayne series is that the reader could look forward to meeting the same cast of characters in novel after novel. The first several books feature Phyllis Brighton, who soon becomes Mrs. Michael Shayne. She dies in childbirth five books later. Halliday says he killed her off to satisfy Twentieth Century-Fox, which wasn't using his books for the Mike Shayne movies because they didn't want a married private eye. Ironically, the studio dropped the series at about this time, so Phyllis's death was unnecessary, although the series markedly improved once Shayne was freed from the domestic restraints of his marriage. Phyllis's role is taken over by Lucy Hamilton, whom Shayne first meets in *Michael Shayne's Long Chance* (1944). She becomes his secretary, sometimes his date, and in her worries about his safety and complaints about his appearance and the look of his office, a kind of mother figure.

Shayne's closest friend and regular drinking buddy over the years is Tim Roarke, a Miami reporter who assists him in a number of ways, including writing stories for his newspaper which further his friend's interests.

Another good friend is chief of Miami detectives Will Gentry, who does things for Shayne no other policeman ever did for a private eye, who is ordinarily portrayed as being at odds with the methods and philosophies of all official police agencies. Gentry has such unflagging confidence in Shayne that he bends and sometimes even breaks the rules in order to protect his friend. Halliday counterbalances Shayne's cozy relationship with the Miami police by including Peter Painter, ambitious pint-sized chief of the Miami Beach detective bureau and Shayne's nemesis for well over forty years. Painter is so bent on pinning every crime committed in Miami Beach on Shayne that he ignores evidence to the contrary right under his nose. Especially in the early novels, Shayne seems to devote most of his time to trying to prove his innocence in the face of Painter's accusations, which usually forces him to solve the crimes Painter, whom he considers a "nincompoop," is too incompetent to solve himself. He does, however, put his animosity aside long enough to rescue Painter from kidnappers in *Murder in Haste* (1961). For a while Shayne moves his office to New Orleans, which eliminates the childish bickering with Painter, but he eventually returns to Miami and resumes his temperamental disagreements with his old adversary.

Brett Halliday was actually only one (albeit the most famous) of many pseudonyms used by Davis Dresser. Others include Asa Baker, Matthew Blood, Don Davis, Anthony Scott, Anderson Wayne, and (with his second wife, Kathleen Rollins) Hal Debrett. Dresser was born in Chicago in 1904 and raised in Texas. After an adventurous youth, highlighted by enlistment in the army at fourteen and a childhood riding accident that left him blind in one eye, requiring him to wear an eyepatch for the rest of his life, he settled down and earned a civil-engineering certificate from Tri-State College in Angola, Indiana. After working for a time as an engineer and as a surveyor, he turned to writing without much success until Mike Shayne came along.

Halliday's account of the origin of Mike Shayne is an interesting one. As a young man employed as a deckhand aboard a Pan American oil tanker, he found himself with a group of fellow sailers in a Tampico, Mexico, waterfront bar. At a nearby table a tall redheaded American sat alone with a bottle of tequila and a glass of ice water in front of him. In a later version of the story, Halliday changed the drink to cognac, Shayne's favorite. As these things happen, a fight soon broke out in the bar, and before long the redheaded American was in the midst of it. In fact, says Halliday, thanks to him he was dragged safely away from the fray and out of the bar. Four years later, then a struggling writer in New Orleans, Halliday bumped into the same man at a bar in the French Quarter. As they were talking, a girl walked over to their table and said to the redhead, "Hello, Mike." He began rubbing his earlobe, and when he spotted the two men who had entered with the girl moving toward him, he got up and left with them.

At this point Halliday's account becomes colored by imaginative myth-making. In one version, he said he never saw the redhead again. However, in an essay entitled "Michael Shayne as I Know Him,"[29] Halliday claims to have actively sought further information about the man, eventually learning that a private detective in Denver by the name of Connor Michael Shawn declared to his wife on his deathbed that he was the man Halliday was looking for. A year later, while writing a novel in a cabin on the Gunnison river in Colorado, Halliday finally met the real Mike Shayne, on vacation from his lucrative private-detective practice in Miami. Halliday would have us believe that he came to act simply as a chronicler of Shayne's real-life activities, cast in the role of a Boswell to the great redheaded detective. Shayne, however, is so modest, Halliday complains, that he has been forced to cut out much of the good stuff when he records his adventures. He even claims to have been best man at Shayne's wedding to Phyllis Brighton.

Obviously Halliday is only attempting to convey the extent to which the character of Michael Shayne came to play such a dominant role in his life and in his writing. Besides, this version is far more romantic than the truth, which is that it took four years and twenty-two rejections before Halliday found a publisher for *Dividend on Death.* The special relationship between Shayne and his creator did produce, however, one of the most unusual and diverting of all the books in the series, *She Woke to Darkness* (1954), in which Halliday himself becomes the chief suspect in the murder of a young woman he met at the annual Mystery Writers of America dinner in New York. He summons his friend Mike Shayne to New York: Shayne repays his debt to his chronicler by proving his innocence and finding the real killer.

Except for some minor changes (the substitution of Lucy Hamilton for Phyllis Brighton and a modification in Shayne's attitudes and methods over the years), the basic formula Halliday employed in 1939 has remained intact ever since, so much so that other writers have been able to slip easily into Halliday's role as chronicler of Shayne's activities with no perceptible effect. Dennis Lynds (as mystery writer "Michael Collins," he will be the subject of a later section of this book), who wrote over eighty Shayne novelettes under Halliday's byline for *Mike Shayne Mystery Magazine* in the 1960s, offers this assessment of Halliday's success: "It is true that Halliday was not a literary stylist, a penetrating psychologist, or a keen analyzer of current society. But he was a writer who knew a good story when he found one, and who knew how to tell that story."[30]

Halliday's writing has been accurately described as "nuts-and-bolts prose."[31] Whenever he attempted to be stylish, he ended up with stale images, as in this typical simile of Shayne's: "I trust you just as far as I could throw a bull by the tail." Instead of going to the trouble of inventing fresh characters each time, he simply recycled familiar ones.

Readers looking for psychological insight or social commentary in the Shayne novels will be disappointed.
However, as Lynds noted, Halliday knew how to tell a fast-
paced story, he knew what his readers wanted, and he gave
it to them over and over again—the daring exploits of a
tough, effective private eye who knew how to get things
done, even if it meant he had to cut some corners to do so.
He left the introspective, brooding thoughts to writers like
Raymond Chandler.

Although he has survived well into the 1980s, Mike
Shayne is not a contemporary figure but a throwback to the
pulp heroes of the 1930s. His ancestor is not the Arthurian
knight errant who inspired the character of Philip Marlowe
but rather the nineteenth-century Western hero who was
transformed into the figures of Race Williams and the Continental Op. Although it is no more than a coincidence, it is
interesting to note that the name given to the hero of Jack
Schaefer's popular 1949 novel, the source of the classic
Western film, is also Shane. In the real world, Shayne would
today be approaching eighty, but in the timeless world of
Halliday's fiction he remains the eternally youthful, peren-
nially successful private-eye hero, the rugged individual who
relies on action rather than thought to get the job done. His
code may be simpler than those of many of his fellow investigators but his record of success is second to none,
thanks to the sheer number of cases he has been involved in
over the years. Even after forty years, it appears that readers
have yet to tire either of his routine victories over evil or his
customary triumphs over Peter Painter.

4

Postwar P.I.s

Prior to World War II, the private eye was confined largely to the pulps and, to a lesser degree but with increasing frequency, hardcover novels. Occasionally he was featured in films. As early as 1931, a film version of Hammett's *The Maltese Falcon* was made, but it wasn't until ten years later, with the release of John Huston's version starring Humphrey Bogart, that the private eye made the successful transition to films. *The Maltese Falcon* ushered in a spate of private-eye movies in the 1940s, ranging from such classic adaptations as Edward Dmytryk's *Murder, My Sweet* (with Dick Powell as Philip Marlowe) in 1944 and Howard Hawks's *The Big Sleep* (with Bogart portraying Marlowe as convincingly as he had Spade) in 1946 to any number of forgettable screen melodramas.

Radio also discovered the private eye in the 1940s, and some of the most popular programs of the day featured detectives. Making their debut over the airwaves at this time were such familiar private eyes as Sam Spade (1946), Mike Shayne (1946), and Philip Marlowe (1947) as well as several new ones created specifically for the radio audience, such as

The Fat Man (by Dashiell Hammett in 1946), Richard Rogue (*Rogue's Gallery,* 1945), Johnny Dollar, Martin Kane, Richard Diamond (all 1949), and three of the most colorfully hard-boiled heroes of them all, Johnny Madero (1947), Jeff Regan (1948), and Pat Novak (1949), all virtually the same character, played by Jack Webb in his pre-*Dragnet* days. In the late 1940s, television began making its first tentative appearances in the American home, and two of the earliest television series were private-eye dramas: *Man against Crime* (with Ralph Bellamy as Mike Barnett) and *Martin Kane, Private Eye* (with William Gargan in the title role), both of which premiered in 1949.

But the most significant development occurred in print as the pulps, which were fast becoming extinct after the war, gave way to a promising new phenomenon, paperback books. Between 1945 and 1946, for example, the number of paperback titles in print jumped from 112 to 353, many of them mysteries.[1] The paperback boom played a key role in expanding the popularity of the private eye in two ways: by making inexpensive reprints of hardcover detective novels available to a mass audience; and by taking over the role the pulps had heretofore played as the chief purveyor of original works designed specifically for a mass audience.

One by-product of the rapid rise of paperbacks was that between 1946 and 1950 alone, a dozen interesting new private eyes were created. Some, like Roy Huggins's Stuart Bailey, showed promise yet never really developed. Bailey's debut in *The Double Take* (1946) was quickly followed by two short story appearances in *The Saturday Evening Post,* but then he disappeared until being resurrected for television on 77 *Sunset Strip,* which ran between 1958 and 1964. Others—for example, Harold Q. Masur's Scott Jordan and Henry Kane's Peter Chambers (both created in 1947) and Sam S. Taylor's Neal Cotten (1949)—enjoyed a modest success. But there also appeared at this time several new private eyes of more than passing interest. Some of them, for example those created by Howard Browne, Wade Miller, and Bart Spicer, earned widespread critical approval, while others, notably those launched by Richard Prather and Mickey Spillane, enjoyed unprecedented popular success. Individually and as a group, these new detective heroes provide ample evidence of the healthy state of the private eye in the years immediately following the war.

Having raised the standards of private-eye fiction to a new level of excellence, Raymond Chandler was a tough act to follow. Writers who sought to imitate his example found themselves in what can only be described as a damned-if-you-do-damned-if-you-don't situation. If their works failed to measure up to the lofty standards set by Chandler, they were dismissed, but if they aped Chandler too slavishly, they ran the risk of being judged nothing more than pale copies of the master.

Paul Pine

(Howard Browne)

One of the first and today still one of the best of those who consciously imitated Chandler was Howard Browne. In four books featuring Chicago private eye Paul Pine, Browne produced some of the finest detective fiction in the Chandler manner ever published. Browne wrote under the pseudonym of "John Evans." Because he himself dropped the Evans byline and published the fourth and final Pine novel under his own name, I will follow his example and refer to him by his real name. In an interesting sidelight to his choice of a pseudonym, Browne says he was surprised to discover after using "John Evans" for some time that it was the same name Chandler gave to his private detective in "No Crime in the Mountains."

After spending two years as an investigator for the Illinois State Attorney's Office, Paul Pine went into business for himself as a private detective in Chicago. He lives in the Dinsmore Arms, a small apartment hotel on the North Side and works out of an office on the eighth floor of the Clawson Building, just west of Michigan Avenue, where his neighbors include a cut-rate dental lab, an obscure correspondence school, a typing service, and "a few doctors and dentists who had flunked the course on how to get into the heavy sugar." Pine is an industrious detective, frequently working on more than one case at a time, although at the rate of thirty dollars a day including expenses, he'll never be a rich man. About his educational background we know little, although he displays a ready knowledge of classical music and has an interest in books, especially mysteries. He mentions reading novels by mystery authors Roy Huggins, William P. McGivern, and Howard Browne, "whoever he is."

By the mid-1940s, all new private eyes were inevitably being compared not only to Philip Marlowe but to the popular stereotype of the detective being promoted by Hollywood films of the day. Consequently, Pine is very self-conscious about being expected to live up to what others think a private eye is and he deliberately seeks to establish his independence from that public image. For example, he once kept a bottle of whiskey in the bottom drawer of his office desk, but because the rash of private-eye movies made him so self-conscious about the practice, he removed it. Pine is especially annoyed to learn others regard him as a womanizer simply by virtue of the popular image of his profession. What bothers Pine so much about Hollywood's version of the private eye is that it unrealistically overlooks "the loneliness of hotel rooms and the gray emptiness of mean streets and the weariness that comes from legwork without results."[2] His impatience at having to compete with the popular image of the private eye boils over when he receives a request for help from a college student who is writing a thesis on the role of the private investigator in modern society: "If there was a place for private detectives," he sputters, "Siberia was it and I would contribute modestly to a fund for that purpose."[3] Pine isn't going to abandon his career simply because he doesn't like the way Hollywood has falsified and romanticized the image of the private eye, but he steadfastly refuses to be influenced by any image of the private detective other than his own, which is an unflinchingly realistic one.

For although like Philip Marlowe he is capable of performing chivalric acts (at the end of *Halo for Brass,* for instance, he lies to the elderly parents of the woman he has been hired to find in order to spare them the ugly truth he had discovered about her) and is a man of high principles ("I work for my clients and my conscience"), Pine possesses a no-nonsense, down-to-earth attitude toward his profession. He never identifies himself with a knight on a crusade for he realizes that his job demands qualities far more mundane and less romantic than a trusty steed or shining armor. In his line of work, he understands that what is required is that you "sat and listened or you stood and listened. And when the calluses got thick enough so you didn't fidget, then you could be a private detective.[4]"

On occasion he succumbs to feelings of self-pity, such as when he sourly remarks that "nobody cared whether I lived or died or moved to Terre Haute," but when he catches himself sounding too much like Hamlet expounding his gloomy "Alas, poor Yorick!" speech, he cautions himself, "Don't run it into the ground, brother." Nobody forced him to become a private detective. If he happens to lead a lonely life, it's because it goes with the job. He has friends, including one who makes repeated invitations to join him in his agency in Los Angeles, but Pine declines the offer because he prefers to work alone. He also knows that the domestic life cannot be reconciled with his profession, and so despite a healthy attraction to members of the opposite sex, he rejects any such prospects for himself. A phone call from the worried wife of a fellow private eye who begs for help in locating her missing husband only confirms his belief that a private eye should commit himself to the monastic life:

> Private dicks had no business being married. Private dicks should live with nothing except a few books and a bottle or two on the pantry shelf and a small but select list of phone numbers for ready reference when the glands start acting up. Private dicks should be proud and lonely men who can say no when the hour is late and their feet hurt.[5]

Despite the tone of the above statement, Pine is not normally as cynical as some of his fellow private eyes. There is more whimsey than bile, for example, in his admission that when he reads the newspaper, he reads Dick Tracy for information and the editorial page for laughs. Because he recognizes that he lives in the real world and not in some "germ-free section of Utopia," he isn't as susceptible to bitter disappointment as a romantic idealist like Philip Marlowe is, although he tastes his share of disillusionment as a result of some of his encounters. "I don't think I'm hard or calloused or bitter," he confesses. "I get wet-eyed in the movies once in a while, and I think kids are wonderful." But then he adds, "after a few years of being lied to and cheated and double-crossed—well, I quit handing out halos. Too many of them were turning out to be tarnished instead of glowing."[6] This admission occurs shortly before his discovery that the woman to whom he made it is herself a killer, a revelation that will only further confirm him in his disillusionment.

Pine is, like Philip Marlowe, the type of first-person narrator who can be judged by the language he uses and by the distinctive way he observes and describes what he sees. An irreverent soul, he is given to wisecracks in his remarks and hyperbole in his descriptions. For example, to his eyes a fireplace is so large "you could have broiled a mastodon in [it]," an ashtray is "big enough to bathe a camel in," a field has "enough weeds to hide the Taj Mahal," and a carpet "the color of a Hanoverian nosebleed" is "deep enough to ambush tigers in." His narratives are also peppered with colorful similes, many of them drawing upon topical political references for effect: For example, he observes that one character's expression "had changed about as much as the *Tribune*'s opinion of Roosevelt." A woman is said to be "as confident and at ease as a Mississippi congressman up for re-election." And he worries that his clients are "as scarce as German generals named Cohen."

In addition to a steady stream of amusing and inventive similes, Browne's prose is also distinguished by strikingly apt physical descriptions that serve as capsule portraits. In quick, economical strokes he captures the essence of one woman by describing her smile as being "as guarded as her eyes and her eyes were as guarded as the Philadelphia Mint" and of another by observing that "she carried her breasts high and insistent, like medals won in combat." In just two sentences he reveals all there is to know about this character:

> She was one of those small birdlike females who are active in church socials and the local chapter of the Eastern Star, and who work up quite a reputation for strawberry preserves. She would go into her eighties and die with patient resignation, knowing in advance that the wings would fit and the harp would be in tune.

One of Browne's greatest talents as a writer, however, one in which he surpasses Chandler, is his ability to create and sustain plots of genuine mystery. In *Halo in Blood* (1946), for example, he deftly weaves three seemingly unrelated occurrences—the funeral of a pauper at which twelve clergymen from different faiths are the only mourners in attendance; Pine's being hired by a client to dig up some dirt in the background of a man who intends to marry his daughter; and another case Pine is working on during which he is

nearly killed while delivering a twenty-five-thousand-dollar
ransom for a kidnap victim with what he later discovers to
be counterfeit bills—into a complex yet convincing web of
events that produces some explosive surprises at the end. In
Halo for Satan (1948), Pine faces another bizarre situation
when he is hired by a Roman Catholic bishop to locate the
man who disappeared after offering to sell him a manuscript
he claims was written by Jesus Christ. In the manner of *The
Maltese Falcon,* the plot involves murders, double crosses,
and the desperate competition of opposing factions (including one led by a dying Chicago gangster who hopes to
insure his passage into heaven by getting the manuscript for
the church) to get their hands on the mysterious object.
Halo in Brass (1949) begins more sedately, with Pine ac-
cepting a seemingly simple assignment to locate the
daughter of an elderly couple whom they haven't heard
from in some time. His investigation, however, unlocks a
Pandora's box as his search for the missing girl turns up a
whole flock of dead women, all of them lesbians.

Paul Pine's final adventure, *The Taste of Ashes* (1957), is a
genuine treasure among private-eye novels. Like Chandler's
The Long Goodbye, published four years earlier, the novel
begins as a mystery but turns into a novel of disillusionment
and self-discovery. Pine is summoned to Olympic Heights, a
quiet little town forty miles north of Chicago, by a wealthy
dowager who wants to hire him to get rid of whoever is
trying to blackmail one of her daughters. Put off by the
woman's officious manner and by the nature of the task she
wants him to perform, he declines her offer and returns to
Chicago. Later that night he receives a phone call from the
worried wife of a fellow private eye who has turned up
missing in Olympic Heights. Reluctant at first to become involved, he finally agrees to return to the town to look for
her husband. He quickly finds him, dead in his hotel room.
When the local police, in the face of convincing evidence to
the contrary, declare his death a suicide, Pine becomes
highly suspicious. What follows is a masterful plot that

produces several more dead bodies, a bountiful share of surprises, and, as he sorts the whole sordid mess out, some
disillusioning experiences for Pine. *The Taste of Ashes* is an
eloquent reminder of what Browne might have accomplished had he chosen to continue writing private-eye
fiction.

Like most of the private-eye writers of his day, Browne
had a pulp background, although in his case it was as both
writer *and* editor. Born in Omaha in 1908 and raised in the
small Nebraska town of Arapahoe, he hitchhiked to Chicago
at the age of seventeen and stayed for the next twenty-four
years. After a succession of odd jobs, he landed a position as
credit manager for a large retail furniture chain, a job he held
for many years, but because he disliked his work so much,
he began looking for an escape and turned to writing. He
sold his first two stories to a Ziff-Davis pulp in 1941, then
was promptly hired to edit the magazine. For the next fifteen years he continued as an editor, although he also wrote
innumerable pulp stories under a variety of pseudonyms.
Paul Pine, however, was an original hardcover creation, not
a character that had its origins in the pulps. (Pine was
modeled after a wise-cracking skip tracer Browne knew in
Chicago by the name of Paul Prye.) Following the
publication of the first Pine novel, *Halo in Brass,* Browne
took a leave of absence from his editing duties and moved to
California to write the next two Pine books, then returned
to Chicago and his editing job.

Despite both critical and popular success, the Pine series
ended after only four books, although Pine made one other
appearance in a story entitled "So Dark for April," published
in *Manhunt* in 1953. There is, however, no real mystery
behind Browne's retirement from novel writing. His original
plan was to write a Pine book each year and Simon and
Schuster was interested enough to back him as a full-time
writer, thus freeing him from his editorial duties. However,
at about the same time Warner Brothers made him an offer
that promised an income Browne describes as being far

beyond what he could ever hope to realize from writing mystery novels. "It took me a full five minutes to make up my mind," he recalls.[7] And so he moved to California, where he eventually wrote over 125 scripts for such television series as 77 *Sunset Strip, Maverick, Mannix, The Fugitive, Columbo,* and many others.

Twenty years after *The Taste of Ashes* was published, Browne began working on a new Pine novel, entitled *The Paper Gun,* in which he planned, among other things, to make observations about the numerous changes that have taken place in Chicago since the 1950s. Midway through the book, however, he abandoned the effort, deciding that "it all seemed so stylized, so repetitive, so tiresomely familiar. I feel that Chander must've felt that way before he wrote *Playback*; Chandler's mistake," Browne concluded, "was going ahead with it."[8]

Browne isn't at all coy about his debt to Raymond Chandler. "Had there been no Philip Marlowe," he concedes, "there would've been no Paul Pine."[9] He says he discovered *The Big Sleep* while writing his first Pine novel and the effect was electric: "His mastery of the English and American languages, his deft handling of description, mood, pace and action, his diamond-hard dialogue, his mind-blowing similes and metaphors—all this and more had a tremendous impact on me. . . . I had no choice but to try to capture the essence of his style." His main worry was that Pine would become nothing more than "a smudged copy of Philip Marlowe," and looking back he acknowledges that in his first book Pine was "a kind of plastic imitation of Marlowe." However, with each succeeding book, Pine became more and more his own man, emerging fully individualized in *The Taste of Ashes,* which Browne admits is "probably as good a detective novel as I'm capable of writing." The sad thing about it, at least to fans of Pine, is that, as Browne confesses, "perhaps in finding him I'd accomplished my purpose and lost the desire to do more books about him."[10]

Like Chandler, Browne demonstrated that a private-eye

novel didn't need incessant action or piles of dead bodies to be effective. He showed that the combination of an engaging and credible private detective, a convincing sense of character and place, and a polished and evocative writing style was an effective recipe for success. Admirers of the Pine novels must be content with but four appearances of the Chicago detective, although they can also take satisfaction in knowing that Browne came closer than most of the many other imitators who sought to capture in their own works the distinctive qualities of Raymond Chandler's fiction.

Max Thursday

(Wade Miller)

In 1947, a pair of young San Diego writers, Bill Miller and Robert Wade, using the name Wade Miller, published the first of six novels featuring a private eye named Max Thursday. The series is noteworthy for two reasons: it was the first to take advantage of San Diego as a fresh setting for a private-eye series and, more importantly, it was among the first to follow Raymond Chandler's lead in employing the private-eye novel as a vehicle for exploring the personality of the detective.

The series began with *Guilty Bystander* (1947), which opens with Thursday being roused by his ex-wife Gloria from a drunken slumber at 4:15 in the afternoon at the sleazy flophouse where he works as house dick. Their son, whom Thursday hasn't seen in the four years since his divorce from Gloria, is missing and his ex-wife wonders if he has any knowledge of the boy's whereabouts. He knows nothing about his son's disappearance and is reluctant, despite the fact that he used to be a pretty good detective, to help Gloria look for him. "I haven't been a detective for a long time," he tells her, "and I haven't the guts or the hunches any more."[11] But old habits die hard, and, since it is his own son who is missing, he has a reason for becoming involved which he cannot ignore. He borrows five dollars from Gloria for a shave, haircut, and a meal and sets out on a search for the missing boy which will turn into a journey toward his own personal rehabilitation.

Before joining the Marines in World War II, Thursday, a tall lean man with a gaunt rugged face, sharp blue eyes, heavy eyebrows, and a prominent arched nose, was a private detective, but he came home from the war with a bad case of what he terms "bum nerves" and began drinking heavily, which eventually cost him his wife and his job. Now he lives in a flophouse where he earns drinking money by keeping an eye on the place for the owner, a tough old woman named Smitty, resigned to a life he cynically describes as one happily involving "no work, no worries, no wife."

Once roused from his lethargy, however, Thursday demonstrates, especially to himself, that he is still an effective investigator. One measure of his increased self-esteem is his success in weaning himself from alcohol. However, despite rescuing his son from his kidnappers, all is not rosy at the end of the novel. For one thing, several people have been killed during the course of the case, including three by his own hand. Even more painful to him is the disillusionment he experiences when he learns that the mastermind behind the kidnapping was his friend Smitty, whom he depended on for aid and support during his time on the skids. In a confrontation at the end of the novel, she pulls a shotgun on him, leaving him little choice but to kill her. The novel ends with Thursday, having emptied his gun into her body, sitting disconsolately, "his fingers spasmodically squeezing the trigger."

Thanks to his rehabilitation in *Guilty Bystander,* when we next meet Thursday in *Fatal Step* (1948) he has resumed his career as a private eye and has even opened his own office, though business is slow. Yet he is still a troubled man, especially by all the killing he was responsible for in *Guilty Bystander*. He admits to having spent many uneasy nights filled with "nightmares of stiffened shapes falling toward him, constantly falling," and he "still didn't dare trust himself with a gun." To make matters worse, his problems aren't private any longer as his exploits have been splashed all over the front pages of a local newspaper, where he has been branded a "licensed killer." This has brought him clients, but the wrong kind, mainly those looking for a hired gun. Now he must overcome a negative public image as well as his own personal demons.

When a client tries to hire him to prove that his murdered son was not guilty of any wrongdoing before his death, Thursday is at first reluctant to take the case. "A murder investigation is no job for a private detective," he explains to the father, then adds ominously, "I don't dare get mixed up in a murder case again. It might be the last time all over."[12] Despite his reservations, however, he takes the case, and in the end not only establishes the boy's innocence but in a showdown with the members of the local gang responsible for the boy's death, prides himself in besting them without using his gun. But his satisfaction turns out to be fleeting, for shortly afterwards he awakens on a stretcher, having been blown through a window in an explosion. He managed to escape death in the blast, but he has not escaped his twin demons of guilt and self-doubt, for he learns that moments before the blast he had once again reflexively emptied his gun, this time into the body of the man with the bomb.

In the next three novels in the series—*Uneasy Street* (1948), *Calamity Fair*, and *Murder Charge* (both 1950)—the personal drama that has heretofore been unfolding is all but ignored. We learn that Thursday has surrendered his gun license and has sold his .45, but other than that little is made of his violent proclivities, and he settles down comfortably into the standard mold of the traditional private eye. It isn't until the final novel in the series, *Shoot to Kill* (1951), that Thursday's private drama once again becomes the focus of the action.

Over the course of the series Thursday has become roman-
tically involved with Merle Osborn, the reporter for the *San
Diego Sentinel* who was responsible for sensationalizing the
killings he committed in *Guilty Bystander*. After a four-year
affair that Thursday expects will one day end in marriage, he
is shocked by Merle's announcement at the beginning of
Shoot to Kill that she wishes to end the relationship. What
pains him most is his discovery of the real reason—she has
fallen in love with another man, Miles Weaver, whom
Thursday dislikes. One night, in a jealous snit, he follows
Weaver from Merle's place to the apartment of his estranged
wife. Moments later, he sees him leave in a rush. Upon investigating, Thursday discovers the reason for his hasty
retreat: Weaver's wife has been strangled to death. Pleased
that he can pin the murder on his rival, he plants a handkerchief belonging to Weaver (which he had fortuitously
picked up by mistake earlier when the two men were at
Merle's apartment) on the body so the police will be sure to
nab him for the crime Thursday assumes he committed.

The following day, however, he discovers that he has
made a terrible mistake—he planted his *own* handkerchief,
which leaves him no choice but to explain to his old friend
Lieutenant Clapp, a regular character in the series, exactly
what he had done. It appears to Clapp that Thursday, acting
out of jealousy, was attempting to frame Weaver. Stung by
embarrassment, and struck now also by the very real
possibility that he might have implicated an innocent man in
murder (after all, he has no real proof that Weaver actually
killed his wife), he feels compelled to do what he can to
clear up the matter by trying to determine the identity of the
killer himself. This places him in the odd position of
working to establish the innocence of the man who is his
rival for the affections of the woman he loves. His final act in
the series is thus a gallant one, as he makes it possible for
Merle to be happy with the man, he is forced to admit, she
really loves.

The Thursday books thus fall into two distinct groups:

those (like *Guilty Bystander, Fatal Step,* and *Shoot to Kill*) in which personal drama is intimately intertwined with the mystery elements; and those (like *Uneasy Street, Calamity Fair,* and *Murder Charge*) which are ordinary, run-of-the-mill mysteries. In *Murder Charge,* for example, because he bears a resemblance to an underworld figure wounded in an assassination attempt, Thursday agrees to the police request that he pose as the gangster for twenty-five dollars a day in order to infiltrate the San Diego underworld. Few private eyes have ever exhibited such a sense of civic responsibility, nor would most ever cooperate with the police to quite this extent. One suspects that the authors had a ready-made mystery available and simply plunked Thursday into the main role. The most effective books in the series are unquestionably those distinguished by the attention paid to Thursday's personal drama, where the interest is not limited to the unfolding of the mystery, but also includes the development of the private eye himself.

Like Paul Pine, the character of Thursday owes much to Philip Marlowe, for although he would have us believe that, like many of the early private eyes, he is in business mainly for the money—"I'm not weighed down with many [scruples]. . . . First, last and always I'm in the business for money. Scruples never earn money"[13]—his actions belie his words. For example, when in *Fatal Step* he is presented with an opportunity to trade some information he has for virtually any figure he wishes to name, all he bargains for is a simple note that will clear the name of his client's son. Moreover, his claim about scruples being unprofitable notwithstanding, he is a man clearly guided by principles. Thus although he contends that "anybody that makes loud noises about ethics like I do isn't any paragon, you can bet,"[14] the reader is invited to view Thursday as a man who, like Marlowe, strives to be a good man in a bad world.

Thursday is an ordinary man, as common, as his name suggests, as one of the days of the week. He doesn't see himself as a hero, just a "run-of-the-mill private cop" with an unpretentious view toward his work. "I'm not tough," he insists. "I just do the only job I know how to do in the only way I know how to do it."[15] Unlike some of his colleagues, who boast about their moral or intellectual superiority to the police, he maintains a cozy working relationship with the San Diego police, especially with Lieutenant Clapp, who treats Thursday like a son. Never does he gloat over beating the police to the solution of a crime, which he often does. He understands that he owes his success to the fact that, unlike the police, he can focus all his attention on a single problem. Also, he often has a stronger personal incentive, such as finding his own son or clearing his name, for getting to the bottom of things.

Thursday enjoys his work ("My business is my pleasure"), yet he is sensitive enough to be disturbed by certain aspects of it. In *Calamity Fair,* for instance, he finds it necessary to sleep with a woman in order to search her apartment, but then feels "grubby" afterwards. "The needle spray didn't wash off the way he felt." Although he enjoys the investigation that leads to the exposure of a salesman who was stealing from his employer in *Shoot to Kill,* he hates the embarrassing scene that follows when the man is confronted with the evidence of his guilt. "Inside he was sick of himself. He could enjoy the work of trapping, but never this inevitable slaughter of another man's pride."[16] Nor is he immune to troubling night thoughts, as in *Calamity Fair,* where he lies awake worrying about the morality of his methods. Thursday is not a hero nor does he feel obliged to live up to the demands of some ideal conception of himself. He simply desires to do the right thing and to control those elements within himself, such as his itchy trigger finger, that he knows to be bad. He is, like Marlowe, a man of conscience who realizes he must struggle to remain vigilant lest he be sucked into the vortex of violence that he must inevitably confront in his chosen profession.

The Robert Wade-Bill Miller collaboration began in high school and continued through San Diego State College, where they edited the *East San Diego Press.* Following service in World War II (both were sergeants in the Air Force), they resumed their collaboration, producing their first book as Wade Miller, *Deadly Weapon* (1946), an excellent private-eye novel which includes one of the most surprising endings in the genre. Following their success with the Max Thursday series (six books over a five-year period, one of which [*Guilty Bystander*] was made into a film in 1950 with Zachary Scott as Thursday) the duo turned to other efforts, both under the Wade Miller byline and under another successful pseudonym, Whit Masterson, which Robert Wade continued to use after the death of his partner in 1961.

The Thursday novels are competently written, skillfully plotted, and fast paced, aided in large part by the authors' characteristic habit of beginning each chapter with the day and time of the events included therein, which imparts the effect of a minute-by-minute account to the action. The portrayal of character in the novels is effective, especially the recurring figures of Lieutenant Clapp, a decent man and concerned father, saddened but still not cynical despite "twenty years of watching people at their bloodiest," and Merle Osborn, a woman who is forced to hide her attractiveness behind a masculine appearance in order to compete successfully in the male-dominated newspaper profession. Probably because two authors were involved in the writing of the novels, they are narrated in third-person rather than the first-person technique used so effectively in most private-eye novels, although the private side of Thursday is nonetheless fully expressed. The dual authorship did, however, produce some oddities. The solution to the crime in *Fatal Step* hinges upon Thursday's discovery that two characters were actually one character disguised as two. A variation on this gimmick also occurs in *Uneasy Street,* where a man is revealed to have been posing as his dead sister as well as himself. Intentionally or not, the authors were in such instances hinting at their own situation of being two authors posing as one.

Although the Thursday series is uneven, the novels provide further evidence of the widespread popularity of the private eye in the years immediately following the end of World War II. The best of them also attest to the special interest that writers, thanks to Chandler's strong influence, began to display in the character of the hero, as he was increasingly being portrayed as the center of interest rather than simply as a solver of crimes.

Carney Wilde

(Bart Spicer)

Carney Wilde is a Philadelphia-based private eye who appeared in seven novels by Bart Spicer published between 1949 and 1959. Like most of the postwar private eyes, Wilde was a veteran who embarked on a career as a private detective following his discharge from service in World War II. Unlike most of his colleagues, however, he was so bitten by the get-ahead bug and became so upwardly mobile that he ceased entirely to function as a private detective. Rags-to-riches success stories are popular in American literature but, as Spicer demonstrated, they can be fatal in private-eye fiction.

After the war, Wilde set up shop in an office decorated with used furniture he purchased from the building superintendent for five dollars. He is kept afloat financially during his tough early days in business by Eli Jonas, a kindly department store owner who put him on retainer to oversee the security in his store. Now, after three years in business, he has reached the point where he no longer needs Jonas's work, but he promises "there would never be a time when I didn't want to work for him."

In most regards Wilde is a private eye in the Philip

Marlowe tradition. He carries a gun, but seldom uses it. He is realistic about the violent aspects of his profession, but tries to avoid dangerous confrontations whenever possible. He refuses to take divorce cases, even when he needs the money, because he finds the work distasteful. He prefers cases in which he has a personal interest, as in *Blues for the Prince* (1950), where he labors to defend the reputation of a dead jazz composer he admires from accusations that his compositions were stolen from another man. A compassionate man, Wilde withholds information from a woman who wants to believe there was a good reason for her husband's thievery. "If it made her feel any better to believe that her Willie was a small-scale Robin Hood, I wasn't going to argue it."[17] A sensitive man, he worries that the world he knows contains "too much dark distrust, too much pain and too much hate" and is distressed by certain aspects of his job, such as being forced to bully a frightened girl in order to get information from her. A loyal man, he will do anything for Eli Jonas and for his good friend Lt. Jack Grodnik, a Philadelphia policeman he admires and respects, including putting his own reputation on the line in order to clear Grodnik of bribery charges that have been leveled at him.

But what distinguishes Wilde from Marlowe and from virtually every other private eye is his rapid rise up the ladder of success. By the time of his fourth appearance in *Black Sheep, Run* (1951), he has achieved his longtime dream—he heads an agency called Carney Wilde, Inc., has a new office and a full-time employee working for him. The following year, in *The Long Green,* his agency employs two men full time and has four others on retainer. In *The Taming of Carney Wilde* (1954) his outfit has grown to twelve employees, he earns $200 a week in salary, and has $8,000 stashed in his personal bank account. By the time of his seventh and final appearance in *Exit Running* five years later, his business has expanded into Wilde Protective Systems, Inc., and he now has two hundred men in his employ.

Unfortunately, his success spelled the end for the series, for in becoming a nine-to-five businessman whose main excitement comes when somebody loots the petty cash, he lost his credibility as a private eye. His motives shift from personal ones to largely business concerns. In *The Taming of Carney Wilde,* his pursuit of a fleeing embezzler is motivated in large part by his desire to protect the reputation of his firm, which was responsible for the security of the bank from which the money was stolen. His transformation from an investigator into a busy executive moves him right out of the fraternity of lonely, dedicated private eyes who devote themselves to accomplishing their personal visions of justice. Instead of justice, Wilde must concern himself with balance sheets, incompetent employees, a fleet of radio cars, a shipload of burglar alarms, and various other equipment installed all over Philadelphia.

As if this weren't enough to bring a halt to his career, Spicer ignores his own hero's warning that "nobody in my racket has any business with a wife" and marries off Wilde in *Exit Running* to Ellen Pomeroy, a beautiful Philadelphia photographer he had met in his previous case, *The Taming of Carney Wilde.* The titles of these, his final two appearances, are certainly prophetic. To make matters worse, his wife is a delicate soul with "an intemperate and unexplainable dread of violence, even of a voice raised in anger," and so he frets about protecting her from every hint of the more violent side of his profession. The combination of Wilde's new domesticity and his ascent to the presidency of what amounts to a large corporation brought the series to a dead end and Spicer wisely abandoned any further Wilde adventures.

Anthony Boucher, who praised Spicer's work for being "as human and even tender as it is hard and tough," credited him, along with Ross Macdonald, with leading the renascence of the tough detective story following the war.[18] As a character, Carney Wilde embodies those qualities one associates with the best of the believable private eyes.

Spicer's novels make good use of setting and atmosphere, especially those (like *The Long Green,* set in Arizona, and *The Taming of Carney Wilde,* whose action takes place on a Mississippi riverboat headed for the Mardi Gras celebration in New Orleans), which move beyond the Philadelphia setting of the other books in the series. And while he largely avoids the wisecracking humor and colorful similes characteristic of the genre, Spicer's straightforward, unadorned prose achieves a quiet grace of its own.

Especially noteworthy is his skill in characterization and his success in developing believable relationships between his characters. For example, his portrayal of Lieutenant Grodnik, a veteran when we first meet him in *The Dark Light* of twenty-seven years on the force, is both credible and humane. Although he gives the appearance of being an indolent fat man, Grodnik is a real pro with a tough, sure mind behind his warm restful eyes, which often lull the unsuspecting into underestimating his abilities. Because of his respect and affection for Grodnik, Wilde cooperates fully with the Philadelphia police. When Grodnik's reputation is threatened by accusations made against him, it is Wilde who works to clear his name. For his part, Grodnik, while never effusive in his praise for Wilde, displays a paternal affection for his friend. He usually calls him "son" or "boy." One of his greatest disappointments comes when his daughter Jane, with whom Wilde had seemed to be developing more than a casual relationship, surprises the two of them by marrying Penn Maxwell, Wilde's chief operative. Grodnik had secretly hoped that Wilde would become his son-in-law.

Spicer's books are also distinctive for their credible and sympathetic portrayal of black characters. In the novels of most of his contemporaries, blacks are either totally ignored or presented in stereotyped roles. Spicer was one of the few writers of his time, especially in the mystery genre, who sought to go beyond the stereotypes. Wilde's clients and several of the key characters in his first two cases are black, and without windy analysis Spicer manages to make telling comments about their plight through his depiction of such characters as Andrew Jackson, Wilde's client in *The Dark Light,* who thoughtfully walks a half step behind Wilde on the sidewalk so he could pretend he didn't know him if he so chooses; Lawrence Owens in *Blues for the Prince,* a doctor who is both nervous and excited because after seven years of practice he is being allowed to treat his first white patient; and Randolph Greene, also in *Blues for the Prince,* an angry young black whose testiness becomes understandable when Wilde learns that despite being a Phi Beta Kappa college graduate, the best job he can find is operating an elevator. Spicer never allows the racial themes to intrude, yet he manages to incorporate and spotlight them quite effectively in his mystery novels.

Bart Spicer was born in Virginia in 1918. He entered the army at the beginning of World War II and, in the manner of his detective hero, rapidly rose through the ranks, eventually attaining the rank of captain. After working as a journalist and as a radio news writer, he turned to fiction, publishing his first novel, *The Dark Light,* Carney Wilde's debut appearance, in 1949. Although he chose to abandon his private-eye hero a decade later, he did not cease writing, continuing to produce fiction until the 1970s. Under the name Jay Barbette, he and his wife Betty Coe also wrote four mystery novels that were published during the 1950s. Although Carney Wilde today is little known, Spicer is another of those underrated authors who deserve recognition for their efforts in striving to accomplish the same ends that writers like Chandler were aiming for: that is, to create believable characters and situations; to extend the boundaries of detective fiction beyond the limited concerns of tough-guy fiction; to elevate mystery writing to the level of serious literature. It is ironic that in achieving his ends so effectively, Spicer moved beyond the mystery genre entirely.

Shell Scott

(Richard Prather)

A leading pioneer in the field of original paperback publication was Fawcett Books which, as distributor for New American Library paperbacks, was contractually prohibited from issuing reprints of its own. However, it was not prevented from publishing original works, and in 1950, under its Gold Medal imprint, Fawcett launched a series of original paperback private-eye novels written by Richard S. Prather that demonstrated the potential of the new venture by eventually racking up sales of over forty million copies.

Prather's detective hero is a tall, thirty-year-old ex-Marine named Shell Scott, who opened an office in downtown Los Angeles following his discharge from service in the South Pacific during World War II. He resides at the Spartan Apartment Hotel in Hollywood, where he keeps his prized possessions: two aquarium tanks for his tropical fish, whose activities he watches to relax; a gaudy yard-square painting of a nude woman he calls Amelia, which he bought at a hock shop; and his books, with a taste that runs to authors like Frank Harris and Henry Miller. His physical appearance is especially distinctive. His inch-long hair is ''as white as sheets bleached in new improved Bleacho'' and sticks up into the air ''as if a small bleached porcupine were curled up on my scalp.'' His white eyebrows look like inverted v's above his eyes. His nose is bent and broken. And a chunk of his left ear is missing, a legacy from a shooting incident. All in all, he is forced to concede, he isn't a pretty picture, though women certainly don't find him unattractive.

A modest man, Scott doesn't fancy himself as any sort of superhero, nor is he afraid to acknowledge his shortcomings. He knows he isn't the smartest man in the world and often admits to being afraid. When a gang of hoods rough him up, he readily confesses that "if things kept going the way they were, the hoods could have the United States. They could have the world."[19] In the presence of a beautiful woman, his confidence often deserts him, leaving him stumbling and stuttering like a tongue-tied adolescent. Scott feels under no obligation to live up to any image, self-imposed or otherwise, of himself as a tough guy or as a knight in shining armor—or even as a Don Juan. He's far too realistic for any of those burdens.

Scott's ancestors aren't the tough guys like the Continental Op and Sam Spade (about his only similarity to Spade is his v-shaped eyebrows), nor the thoughtful, reflective ones like Philip Marlowe, but rather the fun-lovers like Dan Turner and Bill Crane. He is neither a crusader for justice nor a self-appointed one-man avenger of society's evils. In his view the police are perfectly capable of performing their duty and performing it well, and he always has a good word for the police he meets, especially Captain Phil Samson, his best friend and the "best cop I've ever met." He isn't driven by any obsession with money or with compassion for distressed souls. Nor does getting to the bottom of things have quite the urgency for him that it does for some of his fellow detectives. Blithely free of guilt, nagging self-doubts, compulsive anger, or any other such personal demons, Scott is simply a happy-go-lucky private eye who enjoys his work, especially when it brings him into contact with beautiful women—in which case he describes himself as "happy-go-lookie." He doesn't go out of his way looking for women, he just has an uncanny knack for finding himself in situations any healthy man would envy, and he makes the most of them.

In the first several entries in the series, Scott acts like a conventional private eye, his tales sober, straightforward, and unremarkable. What eventually gives the books their distinctive flavor is a combination of the comic tone that begins to emerge and the wildly unconventional situations Scott manages to get himself into. In *Strip for Murder* (1955), for example, his client turns out to be a member of a nudist colony and he has to go undercover, so to speak, to solve the crime. In *The Cockeyed Corpse* (1964), he is sent to a film site in Arizona to investigate the death of an actress, only to find when he gets there that the film in question is an all-female nude Western. In *The Sure Thing* (1975), he is hired to find a Mideast oil sheik's *six* missing wives. To accomplish their goals, private eyes sometimes adopt disguises, but few have ever assumed such bizarre ones as Scott. In *Strip for Murder,* he agrees to pose as the nudist camp's activity director, which requires him to shed his clothes and lead one hundred naked men and women in morning calisthenics. Later in the same novel he actually dons a knight's armor in order to gain entrance to a nightclub with a medieval decor. Seated atop a horse, he even attacks a man with his lance. In *The Cockeyed Corpse,* he is reduced to disguising himself as a rock by hiding inside a fake boulder he finds on a movie set.

His narrow escapes from perilous situations are also carried out with typical Scott flair. In *Way of a Wanton* (1952), for instance, he eludes two men who are chasing him on the set of a jungle movie by grabbing a rope and swinging, Tarzan-style, to safety. Unlike Tarzan, however, he isn't even wearing a loincloth, and his relief is short-lived when he drops, naked, smack into the middle of a scene being filmed on a nearby set. In *Strip for Murder,* again naked, he escapes a nudist colony by grabbing onto a gas-filled balloon. Unfortunately, the winds carry him all over Los Angeles, eventually dropping him at City Hall. Sometimes, Scott's derring-do is more absurd than embarrassing, as in *The Trojan Hearse* (1964), where he rides a demolition ball through the wall of a building while in pursuit of a suspect. In such instances, one suspects Prather of parodying his own excesses.

In addition to the many awkward and disconcerting

predicaments that bedevil him, Scott's lively style of narration is also a source of humor in the novels. Breezy, irreverent, and self-deprecating, his narratives offer an entertaining blend of puns, flippant remarks, and clever word play. Whether skewering the movie industry by calling it "the filmflam crowd," or a fashion designer in the throes of creative imagination by commenting, "Yeah, he sort of throes up, doesn't he?", his attitudes are brashly irreverent. Many of his choicest remarks are reserved for descriptions of the gorgeous women he meets. He describes one woman's assets: "She had what counts where it counts if you count up to two." Another has an "hour-glass figure in forty seconds of swimsuit." A third is a "tomato who had not ripened on the Hollywood-and-Vine." His characteristic propensity for puns is given free rein in *Take a Murder, Darling* (1958) when he is allowed to sit in on an advertising-agency session in which a name is being selected for a new brassiere. He contributes such offerings as "Finders Keepers," "Peek-a-Boo-Boo," and "Dishonesty Is the Bust Policy," though none of these is as catchy as his description in *Kill the Clown* (1962) of a bra called "Booby Hatch," which to him "looked as if the inmates were escaping." Prather's penchant for puns is also freely displayed in his choice of titles, such as *The Scrambled Yeggs, Three's a Shroud, Slab Happy, The Trojan Hearse,* and so on.

Despite his generally waggish attitude, Scott occasionally casts a serious eye on a subject, such as Hollywood and its excesses, although his soapbox harangues of such targets as corrupt labor unions and liberal politicians, represented in *The Trojan Hearse* by a U. S. Presidential candidate named Horatio M. Humble, sometimes become strident. One subject that is never treated flippantly, however, is violence. Death is a very real element in the books, and Scott tries to avoid killing when he can. Although he customarily carries a .38 Colt special, if possible he shoots to wound rather than kill because, as he once confessed, "to see a man killed violently is one of the most bonechilling sights in the world.''[20] He won't hesitate in administering a brutal beating to someone who deserves it, but unlike some of his brethren he takes no special pleasure in the deed. "I wasn't doing it because I enjoyed it," he confesses in the midst of an assault on one character. "I didn't enjoy it.''[21]

Richard Scott Prather was born in 1921 in Santa Ana, California. Following a stint in the Merchant Marines (1942–45) and a brief career as a clerk at March Air Force Base in Riverside, California (1945–49), he turned to writing, publishing his first Shell Scott novel, *The Case of the Vanishing Beauty,* in 1950. All told, he wrote thirty-four Scott novels, including one, *Double in Trouble* (1959), co-authored with Stephen Marlowe, in which Scott is paired with another popular Fawcett paperback hero, Chet Drum. All but a handful of them were paperback originals, first for Fawcett and later for Pocket Books. For over twenty-five years, Prather demonstrated—and his sales figures confirmed it—that he could keep his large readership entertained with his patented blend of crime and frivolity.

Prather's intention was not so much to parody the conventions of private-eye fiction as it was simply to introduce a comic touch wherever he could. The mystery and detection elements are usually handled in a straightforward manner. The humor is introduced either in the predicaments Scott encounters along the way, or in his jaunty telling of the tale. In an introduction to *The Comfortable Coffin,* a collection of humorous mysteries he edited in 1960, Prather complained that we are "beset these days by much designed to make us feel miserable.''[22] In his view, "we are in imminent danger of drowning entirely in misery and tired blood," thanks to a "flood of woe and weeping, of pessimism and Freudian cuckooism" sweeping across the country. By focusing on what he called "the light vein rather than the gory artery," he sought to dispel some of that grim misery in favor of a lightness of touch. While some might be put off by his odd mixture of comedy and murder, disappointed by the lack of verisimilitude in the books, or even annoyed by his refusal to adopt a properly respectful attitude toward the private-eye format, millions of readers found his formula both entertaining and satisfying. While it is true that Scott never develops as a character (he remains thirty years old for the entire series) and that Prather contributed nothing of lasting significance to the genre (his novels are about as serious and substantial as an hour-long television detective drama), the Shell Scott series is nevertheless notable for providing cheerful and entertaining reading for the mass market audience.

Mike Hammer

(Mickey Spillane)

Mickey Spillane's Mike Hammer is the black sheep of the private-eye brotherhood. On the one hand, Hammer's adventures have earned for his creator a level of popular success far beyond the wildest dreams of all but a select few of his fellow mystery writers. On a list compiled in 1967 of all the best-selling books (not just mysteries) published in America between 1895 and 1965, for example, seven of the top twenty-nine were written by Spillane.[23] Personally, Spillane has also become something of a celebrity, playing himself in one film (*Ring of Fear,* 1954) and Mike Hammer in another (*The Girl Hunters,* 1963). He has also appeared in the television series *Columbo* and in recent years has become a featured star along with a bevy of ex-athletes in a series of popular television beer commercials.

On the other hand, the Mike Hammer books have been almost universally scorned by critics, and even by some fellow mystery writers. Reactions have ranged from Raymond Chandler's dismissal of Spillane's writing as unreadable ("Pulp writing at its worst was never as bad as this stuff"[24]) to George P. Elliott's savaging of the Hammer books as "nothing but stews of slime and slop."[25] Even his father is quoted as describing his son's books as "crud."[26] The Hammer series has been labeled both a "perversion"[27] and "the ultimate degradation"[28] of the private-eye tradition. "By most traditional literary or artistic standards," says John Cawelti, "the works of Mickey Spillane are simply atrocious."[29] Anthony Boucher thought Spillane's *I, The Jury* read like "required reading in a Gestapo training school,"[30] and Mike Hammer has been likened to everything from a "homocidal paranoic"[31] to a "plainclothes Nazi."[32] "The most nauseating, and clinically disquieting, thing about these books," in the view of Julian Symons, "is that Mike Hammer is the hero"[33] rather than the villain Symons suggests he really is.

What did Spillane do to earn such vilification? This deafening chorus of derision cannot be explained away simply as a reaction prompted by jealousy at his resounding success or as the all-too-familiar disparagement that often follows in the wake of the immensely popular. Nor can it entirely be accounted for by a distaste for Spillane's right-wing politics. What lies behind the critical outrage is simply a very forceful repudiation of the character of Mike Hammer himself, although ironically enough it is Hammer's character that also in large part accounts for Spillane's enormous popularity.

From the beginning, the private detective has been portrayed as an outsider operating independently of the duly constituted authorities, though most private eyes stayed within the law themselves. Mike Hammer recognizes no law but his own, and while he often cooperates with the police (or at least with his old friend, Captain Pat Chambers of the New York Police Department), he clearly considers himself above the restraints of the law. He doesn't view himself as intellectually superior to the police, as the Holmesian detective does, nor morally superior to their corrupt officials, as

Philip Marlowe does. Hammer is simply meaner than the police. "I don't underrate the cops," he admits. "But cops can't break a guy's arm to make him talk, and they can't shove his teeth in with a muzzle of a .45 to remind him that you aren't fooling."[34] But he can, and he does. Certainly other private eyes have enjoyed the freedom to act without worrying about the restraints of departmental regulations and red tape, but few have taken this as an excuse for the liberties that Hammer takes.

In Hammer's opinion, the law is simply ineffective in dealing with criminals, and thus a man with guts, like himself, must step in and take matters into his own hands. Unlike the police, he doesn't seek convictions, he seeks satisfaction, which means he wants the killer himself. The problem with juries is that they have to be fair, but Hammer doesn't. "I'm the law," he boasts, "and I'm not going to be cold and impartial."[35] Thus he acts, not in the service of community justice, but as a substitute for it, as a one-man, self-ordained judge, jury, and executioner. The titles of his first three books—*I, The Jury* (1947), *My Gun Is Quick* (1950) and *Vengeance Is Mine* (1950)—reinforce his self-appointed role as lone avenger. In pursuit of his prey, Hammer doesn't feel bound by any innocent-until-proven-guilty constitutional niceties. When he's on the trail of a killer, nothing can stop him until he has dispatched the culprit himself, and if this requires him to be more vicious, more cold-blooded, and more violent than the criminal he is after, then so be it.

As long as he retains his private-detective license, which he is in dread fear of losing, he considers himself to have a license to kill, his methods and actions justified in his mind by nothing more than his hatred of criminals. "I hate the bastards that make society a thing to be laughed at and preyed upon," he announces. "I hate them so much I can kill without the slightest compunction."[36] In the case of a powerful enemy like Communism, there are no holds barred. "Kill 'em left and right, show 'em that we aren't so soft after all. Kill, kill, kill, kill!," he cries.[37] However, Hammer's let-them-eat-bullets brand of justice does have its drawbacks. In the first five Hammer books alone, by one accounting, forty-eight people are killed, thirty-four of whom would have lived had Hammer kept his nose out of things—certainly a steep price to pay simply to satisfy his obsession with personal justice.

Violence has always been associated with the hard-boiled detective, but most private eyes have been sensitive to its dangers to the soul. The Continental Op, for instance, fearful about becoming tainted by the violence he unleashed in Poisonville, fretted in *Red Harvest* that he was going "blood-simple" like the natives. But no such concerns trouble Mike Hammer, who is the most violent and most sadistic of all private eyes. The capacity for violence and vigilantism that was present but held in check by even his most bloodthirsty predecessors is unleashed and celebrated in Mike Hammer. It isn't just that he, like many of his colleagues, is required on occasion to resort to violent methods; he goes out of his way to employ violence, and he openly takes pleasure in it. One can perhaps understand, if not totally accept, his obsession with bringing killers to justice. What is troubling are his methods of securing that justice and his total disregard of everything save his own need for revenge. "I loved to shoot killers," he boasts, adding, "I couldn't think of anything I'd rather do than shoot a killer and watch his blood trace a slimy path across the floor."[38]

It is apparent that Hammer's obsession with finding the killer is only an excuse for the unleashing of his own sadism and the satisfaction of his blood-lust. His motivation is not a quest for the truth or even a simple desire to secure the demands of justice. In fact, he almost never has a paying client. Armed with his menacing .45, which he variously but affectionately calls "old betsy," "old junior," and "old ironsides," he is a killer on the hunt, driven by a burning desire for revenge, hatred oozing from his pores like sweat. No amount of blather about his justification in dealing harshly with those who are themselves cold-blooded murderers can excuse his actions or fully account for the thrill he gets from killing his prey.

For Hammer it isn't enough that the killer must die, he must (as in the case of his prey in *My Gun Is Quick*) die "slower and harder than any son of a bitch had ever died before," during the process of which he fully intends to "laugh my god-damn head off." In that novel he is satisfied only after brutally killing his victim with his bare hands in one of the grisliest scenes in private-eye fiction. "[I] took that head like a sodden rag and smashed and smashed and smashed and there was no satisfying, solid thump, but a sickening squashing sound that splashed all over me." In *Vengeance Is Mine,* he kicks a man so hard in the face that his teeth come off on his shoe, and in *Kiss Me, Deadly,* he actually pulls the eyes out of a man's face. Nothing, however, matches the orgy of violence at the end of *One Lonely Night,* where he smashes a hole in the forehead of one man with a rifle butt, snaps another's back, shoots the arm off a third, then allows him to take a good look at it lying on the floor before he blasts him to oblivion. Finally he walks around the room shooting the faces off all the bodies. His reaction: "God, but it was fun. It was the way I liked it."

It isn't just killers who bear the brunt of Hammer's hostility. He hates homosexuals ("hate" is one of his favorite words) and gleefully dumps a pitcher of water on some gays who are arguing under his window. He smashes together the heads of two guys who make a harmless comment as he walks by them with a beautiful woman at his side. He flips a lighted cigarette into the eye of another man who makes the mistake of putting his arm around the woman he is with. He turns the simple act of paying an elevator operator for some information into a hostile one by stuffing the money into the man's mouth. He prevents one suspect from escaping by pounding a four-inch nail through his hand, and he shows his displeasure towards a woman who is a Communist by stripping off her clothes and whipping her with his belt. His method of relating to women he likes reveals a similar sadistic streak. He habitually squeezes them so violently they are left gasping for breath and wincing in pain. Even his manner of displaying affection for Velda, his loyal secretary and true love—faking a punch at her jaw—is tinged with violence. Hammer pushes, pulls, pokes, shoves, rams, yanks, slams, and bullies his way through the most violent series of private-eye novels ever written.

Yet while many critics and readers found his actions repugnant, it is precisely Hammer's bulldozer tactics that caught the fancy of the millions of readers who made Spillane such a best-selling writer. While it would doubtlessly be unfair to suggest that every reader heartily endorsed Hammer's brutally sadistic methods, there can be no denying that there was widespread approval of his attitudes and his decisiveness in dealing with problems that to many seemed impervious to the slow and deliberate movement of due process. Race Williams, it will be recalled, emerged amidst the frustration and confusion that characterized the turbulent years following World War I. Mike Hammer was created under similar conditions following the end of World War II. He embodied his reader's indignation (and paranoia) about such enemies as the Mafia and the Communists, and he provided an escape valve for his sense of outrage and feelings of impotence in the face of such dangers. Instead of dismissing Hammer as a simple personification of violence and vigilantism, perhaps the reader ought to acknowledge, as one critic has suggested, that Spillane's work exposes "the dark side of the American psyche" and recognize that in the character of Hammer he has given us a view "of the nastier side of ourselves that is no less true for being disgusting and horrifying. America the beautiful is also America the hateful."[39]

Not all of Spillane's popularity, however, can be accounted for by Mike Hammer's simplistic solutions to complex problems. His largely male readership was undoubtedly also attracted to the books because of their heavy emphasis

on sex, with Hammer an embodiment of the standard
adolescent male fantasy. Virtually every woman he meets is
an absolute knockout, and, despite the fact that Hammer
himself is far from handsome, women find him irresistible,
surrendering instinctively to his overpowering male-
ness—which Spillane equates with toughness. The women
aren't merely pliable, either, they are downright aggressive,
one after the other eagerly wiggling out of her clothes as
soon as possible and parading around naked in an attempt to
coax Hammer into bed with her.

The easy availability of women is only part of the sexual
fantasy played out in the books. The other half centers
around Hammer's beautiful secretary Velda, who in addition
to being a stunning beauty is also tough (she packs a gun and
has her own P.I. license), understanding, and totally devoted
to her boss. Hammer's attitude toward Velda reveals all the
symptoms of the classic madonna complex, for although he
swears undying love for her and promises marriage (theirs is
one of the longest engagements on record), he refuses to
have sex with her (though poor Velda does her best to
dissuade him). Even when he is reunited with her after a
seven-year absence (during which time he became a drunk
and lost forty pounds because he thought she was dead), he
still refuses to bed her. He has no hesitation about yanking
down the sheets to leer at her naked body, but sex with
Velda is out until marriage. Of course he never allows his
devotion to her to interfere with his sexual activities with
other women, for Hammer is a firm believer in the double
standard: sex is OK for him (and for all the "loose" women
he meets) but is verboten with (and for) the Virgin Queen he
intends to marry. Thus Hammer enjoys the best of both
worlds—all the sex he wants, plus the faithful devotion and
complete understanding of the woman he will one day,
perhaps when he tires of all those other women, make his
wife.

As for the emphasis on sex in the Hammer books, what we
are offered is not the active participation of the satyr but the

leering fascination of the voyeur. The women are all gorgeous creatures with enticing bodies and pneumatic breasts whose sole function is to serve as instruments of Hammer's pleasure, which is largely visual. After feasting his eyes on their naked mounds and clefts, and after being flattered by their seductive pleas, he can love 'em or leave 'em, depending on his mood and the urgency of his business. Although he is seldom the seducer, he is thus always in control and never has to worry about rejection. Whenever he deigns to sample the merchandise, he and his panting partner usually do so offstage, as Spillane is never explicit as far as actual descriptions of sexual activity are concerned. This leering attitude toward sex anticipates the success of another purveyor of lusty fantasies—*Playboy* magazine—which made its debut in 1953 at the height of Spillane's popularity. Like *Playboy*'s, Hammer's sex is uncomplicated, uninvolving, and largely voyeuristic.

Raymond Chandler once observed that the fictional private eye is "an exaggeration—a fantasy," then added, "but at least he's an exaggeration of the possible."[40] In his skillful hands, Philip Marlowe matured into a complex and believable "exaggeration of the possible." Hammer on the other hand is all exaggeration, all wish-fulfillment, whether it be in the form of one's desire to take violent and decisive measures to eliminate complicated problems without giving a damn for the consequences, or in the form of being overpoweringly irresistible to every beautiful woman one meets. According to Spillane, Mike Hammer was originally created as a comic book hero named "Mike Danger." In writing the Hammer novels all he did was transfer his larger-than-life superhero from the comics to what can be described as a comic-book novel, where credibility plays as important a role as it does in a Superman adventure.

Mickey Spillane, the son of a bartender, was born in Brooklyn, New York, in 1918. After a brief stay at Fort Hays State College in Kansas and a stint in the Air Force during World War II, he turned to writing, but unlike an earlier generation of mystery writers who served their apprenticeship in the pulps, he began as a writer of comic books, turning out stories for such comics as *The Human Torch, Captain America,* and *Captain Marvel.* His first novel, *I, The Jury,* was written in only nine days, but it became such a smash success that Spillane, who had not written the book with a series in mind, quickly turned out six more Hammer novels, five of them published between 1950 and 1952. The sixth, *The Twisted Thing,* did not appear until 1966. Following his conversion to the Jehovah's Witnesses in 1952, Spillane retired from writing for the next ten years. He returned to the business in 1962 with *The Girl Hunters,* which was quickly followed by four more titles published over the next eight years, although these were decidedly pale imitations of the earlier Hammer novels. Drastically toned down are the sex (except in *Survival . . . Zero*), violence, and intense, overpowering hatred that energized the earlier books, with Hammer now relying more on detection than confrontation in his war against criminals. Mike Hammer was also featured in a 1983 made-for-television movie, not written by Spillane, in which he discovers he is the father of an eighteen-year-old-girl. As might be expected, both the daughter and her mother die before the end of the film, thus freeing Hammer for future exploits. Spillane also created a James Bond-type espionage agent named Tiger Mann, who appeared in four novels. In recent years, though, his writing has been limited to mystery books for children, which is in a sense a return to his origins, for he started out as a writer of comic books aimed at young readers.

To his credit, unlike some other popular writers who confuse sales with quality, Spillane has never made extravagant claims for his fiction. He self-deprecatingly describes himself as "the chewing gum of American literature."[41] To those who say his work is garbage, he replies, "but it's good garbage."[42] The fact that he has been scorned by the critics doesn't particularly bother him, given his success with readers. "The only award I've ever gotten is the ringing of the cash register from the public."[43] Characterizing himself as a writer rather than an author, he acknowledges that his primary motivation is money: "Creative urge, hell—I get a money urge."[44] Thus the reason for his lengthy retirement from writing at the height of his popularity is not difficult to fathom: "Why write," he asks, "if you don't need the money?"[45]

He has had his defenders, among them novelist Ayn Rand, who said, "Spillane gives me the feeling of hearing a military band in a public park."[46] Fellow mystery writer Michael Avallone placed *I, The Jury* fourth on his list of "The 11 Best Private Eye Novels of Them All," right after Hammett's *The Maltese Falcon,* Chandler's *Farewell, My Lovely,* and Ross Macdonald's *The Way Some People Die.*[47] Yet no one has ever accused Spillane of being a literary stylist. The fact is, he is a lousy writer. *Newsweek* once tartly suggested that his works demonstrate "that the surest way to be widely read is to be unreadable."[48] For all of Hammer's hard-boiled attitudes and tough posturing, Spillane's prose is frequently given over to an overripe, overblown rhetoric, marked by heavy doses of sentimental rubbish and melodramatic claptrap. But what even his detractors have to concede is a powerful narrative drive and a flair for the dramatic ending. "Telling a story is like sex," he explains. "You read a story to get to the end, not to the middle. It's like the satisfaction of an orgasm."[49] He has produced some of the most explosive endings in mystery fiction, especially that of *I, The Jury,* where the beautiful Charlotte Manning performs a provocative strip tease in order to dissuade Hammer from killing her. When he plugs her despite her best efforts, she asks, "How c-could you?" and he replies, "It was easy."

Spillane also prides himself on his speed in writing. "It only takes me two weeks to write a book," he brags.[50] He refuses to revise anything he writes. "Anything worth correcting isn't worth writing in the first place."[51] This attitude may account for his indifference toward plot and language in his books. The reader is thus left to wade through sluggish prose and forgettable plots populated by faceless (though in the case of the females anything but bodyless) characters, all for the sake of getting to the promised kick-in-the-pants ending.

In the end, Spillane offered little that was new, for Mike Hammer is essentially little more than a meaner and more sexually active version of the very first private eye, Race Williams. Two of Williams's most famous pronouncements—"My ethics are my own" and "I never bumped off a guy what didn't need it"—might well have come from the mouth of Mike Hammer, although Hammer's methods of executing his prey are far more extravagantly violent than Williams's favored method of delivering a single bullet between the culprit's eyes. Both private eyes have been known to sleep with loaded guns under their pillows. Both share a starry-eyed devotion to a single woman, although Hammer is far more sexually active than Williams, in this regard resembling more the libidinous Dan Turner. Both share an evangelic fervor in their self-ordained mission of stamping out the scum that is infesting New York City and preserving the republic from threats to its security from foreign powers.

Both writers also display a marked propensity for the melodramatic, illustrated by their habit of giving their villains such names as The Hidden Hand, The Beast, and The Head Tag (Daly) or The Snake and The Dragon (Spillane). For a while, readers were even able to follow the adventures of both heroes at the same time, for the Race Williams stories kept appearing until 1955, though by this time he was totally overshadowed by Mike Hammer. The many parallels between both writers aren't surprising, given Spillane's frank admiration for Daly. "I always liked the Race Williams stories so much," he once confessed. "I used to say that's the kind of story that I'm going to write."[52] A kind of hidden tribute to Daly can perhaps be detected in Spillane's first novel, where the friend whose death launches Hammer's crusade against criminals is aptly named Williams.

Following Spillane, writers were offered a clear-cut choice: they could either heed the example of Raymond Chandler and create a believable human hero whom the reader was invited to admire for his vigilance in struggling to adhere to a strict code of ethical behavior in a violent and immoral world; or they could follow Spillane's lead and create a vigilante hero with whose anger and frustration, and sexual success, the reader was encouraged to identify. Those writers who were motivated by nothing more elevated than the ringing of the cash register found all the encouragement they needed in Spillane's whopping sales figures. Spillane's primary contribution to the private-eye genre has thus been the spawning of an entire generation of Revengers, Executioners, Penetrators, Destroyers, and Lone Wolves who joined Mike Hammer in riding the wave of sex and violence to the crest of popular success.

5

The Compassionate Eye

Although Mike Hammer dominated the private-eye field in the early 1950s, at least as far as sales are concerned, he was hardly the sole influence on the genre. Counterbalancing his iron-fisted, vengeance-driven assault against the forces of evil in the world were a number of private eyes who shed the tough-guy image and bloody methods of their pulp forebears and instead adopted as their credo a readiness to serve their fellow man. While Mike Hammer was hacking his way through the criminal underworld, private eyes like Ross Macdonald's Lew Archer, Thomas B. Dewey's Mac, William Campbell Gault's Brock Callahan, and Michael Collins's Dan Fortune were going about their business with compassion rather than savagery, mercy rather than vengeance. The hard-boiled hero was softening and becoming more humane under the guiding hand of these writers.

Lew Archer

(Ross Macdonald)

Along with Dashiell Hammett and Raymond Chandler, the writer who has made the greatest contribution to the private-eye novel is Ross Macdonald, though when he began writing he labored very much under the influence of his illustrious predecessors. After publishing four novels under his real name, Kenneth Millar, between 1944 and 1948, Macdonald turned out his first private-eye novel in 1949. He published the book under the name John Macdonald so as to avoid confusion with his wife, Margaret Millar, who was writing mysteries under her own name. Later he was forced to change his name to John Ross Macdonald to avoid confusion with John D. MacDonald; then he simply dropped the first name and became Ross Macdonald.

Lew Archer, whose name was taken from Miles Archer, Sam Spade's murdered partner in *The Maltese Falcon,* started out like most of the other postwar private eyes as a tough-talking ("I'd like to mess up your brilliant pan sometimes"), wisecracking, cynical man ("There was nothing wrong with Southern California that a rise in the ocean level wouldn't cure") whose work, which he describes as "peeping on fleabag hotels, untying marital knots, blackmailing blackmailers out of business," is anything but heroic.

Born in Long Beach, Archer attended grade school in Oakland, then returned to Long Beach and became a "junior-grade hood," involved in gang fights and car thefts. A whiskey-smelling plainclothesman who caught him shoplifting a battery from Sears set him straight by warning him where his actions were going to lead. Later he joined the Long Beach Police department, but left after five years because of his conscience. "There were too many cases where the official version clashed with the facts I knew," he explains, though whether he was fired or left of his own volition is unclear. He then opened an office on Sunset Boulevard in Hollywood and became a private investigator chasing after missing persons and straying husbands. But the key event in his personal history is the departure of his wife Sue, who left because she didn't approve of his job or of the company he kept. She still figures prominently in his thoughts, but despite several attempts at reconciliation, he is doomed to remain a lonely man because of the failure of his marriage.

For the first half-dozen books in the series, there is little to distinguish Archer from the other Marlovian private eyes who flourished in the postwar years. But in 1956, thanks to what he termed "seismic disturbances . . . in my life,"[1] Macdonald and his family moved to the San Francisco area for a year while he underwent a period of psychotherapy, an experience that produced some significant changes in his books. First came *The Doomsters* (1958), which he declared "marked a fairly clean break with the Chandler tradition . . . and freed me to make my own approach to the crimes and sorrows of life,"[2] followed by *The Galton Case* (1959), which represented a significant turning away from the traditional hard-boiled tale in favor of a mystery novel with considerable psychological and symbolic overtones. In that novel Archer is hired by an elderly woman to find the son she hasn't seen in twenty-three years. During his investigation he meets up with the missing man's son, who for his own reasons is searching for his father. As Archer continues to plumb the depths of the family's troubled past, the complex interweaving of fathers and sons begins to reverberate with mythic overtones (notably the Oedipus legend) and also produces the kind of convoluted plot that would become characteristic of Macdonald's later novels. Macdonald's complicated plots are no accidents but rather what he terms "vehicles of meaning," their dense complexity embodying his belief that everything—from incidents in the past to crimes in the present and from one family member to another—is part of a single pattern. As he began to gaze inward rather than outward, Macdonald produced novels that were richer, more complex, more satisfying, and more moving.

Macdonald's shift to more highly personal themes in his books was accompanied by a transformation of Archer from an investigator of crime into an interrogator of people, from a questor after justice into a questioner of human behavior. His concern shifts from pursuit of the guilty to attention to the needs of the victims. "Other people's lives are my business," he proclaims. "And my passion. And my obsession, too, I guess. I've never been able to see much in the world besides the people in it."[3] With increasing urgency, Archer devotes his efforts to healing wounds, to bridging gaps between people, to mending fractures in relationships, to assisting the troubled to deeper self-knowledge. No longer a slayer of dragons in the knightly tradition of Philip Marlowe, Archer instead labors to exorcise the demons that lie lurking in the pasts of the characters he meets. For the Op, each case was a job he strove to do well. For Marlowe, a case became a moral crusade. For Archer, a case leads him on an emotional and psychological odyssey into the past and into the self, forcing him to assume the multiple roles of psychologist, marriage counselor, social worker, and clergyman.

As his works became more personal, Macdonald's attitude toward Archer became more complex. On the one hand, he openly acknowledged his intimate relationship with his hero. "Archer was created from the inside out. I wasn't Archer, exactly, but Archer was me." He described him variously as a "welder's mask" enabling him to handle "dangerously hot material,"[4] "protective lead" interposed between himself and "the radioactive material," and an "obvious self-protection which holds the eye . . . while more secret selves creep out of the woodwork behind the locked door."[5] Yet despite Archer's role as an instrument of self-examination, Macdonald at the same time insisted on his

distance from his hero. Unlike Chandler, whose detective
was in many ways a fantasy projection of himself, Macdonald stoutly insisted, "I could never write of Archer [as
Chandler did of Marlowe]: 'He is the hero, he is
everything.' " Macdonald labored to make Archer "a deliberately narrowed version of the writing self, so narrow
that when he turns sideways he almost disappears" because
he did not want the reader to identify too closely with either
his exploits or his attitudes. He intended Archer to be simply
"the lens I look through"[6] and the "consciousness in which
the meanings of other lives emerge."

One can observe a close parallel between Nick Carraway,
the narrator of F. Scott Fitzgerald's *The Great Gatsby* (a
novel Macdonald admitted he reread yearly), and Archer,
especially in their roles as secondary characters who are
primary sources of information about the other characters in
the book. Like Carraway, Archer does have a distinct personality and his attitudes are crucial in molding the reader's
response to the other characters. But because Archer is, according to his creator, "not the main object of my interest,
nor the character with whose fate I am most concerned,"
Macdonald is freed of the need to celebrate his "physical or
sexual prowess" and the burden of making him "consistently funny and charming." One of his main criticisms of
Chandler was that he was too bound up with the character
of Marlowe. He would work diligently to keep Archer's
private life from intruding too noticeably on his dual task of
investigator into and narrator of other people's lives.

In his capacity as investigator into other people's lives, Archer relies not on rugged fists or a deadly .38 but rather on a
sympathetic ear, a compassionate heart, and an empathic
spirit. In *The Zebra-Striped Hearse,* he lists the qualities he
considers essential in a detective: "honesty, imagination,
curiosity, and a love of people." Notice he says nothing
about toughness, courage, a thick skull, or an accurate
trigger finger. These were all right for an earlier generation of

private eyes but for a man like Archer, whose primary concern is the victim rather than the criminal, what is needed is an openness to people and a readiness to offer them assistance. He isn't out to rid the world of evil. Chandler's "detective-as-redeemer" is, in Macdonald's opinion, "a backward step in the direction of sentimental romance." His desire is to minister to the wounded and troubled souls in the world. His credo is a simple one: "The problem was to love people, try to serve them, without wanting anything from them."[7]

What motivates a man like Archer to become so intensely involved in the private lives of the people he meets? It certainly isn't money or even loyalty to his clients, for his efforts serve many who aren't actually his employers. One answer is that he is simply a man of uncommon decency, compassion, and understanding. But there is more to it than this. Archer obviously reflects his creator's personal concerns. The fatherly interest Archer takes in lost and troubled children clearly reflects, as Macdonald has frequently admitted, his own unhappy background: his father moved out when he was three years old, and by the time he was sixteen, by his own accounting, he had lived in fifty different rooms. Himself a problem youth who was set straight before it was too late, Archer is also shown to have a special interest in helping those who might be saved from future trouble by the intervention of a caring person. A divorced man who has suffered the pain of a failed marriage, he has a special understanding of those experiencing similar problems and an affinity for those with whose pain he is able to identify. Because of his divorce, Archer is a loner who needs to fill a void in his own life, and his compulsion to try to patch up teetering relationships in the lives of others can also be seen as a way of atoning for his own failure with Sue. Having experienced disappointment and personal unhappiness in his own life, he has attained both a deeper understanding of his own flawed humanity ("We were all guilty. We had to learn to live with it'') as well as a more profound sympathy for those who suffer, which produces in him an attitude that clearly projects the message, ''I care, I understand.''

The Archer series does not depend for its success entirely on Archer himself or on his special mission. Macdonald's depiction of the Southern California setting, for example, is the equal of Chandler's. Like Chandler, he brought to his portrayal of Southern Californian manners and morals a dual perspective. An American by birth, born in Los Gatos, California, in 1915, he was raised in Canada, which allowed him to give Archer ''the fresh suspicious eye of a semi-outsider who is fascinated but not completely taken in by the customs of the natives.'' Thus we get in the books a satirical put-down of many of the excesses of Southern California society, especially Hollywood, as well as an examination of phenomena which, while not restricted to California, are more noticeably on display there: shattered dreams, broken homes, fractured lives, disappointed hopes. As Archer makes his way through the well-trimmed suburbs filled with affluent people and comfortable homes, he exposes the tragedies and fears, the sadnesses and failures that are the stuff of human suffering everywhere. A novelist of considerable social acumen, Macdonald effectively evokes a specific sense of place, yet although the actual physical setting of the novels is Southern California, it is the social and emotional landscape of American life, especially during the troubled 1960s and 1970s, that is his primary concern.

Macdonald is also a prose stylist without peer in the genre. Recipient of a Ph.D. in English Literature from the University of Michigan in 1951 (his dissertation subject was the English poet, Samuel Taylor Coleridge), Macdonald has acknowledged how the study of literature has influenced his own writing. ''I think I am one of the few American detective story writers who have been fortunate enough to be able to learn from the poets how to handle imagery,'' he said. He is both a master of imagery and, like Chandler, a wizard with the simile, although where Chandler displayed a propensity for the strikingly unexpected comparison, Macdonald aims for the simile that is both surprising *and* meaningful. For example, this line from *The Underground Man*—"A gold wedding band was sunk in the flesh of one finger like a scar"—is startling in its originality yet it also sets off reverberations in the mind thanks to its thematic aptness. It was such stylistic virtuosity as this that prompted novelist Eudora Welty, in her influential *New York Times Book Review* essay on *The Underground Man,* to liken Macdonald's writing to "a stand of clean, cool, well-branched, well-tended trees in which bright birds can flash and perch. And not for show, but to sing."[8]

Macdonald has earned well-deserved popular and critical success with his Archer series. Ever since William Goldman reviewed *The Goodbye Look* on the front page of the *New York Times Book Review* in 1969, where he called the Archer books "the finest series of detective novels ever written by an American," Macdonald's books have been best sellers in hardcover. He has been featured on the cover of *Newsweek* magazine. Archer has been played by Paul Newman twice in films (*Harper* [1966], based on *The Moving Target,* and *The Drowning Pool* [1975]). His work has been the subject of numerous laudatory books and articles. The reason for his elevated reputation is not difficult to understand. He brought to the private-eye story a seriousness of purpose as well as an artistry in execution. By combining the novelist's concern with structure, plot, character, and setting, the poet's attention to language, image, and symbol, and the sensitive man's understanding of the deepest recesses of the human mind and heart, he has fashioned works of art that repeatedly confirm Chandler's contention that the mystery story could enter the realm of serious literature.

Mac

(Thomas B. Dewey)

One of the most consistently satisfying private-eye series features a detective known only as Mac, who appeared in sixteen novels written by Thomas B. Dewey between 1947 and 1970. By fusing the dogged professionalism of Hammett's Op with the knightly attitudes of Philip Marlowe, Dewey created in Mac a figure of uncommon decency, tenaciousness, and unfailing believability.

Mac grew up in the Chicago slums, where he was often involved in gang fights and run-ins with the police. Eventually, thanks to the influence of a local ward heeler, he joined the police force, where he came under the tutelage of a wise veteran named Donovan, who turned him into a good cop. But he became *too* good a cop, getting himself booted from the force for solving a crime that someone with more authority than he did not want solved. With Donovan's help, he obtained a private detective license, and now, fifteen years later, he still remembers his personal and professional debt to his mentor. "He's more of a father to me than the real one I had once," he declares, and the two men retain a close personal relationship throughout the series, even though they work on different sides of the street.

Aside from the above information, we learn very little about Mac as a person. Like the Continental Op, he is a man whose identity is defined almost entirely in terms of his work. He has no hobbies, no outside interests, no friends other than Donovan, no romantic interests, nothing outside of work. One indication of how closely interwoven are his personal and professional lives is the fact that his first-floor flat on the near North Side of Chicago also serves as his office, thus making him always available to clients. He occasionally drops into Tony's across the street for a sandwich and a beer, but that is the extent of his social life. The rest of the time he is either out working on a case or at home waiting for a client seeking help.

Over the years Mac has earned a well-deserved reputation for honesty and integrity. One client hired him after three people named him as the one person they could trust with a million dollars in cash. The most valuable quality a client who hires him gets is his dogged persistence. Mac doesn't rest until he has all the answers he needs, and a client never has to worry about private concerns interfering with his work, for he has none. A good example of his tenacity occurs in *Deadline* (1966), where he races the clock to uncover evidence that will forestall the execution of a young man convicted of murder. Against all odds, and with no cooperation from the tight-lipped community where the crime was committed, he succeeds.

Although he thus resembles Hammett's Op both in his relentless pursuit of the solution to a crime and in his dedication to his work, there is an important difference between Mac and the Op. As an employee of the Continental Detective Agency, the Op felt duty-bound out of loyalty to his employer to do the best job he could do. Mac, who once declined an offer to join a large agency because of his fierce independence, has no organization toward which he feels obligated. His dedication is entirely self-imposed, which doesn't make it any less binding. As he explains to a physician who is treating an injury to his ankle, his responsibility to his work is as serious and as compelling as a doctor's. "Sometimes I have to do my job whether I feel like it or not—like you," he tells the doctor. "I'd like to go to bed and forget [the case]. But I can't quite do it—any more than you could turn me down when I called this afternoon."[9]

Mac also considers his clients to be more than just his employers. Like Marlowe, he becomes a crusader for their welfare. Mac isn't ordinarily a very reflective man, usually keeping his thoughts to himself, but during the course of the series he mentions two dreams of his that serve to illuminate his primary concerns. In the first, a kind of pipedream, he discloses his secret hope, the motivating principle behind all his actions. "Someday you were going to nail all the dirty guys and only nice people would be left. Then there wouldn't be any need for cops and you could retire and live on a farm and get a good night's sleep."[10] This is the romantic idealist side of Mac, characterized by the impulse to make the world a better place for all the good and decent people. In his other dream, a recurring one with a darker hue, he expresses his deepest fear: "The faces and situations change, but the pattern stays the same—some force which terrifies me and against which I am helpless proceeds to commit atrocities against children, while I look on, trying to scream for help, unable to make myself heard."[11] These two impulses—the desire to make the world a better place and the fear that he will be unable to prevent all the suffering that occurs, especially that involving children, the most helpless victims—define the dimensions of his personal crusade.

For no matter what job he is actually hired to perform, it is the welfare of his client that becomes his primary concern. "My client was more important to me than the assignments," is his guiding principle. Sometimes his loyalty is sworn to someone who never actually becomes a client, as in *The Case of the Murdered Model* (1954), where his involvement in a case is prompted simply by information he receives that a murdered woman had circled his number in the phone book, presumably to call him about some matter. Although she never actually contacted him, he feels obliged to solve her murder. In *Death and Taxes* (1967), a gangster confers with him about a case, but is killed before Mac agrees to accept the assignment. No matter—that is enough to earn his involvement.

It is the young, however, who prompt his deepest and strongest personal commitment. In *Every Bet's a Sure Thing* (1953), for example, he is hired to tail a woman traveling cross country to Los Angeles. On the train his attention is drawn to the woman's two young children. It is they who become his chief concern, the job he was hired to do relegated to secondary importance. When the woman is gunned down shortly after arriving in Los Angeles, he takes the children under his wing and at the end of the book even arranges for Donovan's childless daughter and her husband to adopt them. This is only one instance of many in a career-long interest in the young. One can, in fact, trace the history of various youth movements in the U.S. over several decades simply by examining Mac's involvement: *The Mean Streets* (1955), whose title is a conscious echo of Chandler, treats the problem of juvenile deliquency, a matter of pressing concern in the 1950s; in *A Sad Song Singing* (1963), one of the best novels in the series, the action is played out against the background of the folksinging milieu of the early 1960s; in *The Love-Death Thing* (1969), Mac travels to L. A. and finds himself smack in the middle of the hippie scene of the late 1960s.

The particulars of time and place may change (Mac's cases take him from Chicago to southern Illinois, rural Indiana, and even to Los Angeles, where in his final case, *The Taurus Trip* [1970], he relocates his office), but what remains unaltered is Mac's unwavering decency and dedication, especially to the health and welfare of the young. The key to understanding his motivation in this regard can perhaps be found in the events of his own life. His father was killed when he was a boy and it was only the guiding hand of Donovan that helped him turn out all right. His own experience has taught him the importance of having someone in your life who cares about you. His commitment to the young is one way of repaying his debt to Donovan.

Despite his best efforts, however, Mac knows he cannot always insure happiness for those he takes under his wing. Sometimes, as in *You've Got Him Cold* (1958), where he unites a man with the daughter he never knew he had, he achieves positive results. But he can do nothing to prevent the disappointment his client, a seventeen-year-old girl, suffers in *A Sad Song Singing* when he must inform her that her missing boyfriend not only is dead but that he used her as a decoy to allow him to elude some people pursuing him. All he can do is comfort her and guide her through her ordeal, and, noting her condition when she first comes to him, see that she gets a clean bed and some proper food. In situations like this, he operates less like a crime solver and more like a compassionate angel of mercy.

In his cases Mac comes alive, his involvement in the lives of others supplying meaning to his own life. They also bring him into contact with individuals whom he admires and respects, Good Samaritans like the doctor in *Every Bet's a Sure Thing* who treats his ankle injury and who lends him his car, the cab driver in *Death and Taxes* who offers assistance beyond merely transporting him from one place to another, and the fellow private eye he meets in *The King Killers* (1968) who earns his respect when he learns that the man's efforts are motivated by a desire to repay a friend who had saved his life during the war. Mac's affection for such characters is proportionate to the degree that they mirror his own compassionate inclinations. Sadly, though, the relationships he develops with these good souls are always transitory. His oft-repeated compliment, "He was a good man," is matched by the equally oft-repeated lament, "I never saw him again." Mac requires a case in order to be able to exercise the compassion and sympathy that are hallmarks of his character, but once his work is over, he is fated to return, like Philip Marlowe, to a lonely room in a lonely building in a lonely world. Mac all but ceases to exist when his job is done.

His heart may be soft, but in other respects Mac is a tough individual, though unlike some of his colleagues he shows it not by dishing out punishment but by displaying a capacity for taking it. In *Every Bet's a Sure Thing,* he continues on the case despite being hobbled by a painful ankle injury suffered when he was forced to leap from a moving train. In *Death and Taxes,* a brutal beating fails to weaken his resolve to remain on a case. Beyond this, Mac also displays a tough inner core. Though he is attracted to women and a romantic relationship would certainly alleviate his loneliness, he declines all such opportunities for female companionship while on the job, for in his view "hardly ever does it happen that a pass made while working can possibly turn out to be anything better than what in the books they call a fiasco."[12] Mac is a man like the Op, who also stoically keeps all his doubts, fears, and despairs to himself.

Because Mac seldom either pauses to analyze his role as a Galahad-figure or frets at any length about the world's stubborn refusal to measure up to his preconceived standards, we cannot construct a profile of him on the basis of his observations or comments about the manners and morals of his society. As was true in the case of the Op, we must instead pay close attention to his actions, from which emerge a picture of a man of integrity, decency, compassion, honor, and dedication. In a hippie neighborhood in Los Angeles in the late 1960s, Mac notices a sign in a window which reads, "Work Is Love Made Visible," a slogan which might well be taken as his credo, for through his efforts on behalf of those in need of his help, he not only displays his deep affection for his fellow man, he also reveals his love for the tasks he undertakes to perform.

Unlike Chandler and some of his imitators, Dewey chose purposely not to focus too much attention on the personality of his detective. Attention is instead directed to the mystery itself by means of Dewey's generally well-constructed puzzle plots, and to the plight of the characters Mac meets rather than to his own personal crises. It is perhaps for this reason that Dewey never even gives Mac a full name. Though Mac does identify himself in his fifteenth book as Mac Robinson, there is some doubt that this is his real name, especially since it has often been mentioned that he is of Scottish descent. Dewey also purposely forgoes the colorful narrative style used so effectively by Chandler, Browne, and others as well as the witty repartee so characteristic of the private-eye breed. His intention is to avoid anything that might divert attention away from the primary business of the books, which is Mac's relationship with the other characters, not his personality. Although his novels lack the colorful verbal pyrotechnics of some of those in the genre, Dewey's straightforward narrative style nevertheless comes to assume a quiet dignity of its own.

Thomas B. Dewey, no relation to the former Governor of New York, though a distant kin to Admiral Dewey, was born in Elkhart, Indiana, in 1915. After receiving his degree from Kansas State Teacher's College in Emporia in 1936, he did graduate work at the University of Iowa, then worked at a variety of jobs: clerical worker, editor for a correspondence school, administrative and editorial assistant at the U.S. Department of State in Washington between 1942 and 1945, during which time he published his first novel, *Hue and Cry* (1944). In 1945 he began working for an advertising agency in Los Angeles, although he continued writing novels, including the first Mac book, *Draw the Curtain Close* (1947). He left his advertising job in 1952 and the following year published the second Mac novel, *Every Bet's a Sure Thing*. This was followed by fourteen more Mac books over the next seventeen years, as well as another series, this one in a lighter vein featuring a married L. A. private eye named Pete Schofield, who appeared in ten novels between 1957 and 1965. In addition to a gorgeous red-headed wife named Jeannie, Schofield possesses two other items lacking in Mac: a sense of humor and a facility for the wisecrack. In 1971, following the publication of the last Mac novel, Dewey joined the faculty of Arizona State University as an English professor, where he remained until his retirement in 1977. He received his Ph.D. in 1973 from UCLA.

Dewey's books earned high praise from reviewers, and Mac's popularity with readers kept the series alive for twenty-three years. In addition, his influence on younger writers cannot be discounted. Bill Pronzini, who went one step further than Dewey by giving his private eye neither a first nor a last name, credited Dewey with being the biggest influence on his work. Readers today, however, who wish to enjoy Mac's adventures must resort to libraries and used bookstores, though most will find their efforts well rewarded, for in his quiet and unassuming way Mac generates a fictional presence that is as genuine and convincing as that of any private detective who has ever walked the mean streets.

Brock Callahan

(William Campbell Gault)

William Campbell Gault is the last of the private-eye writers to have served his apprenticeship in the pulps. Born in Milwaukee, Wisconsin, in 1910, he sold his first story to the pulps in 1936, and over the next sixteen years, until their disappearance in the early 1950s, he sold hundreds more, mostly mysteries and sport stories. In 1952, with the pulp market gone, he wrote his first novel, *Don't Cry for Me,* which won an Edgar Award as the best first mystery of the year. Three years later, in *Ring around Rosa* (1955), he published the first in a series of novels that featured Los Angeles private eye Brock Callahan. Gault solved the problem of carving out a unique identity for his private detective by drawing upon his interest in both mysteries and sports. By making Callahan a former professional football player who becomes a private detective, he created a fresh and original addition to the private-eye fraternity.

Like Lew Archer, Brock (The Rock) Callahan grew up in Long Beach, the son of a policeman who was killed in a shootout with hoodlums. He attended Stanford University, where he became an All-American football player, then joined the Los Angeles Rams, where he played guard for nine

years, earning All-League honors several times. But the
career of a professional athlete is only temporary, and
following his retirement from the sport he had to select a
new occupation. Eager to capitalize on his well-known
name, but unwilling to accept any of the high school
coaching jobs offered to him, he chose to follow in his
father's footsteps and enter police work, though his independence led him into business as a private detective
rather than as a member of the regular police force.
(Callahan isn't the only former L. A. Ram to have become a
detective. The Rev. C. P. Randollph, a former quarterback
for the Rams, deftly combines the dual careers of minister
and detective in a recent series of novels written by Charles
Merrill Smith.)

Gault uses Callahan's football background as a meaningful
element in his character. Unlike most of his private-eye
colleagues, Callahan must frequently question whether he is
really suited to his new career, moving as he has from a line
of work in which he was recognized as a skilled professional
to one in which he is considered a rank amateur. He knows
only too well that being the son of a cop and knowing a few
policemen "didn't make me any Philip Marlowe." Besides,
as a lineman he was trained to rely on brute force, not on his
brains like the quarterback. Now he must learn to use his
head for something other than a battering ram—though it
helps considerably that he graduated in the top ten percent
of his class at Stanford.

The transition from the simple demands of the football
field, where his biggest worry was stopping the Bears, to the
dangerous realities of the mean streets, where he has to contend with matters of life and death, is an uneasy one. Life on
the playing field was easier because "we knew what we
were supposed to do and the scoreboard was always there to
tell us if we were doing it."[13] Life as a private eye is far more
complicated and uncertain, for he must develop his own inner scoreboard to tell him whether he is doing the right
thing. In this regard he is aided by his Catholic upbringing,

which left him with a conscience that constantly reminds him to do the right thing. Among the many pleasures of the series are watching Callahan convert those qualities that produced success on the football field—pride, persistence, self-confidence, dedication to hard work—into virtues in his new endeavor and observing him adjust to the demands of his new profession without compromising the honesty and integrity that are firm components of his character. He is careful, however, not to allow another quality that contributed to his success on the field—physical violence—to dominate his post-football work. Though he takes no guff from any man, he never throws his weight around or needlessly bullies people.

Another by-product of his football career is something few other private eyes have—a public reputation. This works both to his advantage and his disadvantage. On the one hand, it was what prompted him to open his office in the wealthy environs of Beverly Hills, where he hoped to cash in on his highly recognizable name. On the other, because he lacks the anonymity most other private eyes enjoy, he often finds his work impeded by people he intends to interrogate who are more interested in his views about the new Rams quarterback or the team's chances in the upcoming game against the 49ers than in providing him the information he seeks. Callahan's association with the Rams also serves another valuable function—it places him in the context of the real world. References to the game in which he nailed Otto Graham for a forty-six-yard loss or to the fact that his jersey sits in the Football Hall of Fame serve to convince the reader that he is something more than a mere fictional creation. Stepping from the sports pages to the pages of a mystery novel as Callahan has done helps to establish his credibility as a character.

Callahan also has something else most private eyes lack—a steady girlfriend, though she brings him as much grief as comfort. Jan Bonnett is a highly successful Beverly Hills interior decorator, a savvy businesswoman who knows how to make the most of her wealthy clientele. She specializes in rich customers with expensive tastes. Although Callahan serves the same clientele, as a man of simple bourgeois tastes (he lives in Westwood, drives a beat-up old car, and ordinarily drinks only beer) he lacks, according to Jan, the proper respect for money. This is a source of constant friction between the two. Jan disapproves of both his profession ("I wouldn't be happy married to a man content to wash other people's dirty linen for day wages"[14]) and his reluctance to milk his trade the way she milks hers (she calls him an "economic idiot"). To make matters worse, she is also a moody and mercurial character, which presents Callahan with another problem, for though he would like to marry her, and though he aims to remain faithful to her, he is also susceptible to the charms of other women. "I am monogamous by instinct," he insists, then adds, perhaps by way of rationalization, "but Jan is emotionally erratic, with long barren stretches for which I must maintain outside sources."[15] This situation allows him to enjoy a modestly active sex life, though his bedroom exploits are never trumpeted about, only presented as the normal affairs of a handsome man in his profession.

Although his romantic prospects with Jan would undoubtedly improve if his bank balance were healthier, Callahan's unwavering integrity and lofty principles prevent him from selling out just to be successful. "No man in my trade can afford lily-white ethical standards," he insists. Yet though he concedes he may cut a corner here and there, he never does anything illegal. He declines all shady job offers. "I'm always for rent but never for sale." In *Come Die with Me* he even refuses to charge a wealthy prospective client any fee until he first investigates to see whether or not he can help her. When a case interests him for personal reasons, he also refuses to charge a fee. His readiness to accept what he calls "charity cases" is another source of irritation to Jan, especially when several of them involve clients who could easily afford to pay a steep fee. Callahan's disdain for money is deep-seated. What is important to him is the quality of a man's character, not his bank balance. One of the reasons for his love for football is "That was one place where money didn't talk. A poor man can be something on a football field, looked up to."[16] When his wealthy aunt asks him what being honest ever got him, he replies without hesitation, "inner peace." "I may not be much," he concedes, "but I'm my own man."[17]

Burdened also with what he calls a "pathological compulsion to always protect the lambs," Callahan, in the concern he displays for the health and welfare of his fellow man, lives up to the standards of compassionate and concerned behavior established by such contemporaries of his as Mac and Lew Archer. Though he does not enter into other people's lives to the degree that Archer does ("I'm not a priest," he tells a young man who begins confessing his secrets to him), nor is he driven to fill a void in his own personal life by completing himself through others, he is admittedly a sucker for the underdog and a champion of those in distress. "I work for all the lambs, no matter who pays me."[18] Whether it is a promising young Ram quarterback in trouble (*Day of the Ram*), an eleven-year-old boy whose father is missing (*County Kill*) or a former teammate whose marriage is foundering and whose three-year-old child he fears will suffer if it breaks up (*Dead Hero*), Callahan puts financial considerations aside in order to do what he can to assist the needy, thus behaving, referring to both his romantic inclinations and his football physique, as a self-styled "knight with piano legs."

A prolific writer, Gault wrote, in addition to hundreds of pulps stories, a total of twenty-four crime novels, including a six-book series of paperback originals for Fawcett, featuring a Los Angeles private eye named Joe Puma, which appeared between 1958 and 1961, in the midst of the Callahan series. *Shakedown,* an Ace paperback novel Gault wrote in 1953 under the name "Roney Scott," featured a detective named Joe Puma, but all he retained when he began the Fawcett series in 1958 was the name of the main character. Puma and Callahan are cut from the same cloth. Although he lacks Callahan's football background and is Italian rather than Irish, Puma shares with Callahan everything from size (both weigh around 220 pounds), taste in beer (Einlicher), and daily rates (one hundred a day, plus expenses) to a code of behavior distinguished by rugged honesty and solid integrity.

In 1963, following the publication of the seventh Callahan adventure, *Dead Hero,* Gault retired from mystery writing to devote himself exclusively to the more lucrative field of writing for the juvenile market. "Though they weren't as much fun to write," he said of his juvenile novels, "they stayed in print much longer, earning me considerably more money"[19] than his mysteries had. All in all, he eventually produced a total of thirty-four juvenile books, most of them about football or auto racing.

Then in 1982, after a nineteen-year hiatus, Gault resumed his mystery-writing career by publishing two new Callahan novels, *The Bad Samaritan* and *The Cana Diversion,* both of which appeared in a series of original paperback mysteries put out by Raven House. Gault also wrote two additional Callahan novels for the same publisher, but with the demise of Raven House the fate of those two books is uncertain. According to Gault, he offered the title *The Bad Samaritan* to his friend and fellow Santa Barbara resident Ross Macdonald. Macdonald, who dedicated his final novel to Gault, declined the offer, so Gault felt obliged to write the book himself. Although nineteen years have passed since the publication of his last adventure, only a few months have elapsed in Callahan's life. He is still essentially the same character he was in *Dead Hero,* though some major changes in his life are about to occur. For one thing, Homer Gallup, the rich Texan who was once married to his Aunt Sheila and for whom he worked in *Vein of Violence* (1961), dies and leaves Callahan half his estate. Suddenly a rich man, he promptly marries Jan Bonnett, who no longer has any reason to carp about his financial affairs, and the newlyweds move to the quiet little community of Montevista, a suburb of San Valdesto located ninety miles north of Los Angeles. But the life of a retired rich man bores him, and when he starts worrying too much about the neighbors' dogs messing up his lawn and finds himself drinking too heavily, he knows he has to do something. The murder of a local resident and the request of another to find her missing daughter give him an excuse to return to action once again. He solves the murder, returns the missing girl to her mother, and even has an opportunity to play Good Samaritan to a couple of teenagers he picks up on his way to Los Angeles. He talks them into returning to their parents and even buys their bus tickets home. Freed from financial concerns, he is able now to devote himself to the kind of work he has really been interested in all along—aiding those in distress, protecting the lambs from the threats of the menacing wolves in the world.

The Cana Diversion presents an especially interesting situation as Joe Puma, the hero of Gault's other private-eye series, also turns up in the San Valdesto area, having himself recently moved there from Los Angeles. Unlike Callahan, Puma hasn't been fortunate enough to have a wealthy relative die and leave him money, so he has had to scramble to stay in business. He also isn't even lucky enough to stay alive, for he is murdered one night, which brings Callahan in from the sidelines once again. Puma may not have been a saint, but he was a friend and, more importantly, "one of ours," and as Sam Spade made clear years earlier when his partner was killed, it isn't good for business to let the murder of a fellow private eye go unsolved. Because he is also concerned about Puma's wife, whom he helps get a job, and son, who is about to enter law school, Callahan solves his murder without letting them know anything about the shady dealings Puma had become involved in.

Though he no longer has to eat meals at a lunch counter, since his wife hires a cook who can make Irish stew the way his mother used to do, and he has more time for golf and cocktail parties, Callahan's attitudes toward the wealthy remain unchanged. The life-style of the idle rich, which he sourly describes as comprising nothing more than "chitchat, persiflage, gossip and merriment, filling the void of the days before the big sleep," bores him. He uses his leisure time to picket the site of a proposed nuclear power plant and to work on cases—like the murder of Puma—that interest him personally. He still drives a fifteen-year-old Mustang, and his elevation to the country-cub set hasn't diminished his sympathies for the underdog. He continues to rail, as he has always done, against the wasteful materialism of his fellow countrymen and the inequalities of the American judicial system. Unlike Carney Wilde, Callahan is not tamed by marriage or success, and Gault proves that it is possible to marry off your private eye without destroying either his career or his believability.

As a writer Gault demonstrates several of the virtues and few of the defects of the pulp veteran. His stories are narrated at a crisp, sure pace with plenty of action to keep them moving, yet with care also taken in the depiction of character and creation of mood, setting and atmosphere. He isn't given to similes and poetic images in the manner of Chandler and Macdonald, though he does resemble both writers in his jaundiced attitude toward Southern California, from Los Angeles (which Callahan likens to a "creeping fungus") to the cozy insular environs of wealthy San Valdesto (which he describes as "a town with a minimum of smog and a maximum of rich people, a retreat from reality"). A man of honesty, integrity, and proletarian attitudes, Callahan displays an instinctive repugnance for the phony and the pretentious, a disgust for everything from professional wrestling (which to a former athlete like himself is an utter debasement of sports competition) to what he calls the "thespian fraudulence" that permeates the entire Los Angeles area, making it difficult to separate the genuine from the artificial.

In the character of Callahan, Gault has fashioned a

thoroughly believable detective hero, one who is humanized by being portrayed, thanks to his background, ethics, and values, as a man uneasy in his profession, constantly examining and evaluating his actions. He is never as certain of himself and his mission as such superhero private eyes as Mike Hammer. As a man with thoughts and opinions about many different topics, he also impresses us as a well-rounded individual who cares about his world and the quality of life lived therein. And thanks to his having been freed from the necessity of making a living in his most recent appearances, he can concentrate on the quality that aligns him most closely with his contemporaries—concern for the distressed. Brock Callahan is a welcome addition to the Good Samaritan squad of private eyes.

Dan Fortune

(Michael Collins)

Writers of private-eye fiction are a diverse lot, coming as they do from a wide variety of different backgrounds. A good example is Dennis Lynds, who was a chemist and an editor of scientific journals before becoming a writer. Born in St. Louis in 1924, he grew up in New York, served in the infantry in Europe during World War II (earning both the Purple Heart and three battle stars), and returned home to complete his education, first at Hofstra (where he received his B.A. in 1949), then at Syracuse (where he earned his M.A. in 1951). Between 1951 and 1965, he was employed primarily as an editor of chemical publications (*Chemical Week, Chemical Engineering Progress, Chemical Equipment*). During this time he also began writing, placing his short stories in several prestigious publications (*Minnesota*

Review, Hudson Review, New World Writing), though he also cranked out some eighty Mike Shayne novelettes under the Brett Halliday byline and eight Shadow novels under the Maxwell Grant byline. He also published two novels under his own name, *Combat Soldier* (1962) and *Uptown Downtown* (1963). But his most distinctive and impressive body of work began in 1967 when, under the name "Michael Collins," he published *Act of Fear,* the first of eleven novels featuring New York private eye Dan Fortune.

Dan Fortune—the original family name was Fortunowski, before his father, the son of a Polish immigrant, Americanized it—was born and raised in the Chelsea district of New York City, the son of a cop who was booted from the force for nearly killing a man he discovered with his wife and who shortly afterwards deserted his family. Between his younger days in New York and his return in his mid-40s to open an office in Chelsea as a private detective, Fortune lived a vagabond existence in such faraway places as San Francisco, London, Paris, Tokyo, and Amsterdam, where he worked, in addition to a stint in the Merchant Marines, as a waiter, farmhand, actor, and newspaperman. Along the way he also attended several colleges.

The single most important physical feature about Fortune is a missing left arm, lost at seventeen when it was damaged beyond repair while he was attempting to loot a ship. Though it earned for him the nickname "Danny the Pirate" in the neighborhood, he wisely decided that the life of crime was not for him. When he returned to Chelsea after an absence of several decades, it wasn't as a lawbreaker but as an enforcer of justice, private variety. His decision to become a private detective was prompted by many factors, although as is the case with most of his colleagues, money wasn't one of them. Fortune is an independent man and being a private eye allowed him to set his own conditions of employment. "One of the few things I was proud of," he announces, "was that I'd never worked for a corporation, big or small, never run for the 7:10 train every day, never done work I didn't want to at the moment."[20] He also possesses an inquiring mind, and an unsolved murder is like a mountain—it represents a challenge he feels compelled to meet. He is also motivated by a sense of justice. In *The Brass Rainbow* (1969), for example, he works to clear the name of a local two-bit hood because he is bothered by how easily the police, simply because of the man's shady reputation, conclude he is the guilty party. Finally, like most of his private-eye brethren, Fortune is prompted by private reasons. Once he takes a personal interest in a case, he sees it through to the end, driven by a strong commitment either to his client or, as in *Night of the Toads* (1970), simply to the memory of a dead woman who comes to impress him.

Working as he has at so many jobs over the years, Fortune has reached an important conclusion: "I never found work worth doing for its own sake," he admits. "The best I found was trying to solve other people's problems."[21] Though he acknowledges he makes his living from other people's troubles, he also understands that "maybe it's better to make your living from other people's troubles than from other people."[22] He often displays the same dedication to work that the Op did, though ordinarily it isn't work for its own sake that drives him. Like Mac and Lew Archer, he has discovered that being a private detective gives meaning to his life while it also offers him an opportunity to satisfy a basic urge to help others.

Like Brock Callahan's football background, Fortune's missing arm is used by Collins as something other than a simple identifying gimmick. To Collins, by the way, belongs the distinction of having created not one but *two* one-armed protagonists. Prior to the Dan Fortune books, he wrote a series of short stories in the 1960s for *Mike Shayne Mystery Magazine* which featured a one-armed character named Slot-Machine Kelly. The missing arm is an inventive conversation piece, as Fortune concocts a variety of colorful explanations for its absence, everything from having lost it during the Normandy invasion to surrendering it to sharks in Vietnam. It has also helped shape his character. A constant reminder of his vulnerability, it has made him a cautious man. It has forced him to rely more on his wits than on his physical strength, which has prevented him from adopting bullying tactics. Because he has had to learn to do many things in two steps rather than one, it has taught him the virtue of patience. The arm can also even be seen as a symbol of certain of those qualities—alienation from society, an incompleteness of self that demands participation in other people's lives—that are typical of the private eye's lot in life.

Although in many ways Fortune is more fully developed as a character than, say, Lew Archer, he is like Archer a man who enjoys very little in the way of a private life separate from his work. For the first several books in the series, he enjoys a romantic relationship with Marty Adair, an aspiring actress who dances semi-nude in clubs while awaiting her big break. But she tires of their relationship and announces her desire to marry another man. "With you I'd drift on and on without tomorrow," she complains. "Two castaways in a lifeboat."[23] Five years later, in *The Slasher* (1980), she summons him to California to investigate the murder of her second husband's niece. They sleep together once for old times sake, but that's it. To assuage his loneliness, Fortune engages in a few fleeting affairs, but his sex life can only be described as modest. There is virtually no sex in the Fortune books, which is ironic, considering that their paperback publisher is Playboy Press. Fortune seems to have only two friends: Joe Harris, a Chelsea bartender, and Captain Gazzo, a New York policeman who, because he once had an affair with Fortune's mother, takes a special interest in him. But Gazzo is killed in *The Night Runners* (1978) and Harris drops out of sight, which relegates Fortune to the kind of monastic life that is common among men in his profession. In fact, as the series continues, Fortune, who had earlier maintained separate living and working quarters, combines both into a single location when he moves into a third-floor loft on Twenty-second Street just off Eighth Avenue.

Fortune is a knowledgeable man, especially when it comes to music, as evidenced by his intimate familiarity with works by Bartok, Sibelius, Mahler, Shostakovich, and Nielsen, among others. He is interested in literature, and his narratives refer to such writers as Sean O'Casey, Maxim Gorky, and Isaak Babel. He is also a student of human behavior, and this, coupled with his experience as a private detective, has given him an understanding of, and a tolerance for, human weakness. For instance, he allows a woman who murdered her husband to go free because he recognizes that she acted in response to the heated emotions of the moment and will never kill again. Besides, she has young children and he believes she will be a good mother to them. Fortune finds it difficult to work up much hatred for any killer, realizing that most of them are creatures who act more from fear than from hate or greed. He is even able to extend tolerance toward his father, the hatred he once felt for the man for deserting his family now replaced by an understanding of the forces that drove him to act as he did. One item for which he has no tolerance, however, is the evil of Naziism. In *The Slasher* he refuses to cooperate with the CIA which, for reasons of its own, is anxious to keep a lid on his discovery of a former Nazi war criminal now living in Los Angeles. In his view, that is one evil that cannot be ignored or forgotten.

Although he possesses ample amounts of intelligence, sensitivity, and understanding, he is lacking in at least one area—he has virtually no sense of humor. His tales are devoid of wisecracks and witty remarks, his prose as serious and sober as he is. The books also lack the colorful and poetic descriptions characteristic of Chandler and Macdonald. Rather than striking similes Fortune favors comments and observations of a philosophical or sociological nature. Instead of aiming for a fresh and startlingly original way of describing the expression on the face of a person who has just been informed that someone he knew has been killed, for example, he pauses to analyze the factors that lay behind such an intense response. Fortune also regularly interrupts his narratives to interject comments on such diverse subjects as the correct way of pouring beer to insure a proper head and the desperate plight of those who inhabit the poorest sections of our cities. His pronouncements range from the trenchant ("No one lives in a smaller world than a city man") to the trite ("Who can say for sure what goes on inside the mind of a man, any man?"), and he sometimes displays a tendency to overstate the obvious. More often than not, however, Fortune rewards the reader with the sort of thought-provoking comment that shows him to be a man deeply concerned about the world and curious about its inhabitants and their behavior.

Fortune's debut appearance in *Act of Fear*, a novel which earned an Edgar Award as the best first mystery of 1967, established the pattern for the rest of the series. Two seemingly simple incidents—the mugging of a policeman and the disappearance of a neighborhood youth —inexorably lead Fortune to a far more serious matter, in this case a deadly dispute between rival factions within the Mafia. Whether hired initially simply to identify the name of a woman shown in a photograph (*The Silent Scream*), discourage the Broadway producer who has been making passes at his girlfriend (*Night of the Toads*), learn why a large corporation is unwilling to renew its lease for a parking lot a man operates on their property (*Blue Death*), or find the brother of a Connecticut businessman who is off on another of his gambling binges (*The Night Runners*), Fortune invariably moves from the routine to the unusual as his investigations bring him up against an odd assortment of characters, including a demented Chinese immigrant, Lithuanian freedom fighters, Bolivian revolutionaries, an Israeli pilot, a fugitive Indian, assorted Mafia hoodlums, and an eighty-year-old woman known as "Mother Death" for her role in Hitler's Third Reich.

There are few private-eye writers who take the care to construct the kind of intricate puzzles that Collins does, with the result that the reader's attention is focused more on the question of the identity of the killer than in the novels of most of his colleagues. But while plot is clearly a matter of considerable importance to him, it is not, as it is in the classic whodunit, the main concern, for he is far more involved with people than with puzzles, far more interested in exploring the complexities of human behavior than in shuffling the pieces in a puzzle. His elaborately constructed plots provide the satisfaction of a well-made puzzle, yet they are only the skeletons around which his thematic concerns are draped. Collins is very specific about his intentions:

> I write about people driven to violent actions by forces from inside and outside. The forces of the world in which they live. A real world. Our world. If anything distinguishes my books particularly from other books, it is that I write what could be called *socio-dramas*. I want to understand and show what made these people as they are, what created the pressures that will explode within them. What made them, then, act in a crisis as they acted, and what made violence their ultimate solution. [24]

He also insists that whether he writes under his own name or one of his many pseudonyms—Carl Dekker, Mark Sadler, William Arden, John Crowe—or whether he is writing "serious" literature or a crime novel—in his view "a novel is a novel, and 'genre' novels are no less novels than sonnets or ballads or sestinas are poems"[25]—he writes for the same purpose: "to know what makes our world tick—your world and mine—in all its strengths and its weaknesses, its hopes and its horrors, its everyday streets and its hidden corners."[26] Because a crime novel by its very nature focuses on a specific act of violence that is anti-social, it is his contention that "a society and its people, its pressures and its codes, its horrors and its hopes, can be seen in sharp outline"[27] at such moments. More than any other of his private-eye writing contemporaries, Collins is interested in the roots of human behavior and in understanding man not just as a psychological being but also in his social, political and philosophical dimensions as well.

Given his interest in the sociological aspects of crime, it isn't surprising that Collins devotes careful attention to setting in each of his books. The early novels make especially effective use of the Chelsea neighborhood, where Fortune is as much at home as Natty Bumppo in the wilderness. "The

city is my land," he declares. "I know how to hunt through
the solitary rooms and the faceless river of humanity,
through the forest of stone and the glare of neon, through
the shadows and the silence."[28] Collins paints a vivid picture
of the city and its people, going beyond the neon and glitter
to get at the distinctive flavor of Chelsea and its surrounding
neighborhoods. Realizing the limitations of a single setting,
Collins gradually extends the landscape of the series west-
ward into New Jersey, with its contrasting slums and well-
tended suburbs, and north and eastward into the wooded
communities and sloping lawns of Westchester County and
Connecticut. In recent novels, Fortune's cases have even
taken him to Southern California and to the mountains of
Arizona, but it is the neighborhoods of New York where he
is most at home and which provide the novels with their
convincing sense of place. Although Dennis Lynds has lived
since 1965 in Santa Barbara, California—also the home of
Ross Macdonald and William Campbell Gault—Collins,
whom he describes as an alter ego rather than a pen name,
has remained a New Yorker. "When I decided to write about
Dan Fortune, his city and his people," he explains, "I knew I
needed Michael Collins—the perpetual New Yorker no matter where he is."[29]

In the final analysis, Collins is a writer who adroitly uses
the private-eye format to fashion mystery novels that are
also probing studies of character with a decided
philosophical and sociological bent. While there is nothing
particularly original about the manner in which Fortune
goes about his business, and while the novels are seldom
elevated by stylistic flights of fancy, Collins has in his serious
and sober manner produced a body of work impressive for
its consistency and its humanity. By examining the issues of
crime and violence from many angles, from the
philosophical to the psychological, Collins aims to offer a
deeper understanding of what it means to be human, which
is, after all, what all good literature is really about.

6

After Archer

In 1972, the private eye celebrated his fiftieth anniversary as one of America's most popular heroes, yet despite the important contributions of dozens of able writers, it was largely three of them—Dashiell Hammett, Raymond Chandler, and Ross Macdonald—who, at least in the public mind, were identified with the genre and largely credited with shaping it from its infancy through its maturity. As Macdonald's career drew to a close in the 1970s (his final novel appeared in 1976) the inevitable question arose: Would there be a new name added to the Hammett-Chandler-Macdonald triumvirate, someone capable of carrying on and perhaps even modifying the tradition as his notable predecessors had done? While it may be too early to make a definitive judgment, the generally accepted leading candidate as *the* contemporary successor to the tradition that began with Hammett is novelist Robert B. Parker.

Spenser

(Robert B. Parker)

Because I have already written extensively about Parker's fiction in a previous volume in the *Recognitions* series (*Sons of Sam Spade* [1980]), I will comment only briefly on his work here. In the character of Boston private eye Spenser (no first name), he of the bulging biceps, quick wit, and smart mouth, Parker has created a hero who combines the two-fisted toughness of the early pulp heroes, Marlowe's knightly inclinations, and Archer's passionate concern for the welfare of the young with several of his own unique features. A former heavyweight boxer and a weightlifter, Spenser is also a gourmet cook and an educated and highly literate man. A muscular man, he is ready (and often eager) to throw his considerable weight around. He is also deeply sensitive to the feelings of others and is himself not afraid to show his emotions. An iconoclastic and often flippant in-dividual, he is also deadly serious about himself, his work, and his relationships. He is, in short, a complex individual trying to make his way through a complicated world.

Parker has revitalized and enriched the genre in several ways. For one thing, he has rediscovered the value of humor. Spenser is an irreverent soul and his narratives are liberally sprinkled with wit and wisecracks. There are few private eyes as entertaining as he is. Yet underneath the levity Parker addresses several issues—the importance of love between man and woman, husband and wife, parents and children; the desirability of maintaining a coherent code of ethics in an uncertain world; the need for honorable behavior in a dishonorable world—that add considerable substance to the sheer entertainment the books offer.

Another of Parker's contributions is the use of recurring characters for thematic purposes rather than as simple or-naments. Private-eye novels routinely include policemen against whom the detective can measure and evaluate his actions, behavior, and motives. Parker chose to address the issue. from the opposite direction by including Hawk, a tough yet engaging black man who, when he isn't helping his old friend and former sparring partner out of one perilous situation after another, is a legbreaker for the mob. Hawk represents the darker side of Spenser. A man whose code excludes feelings and ethics, Hawk is a reminder to Spenser of what he would become if he were to abandon his ethical code and act upon his violent inclinations without any concern for their moral implications.

More importantly, the series also features in a prominent role the character Susan Silverman, a highly intelligent and independent woman whose function is to provide something more substantial than a mere romantic interest for Spenser. Although she occasions much of the light-hearted sexual banter in the series, her primary purpose is to question and define Spenser's behavior. A guidance counselor and more recently a doctoral student in psychology, she uses her training to explain and interpret Spenser's behavior to him. A far cry from Mike Hammer's Velda, she regularly challenges Spenser's actions and attitudes, helping him in the process to mature as a person.

Since his debut in *The Godwulf Manuscript* in 1974, Spenser has appeared in eleven novels and solidly established himself as a convincing and thoroughly engaging contemporary character. As a detective who both questions as well as embodies many of the essential features of the hard-boiled hero, he is a welcome addition to the private-eye tradition. As a man who struggles to adapt to the new demands and expectations of his time, especially those involving masculine identity and the changing male and female roles, he is a valued addition to contemporary literature.

But while Parker has enjoyed the widest critical and popular acceptance, he is certainly not the only serious pretender to the throne as the "new Chandler" or the "new

Macdonald." The decade of the 1970s saw the emergence of several new series, each providing its own distinct pleasures and also offering the promise of continued development, perhaps even lasting significance. In the hands of such talented newcomers as Bill Pronzini, Michael Z. Lewin, Joseph Hansen, Arthur Lyons, and Lawrence Block, the private-eye novel is being updated and revitalized for a contemporary audience.

Nameless

(Bill Pronzini)

Despite their disappearance from the scene in the early 1950s, the pulps continued to exert a significant influence on the genre. A good example of this is the series of detective novels by Bill Pronzini that feature a private eye whose hobby is collecting pulps and who has spent his entire thirty-year investigative career trying to emulate the pulp detective heroes. The pulps, which gave birth to the earliest private eyes in the 1920s, thus also served as inspiration for one of the most recent additions to the ranks.

Only once identified by name (in *Twospot* [1978]), a novel Pronzini co-authored with Collin Wilcox in which his detective is paired with Wilcox's Lt. Frank Hastings, he is called Bill), Pronzini's private eye has come to be known simply as Nameless. His decision to leave his private eye unnamed has led to much speculation, though Pronzini himself offers a simple explanation for the matter. "The damn detective doesn't have a name because when I began the series in 1968 I couldn't think of one that suited him."[1] When a few years later he dediced to move his private eye from short stories to novels, he tried again to come up with an appropriate name, but once he realized that his hero so closely resembled himself ("He was me; I was him"), he decided not to give him one. Rather than saddling his detective with a name like Sam Spadini or Philip Marlozzi (like his creator, Nameless is Italian), or calling him Bill Pronzini ("Bill Pronzini may be an okay name for a writer," he conceded, "but it's a lousy name for a private eye"),[2] he elected to avoid the entire problem by omitting his name altogether.

In many ways Nameless resembles another famous unnamed private eye, Hammett's Continental Op. Both live and work in San Francisco. Both can be described as no longer young (Nameless is fifty-three in his most recent cases) and no longer thin. A self-styled slob, Nameless admits to a beer belly and "a gray plodding shaggy look." But there the similarities end, for unlike the Op, whose character was defined almost exclusively in terms of his work and whose private side was seldom glimpsed, Nameless has one of the most fully developed personal lives of all private eyes. Just because he lacks a name doesn't mean he lacks a personality.

One of the oldest fictional private eyes in the business, Nameless was born and raised in San Francisco. He began his investigative career in Military Intelligence during the war. Following his discharge from the army, he joined the San Francisco Police Department, where he served for fifteen years, until one day a case he was investigating in which a man had hacked his wife and two young children to death with an ax drove him from the force. He opened an office as a private detective near the Tenderloin district, where he remained until recently relocating to more modern quarters near the Hyatt Regency Hotel. He lives in a cluttered flat in Pacific Heights, filled with dirty dishes and dustballs under the furniture, evidence of his sloppy personal habits.

The most important item in his apartment, however, is his collection of pulp magazines, which increases over the course of the series from 5,000 to 6,500 copies and which is the only thing he keeps neat and orderly. His fascination for the pulps began when he was a young man and has resulted not just in his impressive collection but also in his career choices, first as a policeman and then a private detective, for he freely admits to being driven by a desire to emulate the great pulp heroes of the past. His fantasy of being a pulp detective once cost him the love of a woman who finally tired of what she called his adolescent obsession with dead heroes. Stung initially by her charge, he finally concluded there was nothing wrong with trying to follow the example of men who were true champions of justice. Now he proudly displays a blown-up reproduction of a *Black Mask* cover on his office wall, carries copies of pulps with him to read on the job whenever he has the chance, and even has dreams at night in which he goes after prohibition rumrunners with Jo Gar and Steve McBride and plays poker with Race Williams and Max Latin. The pulps even occasionally assist him in his work. The cover of a *Detective Fiction Weekly* magazine he sees in a bookstore window gives him the clue he needs to solve the crime in *The Snatch* (1971), and a paperback mystery by a pulp veteran provides the key to the solution in *Undercurrent* (1973). In *Hoodwink* (1981) he even gets to attend a convention of pulp writers, where he solves the murder of one of the guests and meets and falls in love with Kerry Wade, the daughter of two veteran pulp writers.

Despite his oft-repeated desire to emulate his pulp heroes, there is at least one important difference between Nameless and the Op, Race Williams, Max Latin, and the rest of the tough-guy heroes. Instead of the rugged hard-boiled attitude that his pulp forebears adopted toward the world, Nameless wears his heart on his sleeve, the icy reserve that characterized their outlook replaced in his case by a free and open display of emotion. Unlike the pulp tough guy who masked his hurt behind a cynical wisecrack, Nameless is a brooding, hand-wringing worrier who freely bares his soul to the reader. Unlike Philip Marlowe, whose frequent bouts with despair could be traced to disappointment at the failure of the world to measure up to his idealistic expectations, Nameless's disappointments are largely personal. Unlike Lew Archer, who is deeply moved by the troubles of the people he meets, Nameless worries about his own problems. He is unable to offer the kind of personal commitment to his clients that many of his colleagues do simply because he is so absorbed in his own miseries.

Life may be a series of emotional ups and downs for most people, but for Nameless it seems there are only downs as he worries about his job, his friends, his health, his love life, his lot in general. His self-preoccupation reaches its zenith in *Blowback* (1977), where he faces a terrifying personal crisis—a cancer scare. A two-pack-a-day smoker for several years, he has become increasingly bothered by a severe cough. Fearful of doctors and wary of learning the possible truth about the reason for his cough, he has put off having a checkup. Finally, though, he submits to an examination and learns that he has a lesion on his lung. He spends the entire novel in an anxious state, worrying whether the lesion is benign or malignant. The novel ends with Nameless on his way into the doctor's office to find out the results of the tests.

Blowback is a crucial book in the series for it represents Nameless's resurrection from the dead. "Private Eye Blues," a short story Pronzini published two years earlier, was intended to be the finale to the series, with Nameless learning that he had terminal lung cancer. Several months after completing the story, Pronzini had second thoughts about ending the series and when he turned "Private Eye Blues" into *Blowback* (a common practice with Pronzini, for most of his novels began as short stories which were later expanded or combined to form the novels), he retained the medical crisis that haunts Nameless but changed the prognosis. That the lesion is benign rather than malignant isn't revealed, however, until his next appearance, *Twospot,* published in 1978. What remains unchanged, however, is Nameless's close brush with death and the en-

counter with his own mortality. The first thing he does is
give up smoking permanently.

After *Blowback,* there occurred a significant shift in focus
in the series as Pronzini began to fashion plots of a far more
puzzle-type nature than heretofore. The unraveling of these
baffling mysteries is often ingenious, but the shift in focus
adversely affects the novels as private-eye adventures. For
example, *Scattershot* (1982) begins promisingly as a novel
about a typical week in the life of a private eye as Nameless
takes on three separate but seemingly routine assignments.
One is to find a woman in order to serve her with a sub-
poena. Two is to follow a man to see if he can confirm his
wife's suspicions about his infidelity. Three is to guard some
valuable presents during a wedding reception. But each case
quickly turns into a puzzle of a locked-room nature, with
Nameless darting from one case to the next, miraculously
solving each stupefying mystery. Readers of the Nameless
stories and novels that appeared between "The Private Eye
Who Collected Pulps" (1978) and *Scattershot* might well
have wondered, to borrow the title of one of Nameless's
recent short-story adventures, "Where Have You Gone, Sam
Spade?"—for he began to operate less like his pulp forebears
and more like Sherlock Holmes, solving crimes by the use of
ratiocinative skills almost exclusively. By relying more
heavily on the puzzle formula, Pronzini may have simply
been attempting to broaden his audience to include fans of
the John Dickson Carr school of mystery fiction. But in so
doing he downplayed or ignored features like colorful
writing, striking characters, a sense of menace and careful attention to mood and atmosphere that are traditionally
associated with the private-eye genre in order to concentrate all the attention on the construction of the puzzle
and the ingenuity of its solution.

In *Dragonfire* (1982) Pronzini abandoned the locked-
room puzzle plot and returned to the traditional private-eye
tale with considerable success. Nameless and his friend of
thirty years, Lieutenant Eberhardt, are both shot by a

mysterious Chinese assailant while relaxing at Eberhardt's home. As his friend lies in a coma in the hospital, Nameless sets out to find the gunman. Operating again like a private detective rather than an intellectual sleuth, he eventually tracks the culprit down, though his investigation also presents him with yet another personal crisis: he uncovers evidence that seems to prove that Eberhardt has taken a bribe. Nameless's problems, which in addition to worries about Eberhardt's health and honesty also include concern over the suspension of his license and his on-again, off-again relationship with Kerry Wade, are deftly integrated into the action in *Dragonfire,* giving him a compelling personal reason for getting to the bottom of things—unlike the situation in his previous few cases, where the crimes existed more to provide an intellectual challenge than to serve as the impetus for a personal crusade.

What gives the Nameless series its consistency, despite the awkward shifts in focus, is the very human figure of its main character. Nameless is less fervently the idealistic crusader and less inclined to the swaggering postures and tough heroics that characterize many of his younger colleagues. His intensity usually comes out only in the display of his emotions as he faces one personal crisis after another—fears about his lungs, disappointment at the several failures in his relationships with women, anger at the attempt on his and Eberhardt's life, distress over the suspension of his license. Unafraid to express his feelings and to admit his worries, Nameless emerges as a less-than-perfect man with whom the reader comes to share a deep rapport rather than a superhero whose dazzling exploits one is expected to admire.

Bill Pronzini was born in Petaluma, California, in 1943. Before becoming a full-time writer in the late 1960s, he attended college for two years, was a sportswriter for his hometown newspaper, and worked at a variety of other jobs. His first story was published (in *Shell Scott Mystery Magazine*) in 1966. The first Nameless stories began appearing two years later, and his first two novels, *The Stalker* (a suspense novel) and *The Snatch* (the initial Nameless novel), in 1971. Since then he has been, like his pulp-writing antecedents, a busy and prolific writer. In addition to the Nameless stories and novels, he has written hundreds of short stories (including Westerns and science-fiction tales), several novels of suspense, horror, and adventure under his own name and under several pseudonyms (Jack Foxx, Alex Saxon), has edited over a dozen anthologies (including a recent collection of pulp detective tales) and has also been an active collaborator (in addition to the Nameless novel he co-authored with Collin Wilcox, he has written short stories with Jeffrey Wallman under the name "William Jeffrey," novels with Barry N. Malzberg, and even a political thriller with columnist Jack Anderson). He also served as the first president of the Private Eye Writers of America, an organization founded in 1982. Although neither a brilliant stylist nor an innovative writer, Pronzini is a solid professional who turns out a steady stream of dependable work. Like Nameless, his work isn't flashy, but it is always reliable and honest.

Albert Samson

(Michael Z. Lewin)

For Michael Z. Lewin, the combination of an unlikely setting—Indianapolis—and a breezy narrative style proved to be a successful recipe for a fresh reworking of the traditional detective novel. His private eye, Albert Samson, whose name suggests his role as a lineal descendant of Sam Spade, is both the cheapest and the poorest among the thirty or so detectives listed in the Indianapolis telephone directory. Always on the verge of going out of business, he is reduced at one point to placing a newspaper ad offering a 20 percent discount during his "Gigantic August Detective Sale." But though he may be at the bottom of the economic scale, when it comes to those Galahadian virtues of perseverance, dedication, and commitment that are the hallmarks of his trade, he can be numbered among the noblest members of his profession.

Samson was born in Indianapolis, but left to attend college. He dropped out of the first one he attended, flunked out of the second. He later moved to New York City, got married and then divorced, worked as a security guard, and finally, seven years prior to his debut appearance in *Ask the Right Question* (1971), returned to the town of his birth and opened his own private-eye agency. His father, now dead, was a guard at the Marion County jail in Indianapolis. His mother runs a local luncheonette, which he visits regularly to play the pinball games. He also has a daughter, a seventeen-year-old girl whom he had not seen in the twelve years prior to her sudden appearance on his doorstep in *The Silent Salesman* (1978). He makes the most of the situation by obtaining a license for her to act as his assistant, the two of them joining forces to become, at least temporarily, the first father-daughter team in the genre.

It isn't difficult to see why Samson is usually perched on the edge of economic disaster. His fees are shamefully low (only thirty-five dollars a day in 1971), and in the service of his clients he frequently spends money on travel and information for which he is never reimbursed. His clients are seldom rich (in *The Way We Die Now* [1973] he receives a retainer of one dollar, which he accepts in the form of four quarters) and often reluctant to pay (his client in *The Silent Salesman* argues about an eighty-two-dollar bill, eventually talking him into settling for forty dollars in cash). To make ends meet, he lives in a combination office-apartment and accepts a variety of odd jobs, such as composing crossword puzzles and doing carpentry and photographic work. By most economic measures, Samson is a failure.

But the private eye has never been one to measure his success by his bank balance. Judged by the standards that count, Samson is a worthy member of his profession. Armed with a notebook (a carry-over from a brief fling at a journalistic career) and blessed with a willingness to do the sort of dogged investigative work that requires digging through bank records and poring over microfilm copies of old newspapers (the kind of work that leads him at one point to complain, "this can be the dullest job in the world"), he goes about his business with persistence and determination. Like most private eyes, he develops a strong commitment to his clients, though he recognizes an even higher one to the truth. When a woman dismisses him in *The Silent Salesman* after he accomplishes the specific task she had hired him to perform, he refuses to leave the case until he has satisfied his own curiosity. Pressure from both the Indianapolis police and the FBI to end his investigation also fails to deter him until he has the answers he seeks. In *Ask the Right Question,* an offer of fifty-thousand dollars to drop the case he is working on also fails to dissuade him. His indifference to such financial incentives allows him to continue behaving like an "indigent anachronism," a man compelled to seek the truth before money.

As a character, Samson is an interesting blend of silliness and seriousness, a man whose moods alternate between the humorous and the self-pitying. On the one hand, he projects a flip, devil-may-care attitude. He's the sort of fellow, for example, who hums "Me and My Shadow" while tailing a suspect and who cavalierly tosses aside a parking ticket he discovers on the windshield of his '58 Plymouth, complaining in mock disbelief, "Is there no respect for age in this country?" His narratives are filled with jokes, wisecracks, puns, inconsequential digressions, and at times downright silly remarks (e.g., "On cue the cuckoo coo-cooed six").

But make no mistake about it, Samson is serious about his

work and, despite the sometimes frivolous tone of his narratives, worried about his plight. The humor serves as a masking device, a way of keeping his suffering at bay. For example, he is able to turn concern about his economic plight into a joke when the thought that he might have to boil his shoe and eat it—à la Charlie Chaplin—produces the remark, "The last of the last shoe hadn't tasted sole good." Sometimes, however, his worries get the better of him and his humor gives way to self-pity. The innocuous comment, "It was going to be one of those days," assumes a darker hue when it is followed by the bleak pronouncement, "Mine was one of those lives." Such outbursts are rare, especially as Lewin over the course of the series gradually modulates Samson's moods, finally achieving in *Missing Woman* (1981) just the right balance between the laughter and the sadness.

Because he never forgets that he is writing mystery novels rather than biographies of Albert Samson, Lewin takes care in the construction and composition of his books. He makes effective use of the Indianapolis setting, frequently including references to local streets and landmarks, without allowing the specifics of place to intrude too much. Oddly enough, however, even though the action of one of the Samson books occurs during May, there is no mention whatever of the city's most famous event, the month-long celebration leading up to the running of the Indianapolis 500. In addition to being a skilled creator of character (except in the case of Samson's girlfriend, a shadowy figure whom he regularly refers to only as "my woman"), Lewin also writes crisp, believable dialogue, constructs inventive plots, and maintains a nice balance between action and introspection.

Michael Z. Lewin was born in Springfield, Massachusetts (also the birthplace of fellow private-eye writer Robert B. Parker) in 1942, raised in Indianapolis, and educated at Harvard, where he was a chemistry and physics major. He received his degree in 1964, then studied chemistry for a year at Cambridge University in England, where, since 1971, he has made his home. Between 1966 and 1969, he taught high-school science, first in Bridgeport, Connecticut, then in New York. While at Harvard, he developed an interest in writing and, while studying in England, thanks to a gift of a Raymond Chandler novel from his wife-to-be, a liking for detective fiction. In 1969, to amuse himself he began writing what was intended to be a short take-off on the private-eye story. A year later the work had grown to novel length and, though it still contained plenty of humor, it had become something other than a mere spoof. The book was published in 1971 as *Ask the Right Question,* Albert Samson's debut appearance.

Although Samson is differentiated from his fellow detectives by virtue of his home base of operation, his unique brand of humor, and even the presence of a teen-age daughter, he is squarely in the tradition of the American private eye. However, by creating a hero who is one of the most obscure detectives in a quiet place like Indianapolis, which Samson describes as "the biggest small town in the country," Lewin manages to de-mythologize him, despite the heroic connotations of his name. Like the Op, Samson emerges as a kind of modest Everyman, going about his business with dedication and without fuss. But as Hammett so well demonstrated with his anonymous protagonist, it is just such unassuming virtues that often result in quietly heroic accomplishments.

Dave Brandstetter

(Joseph Hansen)

Almost from the moment when Carroll John Daly and Dashiell Hammett created the private-eye genre with their tales about Race Williams and the Continental Op, writers began searching about for ways to differentiate their private detectives from those of other writers. As the years passed and the number of private eyes increased, the problem of finding a credible individualizing feature became increasingly difficult. Yet as we have already seen, in recent years several writers have come up with clever and creative innovations: Michael Collins with a one-armed detective, William Campbell Gault with a football-player-turned-private-eye, Bill Pronzini with a nameless hero. But no one in the history of the genre has had the daring to do what Joseph Hansen has done: make his private eye a homosexual. With skill and subtlety, he has created a unique individual who is both a first-rate investigator and one of the most interesting series characters in the recent history of the genre.

Dave Brandstetter is not in the narrow definition of the term a private eye. He is a death claims investigator, first for Medallion Insurance Company and later for other firms. Unlike most private eyes, he does not work for individual clients, nor is he usually involved in crimes such as kidnapping, blackmail, or theft. His business is always death, and usually murder. Whenever a policyholder dies under suspicious circumstances, he is brought in to investigate, ostensibly to determine if his company is obliged to pay off on the deceased's insurance policy. Once on a case, however, Brandstetter is as tenacious, indefatigable, and relentless as any private eye.

Skeptical by nature, Brandstetter never accepts what anyone tells him as the truth without checking out the facts for himself. He tirelessly searches rooms, digs through closets and paws through desk drawers and wastepaper baskets, searching for anything the police might have overlooked. It isn't that he is in competition with the police, but they tend to accept the evidence at its face value, and he knows evidence can be, and often is, planted to lead the casual investigator off the trail. Brandstetter also knows the police don't have the luxury he has of sticking with a case until all the questions are answered. "The police are busy," he explains. "I'm not busy."

Because he does not work for a client the way most

private eyes do, Brandstetter's motivation differs from many of them. Basically, his job is to save his company money. Since his loyalty is not owed to any of the individuals involved in the case, he is free to treat everyone with the same degree of skepticism. It soon becomes apparent, however, that Brandstetter's loyalty to the truth takes precedence over any obligation he feels toward his company. It disturbs him when a case doesn't quite add up right, and he cannot rest until he finds out why. If it happens that as a result of his efforts his company must still pay off the claims, it doesn't bother him at all. The truth is worth it.

In his quest for the truth, he never carries a gun or employs threats or strong-arm tactics—though he isn't immune to such attacks from others, ending up in the hospital at least three times because of injuries suffered in the line of duty. His favorite mode of inquiry is the question, though he never assumes the father-confessor role Lew Archer often plays. He isn't interested in earning anyone's confidence or in assisting troubled individuals to a better understanding of themselves. He is interested only in the truth, and with polite yet unremitting probing, the relentless Brandstetter usually manages to extract the information that sooner or later will lead to the truth.

Hansen's decision to cast Brandstetter in the role of insurance investigator would by itself be sufficient to differentiate him from most other private eyes, but his shrewd investigative skills comprise only the public side of his personality. More important—and the source of the true originality of the series—is Brandstetter's sexual orientation as a practicing homosexual. The private eye, as least up through Mike Hammer, has typically been portrayed as a macho hero, physical in his approach, tough in his actions, and something of a ladies' man. Writers like Thomas B. Dewey and Ross Macdonald were among the first to demonstrate that a private eye did not have to be macho to be both effective and popular with readers. But the most radical departure from the he-man image of the private eye is Hansen's.

As a distinguishing trait, Brandstetter's homosexuality has much more significance than the lack of a name or a missing arm might have. It is one of the most important facts about him, albeit not the *only* important thing about him. Here is a man who has a well-earned reputation as one of the best men in his profession. His accomplishments have been featured in magazine articles, and he has even made an appearance on the *Tomorrow* television show. He *also* happens to be homosexual, comfortable and well-adjusted in his private life. Hansen acknowledges taking special pleasure in having made Brandstetter an insurance investigator, for in his view, "Few institutions are more anti-homosexual than the big American insurance companies."[3] That Brandstetter has proven to be one of the most effective investigators for his company for twenty-five years allows Hansen to make the point, quietly but insistently, that a man's sexual preference has nothing to do with his success or failure in his profession, even in one which in his view is notoriously intolerant toward gays.

Hansen's avowed purpose in the Brandstetter series is "to deal as honestly as I know how with homosexuals and homosexuality as an integral part of the fabric of contemporary life, rather than something bizarre and alien."[4] To this end, he sought "to stand on their heads a lot of received opinions about homosexuals."[5] Thus his homosexual characters are neither effeminate nor swishy. No one ever deduces Brandstetter's homosexuality from his appearance. When a character once asks him, "Do I look like a fag?" he replies, "I don't know what a fag looks like. . . . And neither does anyone else." They aren't promiscuous: Brandstetter's relationship with Rod Fleming lasted for twenty-two years. Following Fleming's death, the number of sex partners he has falls far short of the average for most heterosexual private eyes. The stability of Brandstetter's relationships is pointedly contrasted with those of his father, who has been married *nine* times. Gay characters in the series are found in all walks of life: they include a bank vice-president, a former professional boxer, and a Grand Prix auto racer. And they are as susceptible to the same feelings—pain, loneliness, and jealousy—and have the same need for love and understanding as heterosexuals. Brandstetter and his friends are shown to be different from heterosexuals only in their choice of bed partners.

Hansen is one of those writers who intends his series to be more than a collection of isolated novels. To appreciate fully the portrayal of his protagonist, the books should be read in order, for Brandstetter's character develops progressively over the course of the series. When we first meet him in *Fadeout* (1970), he is grieving over the death of Rod Fleming, his lover for twenty-two years. In his next appearance in *Death Claims* (1973), he and Doug Sawyer, a man he cleared of suspicion of murder in *Fadeout,* move in together. After a series of stresses and strains, their affair ends three years later. In *Skinflick* (1979), Brandstetter's father dies, which forces him to leave his job at Medallion Insurance. Though president of the company, his father had warned him that once he was gone, he would be booted out of the company because of his sexual orientation. So after twenty-five years as one of Medallion's top investigators, Brandstetter is reduced to taking jobs for smaller companies on a free-lance basis. In *Gravedigger* (1982), Cecil Smith, a young black Brandstetter had a brief affair with in *The Man Everyone Was Afraid Of* (1978), shows up again and becomes his new lover and sometime assistant in his investigation. As he encounters changes and disruptions in his life—the loss of a lover, the collapse of a relationship, the death of his father, the termination of his job—Brandstetter emerges as a fully-drawn individual who commands our respect, our understanding, and our sympathy as he faces the inevitable problems of life with dignity, courage, and good humor.

If Hansen were simply writing polemical novels about the plight of the homosexual in American society, his books would appeal to only a limited audience. One reason for his widespread popularity is his success in incorporating homosexual characters and themes into novels that are, first and foremost, outstanding mysteries. He thus manages to broaden his audience to include homosexuals who might not ordinarily read mysteries and mystery readers who might not ordinarily read about homosexuals. The key to his success in this regard isn't simply the sympathetic portrayal of his homosexual main character nor his ability to construct complicated plots. The secret of his success is that he is a writer of considerable skill and imagination.

Foremost among his talents is a genuine sensitivity in the creation of flesh-and-blood characters. In peopling his books with characters ordinarily not found in mystery fiction—or if they are, they are treated as stereotypes—Hansen sought to make them credible without either sensationalizing or glamorizing them. As a result, his gay characters are ordinary human beings, with nothing exceptional about them but their sexual preference. Because his main character and most of his friends are homosexual, there is a higher percentage of gays in the series than would be found in the population at large, though Hansen is certainly not interested exclusively in gays. First, last, and always, he is interested in the humanity of his characters, whatever their sexual orientation, and when he takes a risk and creates an unusual character like the transvestite in *Skinflick* or the young cerebral palsy victim in *Fadeout,* he always shows the human being dressed in the women's clothing or imprisoned in the crippled body. Adopting neither a sentimental nor a cynical view of mankind, Hansen simply aims to populate his books with human beings rather than puppets who are merely functions of the plot. This is the only way the mystery can hope to transcend its plot and become a serious novel about real people, which is what Hansen's books are.

Hansen elected to narrate the Brandstetter books in third-person rather than use the first-person technique customary in private-eye fiction, a choice which not only reflects his preference as a writer but one which also enables him to present Brandstetter from the outside rather than from within, an external perspective proving to be the most effective in rendering Brandstetter's homosexuality in a straightforward and nonapologetic manner. It also frees Hansen of any need to employ style as a way of depicting the character of his private eye. There are few similes in the novels and those that appear (e.g., "She had a voice to holler up field hands against a prairie wind") are usually a reflection of Hansen's own South Dakota background rather than Brandstetter's personality.

According to Hansen, at an early age he learned from the writings of Gertrude Stein "that every word contains a small charge" and that consequently "words must be used with great care."[6] As a result, his own prose is lean and economical, reminiscent of Hammett's, though without Hammett's descriptions of violence. Yet despite its understated quality, it is anything but flat and colorless. Hansen reveals a painter's eye for the colors in a scene (especially striking are his descriptions of the natural flora of Southern California) and a poet's scrupulous attention to the selection of exact and appropriate nouns and verbs. He is also a skilled handler of dialogue, avoiding the flashy and dramatic in favor of the natural cadences of real speech. Hansen is one of those mystery writers like Hammett, Chandler, and Macdonald, among others, whose style contributes immeasurably to the pleasure one receives from their books.

Joseph Hansen was born in Aberdeen, South Dakota, in 1923. Ten years later, driven by the dustbowl conditions of the time, his family moved to Minnesota for three years, then made the long trek to California. Married in 1943, he and his wife moved to Hollywood, where he began a lengthy period of apprenticeship that would in 1970 finally result in the publication of *Fadeout,* the inaugural Dave Brandstetter mystery. Because of the novel's unconventional subject matter, it took him three years to find a publisher. During these years, with a wife and daughter to support, Hansen took a variety of odd jobs. He worked in libraries and bookstores and, for over ten years, for a Hollywood film-processing plant, sang folk songs on a radio program, even cut two albums of songs, wrote television scripts for *Lassie*, edited a little magazine, and turned out several paperback novels about homosexuals under the name James Colton. At the same time, he also published poetry in such prestigious magazines as *The Atlantic Monthly, Harper's, Saturday Review* and *The New Yorker* and dedicated himself to learning the craft of fiction. His efforts paid off handsomely, for in the Brandstetter books he has produced novels notable not only for their sympathetic portrayal of homosexual characters but for their effective blending of the elements of good mystery writing with a mastery of form and style.

Jacob Asch

(Arthur Lyons)

One of the toughest and most authentic of all the recent private eyes is Arthur Lyons's Jacob Asch, who made his debut in 1974 in *The Dead Are Discreet*. Asch is representative of a recent trend toward a new ethnicity in the private-eye novel—he is Jewish (actually half-Jewish, for his mother was Episcopalian). His father was a tailor and at one time operated out of an office in the middle of the L.A. garment district. But as the series has developed, it is clear that Lyons isn't interested in using Asch's Jewishness to the degree that a writer like Roger L. Simon does with his private eye, Moses Wine. What stands out in Asch's character is not his religious or ethnic identity but a toughness of character that has been missing from the private-eye hero in recent years, a quality reminiscent not of Mike Hammer's bully-boy

pugnaciousness but rather much closer to the original hard-
boiled attitude associated with characters like Sam Spade
and the Continental Op.

Asch became a private detective more through circumstances than through choice. For nine years he was happily employed as a reporter for the *Chronicle,* until his
refusal to identify a news source landed him in jail for six
months when a judge had him locked up for contempt of
court. Though he later confesses he was often tempted to
buy his freedom by supplying the name of his source, the
public support he received for his fight for First Amendment
rights made that all but impossible. In addition to the jail sen-
tence which has left permanent emotional scars, Asch's actions also cost him his career, for his publisher not only
failed to back him, he made sure no other newspaper would
hire him when he was released. So he was forced to take his
reporter's instincts and snooper's nose elsewhere and find
himself a new line of work. He decided to become a private
eye and opened an office in Los Angeles.

Although Asch works the same Southern California turf
that Philip Marlowe and Lew Archer did before him, the
territory has undergone a dramatic change since their time.
The seamy side of L.A. that was only faintly hinted at by Arthur Geiger's porno bookshop on Hollywood Boulevard in
Chandler's *The Big Sleep* is openly on display everywhere in
Lyons's novels as whorehouses, sex shops, massage parlors,
rough-trade gay bars, and the like hawk goods and services
catering to the basest of human desires. And the innocent,
troubled, and vulnerable souls that made up Archer's clientele have been shoved aside by the hookers, nude dancers,
dopers, pedophiles, necrophiliacs, Satan worshippers, and
occult fanatics that share the stage with the normal characters in Lyons's books. Asch's world is harsher, more perverse,
more threatening than that portrayed by any of Lyons's
predecessors. The Hollywood that still retained a vestige of
glamour for Chandler has become for Asch a place of
"heroin dreams and Laverne and Shirley nightmares," the
glamour once projected by the glittering neon lights of the

city now replaced by the squalor that is evident in the harsh light of day. The Hollywood he sees reminds Asch of a "man in the advanced stages of syphilis who has been caught with his pants down."

Death is also a gruesome presence in Asch's world, with several victims coming to particularly horrible ends. In *The Killing Floor* (1976), Asch discovers a woman hanging upside down from a hook in a slaughterhouse, her throat slit from ear to ear. In *Hard Trade* (1981), a female client is pulverized by an automobile that intentionally runs her down as she is crossing the street to meet Asch. Another woman, six months pregnant, is blown to bits in a car explosion in the same novel. The pungent odor of death also wafts through the novels. In *All God's Children* (1975), Asch enters an apartment and is nearly bowled over by the stench of a rotting corpse, left there by the killer who had purposely turned the temperature of the room up to ninety degrees before leaving. In *The Killing Floor,* he finds the body of a man he has been searching for rotting in the trunk of his car. In *Castles Burning* (1979), he can even hear the maggots busy at work on a corpse that has been left to decay in a drainage ditch. The effect of all this grim horror is to remind the reader that murder is never pretty.

Raymond Chandler once honored Dashiell Hammett for bringing crime out of the tearoom and into the alleys where it belonged. Lyons follows Hammett's example and creates a harsh and brutal world where murder is vicious and shocking and where the end products of crime are decaying corpses rather than wounded psyches. An artist in *Castles Burning* tells Asch he doesn't want people to be tranquil when they view his paintings, which strike Asch as having a "cold, vicious beauty." The same phrase can be used to describe Lyons's novels, which share with Hammett's an attempt to fashion a poetry of violence by scrupulously avoiding any temptation to sanitize death. "This is not an age for Agatha Christie," Lyons insists. "When somebody dies in my books, the bodies smell."[7]

The special tools of Asch's trade are a badger-like persistence in digging through documents and records searching for facts and an expert interview technique, skills perfected while he was a reporter. Unlike Lew Archer, whose questioning revealed him to be a caring and sympathetic listener, Asch is really a master of deceit. The sympathy he projects is largely fake, feigned as a way of extracting the truth. To a divorced mother, he talks knowingly about his non-existent children. To a man with a bad back, he lies about his own back problems. To an antique dealer, he displays a phony expertise gleaned during a brief stopover at the library on his way to the dealer's shop. He employs whatever approach seems necessary to earn his subject's trust, not because of any desire to help the individual, but because of a desire to obtain whatever information that individual can provide him. Asch's credo—"My life had always been dominated by facts—facts and the truth facts told. Facts had always come first, they had been my primary passion, and people had always run a poor second"[8]—offers an interesting contrast to that of Archer, who insisted, "Other people's lives are my business. . . . And my passion. And my obsession, too, I guess."[9] It clearly isn't compassion that motivates Asch, just a simple demand for the truth coupled with a willingness to do whatever it takes to reach that goal.

As a child, Lyons admits, his hero wasn't The Lone Ranger but figures like Paladin and Peter Gunn, men who fought hard but who also expected to be rewarded for their efforts. He rejects the notion that the private eye must be a knight errant. Asch, for one, is anything but Sir Galahad. In *At the Hands of Another* (1983), he refuses to rush to the aid of a former girlfriend who seeks his help in proving her husband died accidentally rather than by his own hand, especially when her lawyer insists that he will have to work on a contingency basis rather than for his regular fee (two hundred dollars a day). When she comes up with the cash, he agrees to take the case. It isn't that he is obsessed with money, but he knows that he is engaged in a job, often a dirty one at that, and not a crusade, and he expects to be paid for risking his neck. Asch entertains few illusions about the nobility of his work. He is, he knows, just a guy "who can wade through it up to his eyeballs and not puke from the smell." He has his principles, which include loyalty to a client and a refusal to be bought off once he's on a case. But anyone who can describe his work as "throwing a lot of shit on the wall and hoping some of it sticks" is a man who has a clear and open-eyed attitude toward the work he does.

The usually tight-lipped Sam Spade offered the reader a rare glimpse into his philosophical outlook when he related to Brigid O'Shaughnessy the story of Flitcraft, the man whose life was profoundly altered by his chance encounter with the randomness of existence when he was nearly killed by a beam falling from a building. Asch, like Spade, is no philosopher, though he admits to having read Albert Camus, but he has had his own encounter with the precariousness of existence. In his case, it came one day while he was driving down the freeway and realized he was looking up at every overpass to make sure some twelve-year-old kid wasn't waiting to throw a rock at him. Like Spade, he has learned how to adjust to this perception by adopting a hard-boiled attitude toward existence, one that leaves little room for sentimentality or false optimism. He isn't as subject to disillusionment as some of his more idealistic colleagues, for he never expects things to be better than they are. It doesn't surprise him, for example, to discover that the governor of California is a pederast or that the crusading politician for whom he worked in *Hard Trade* sells out in order to run for the governorship himself. He is a realist, wised up to the ways of the world, and he lives his life according to those principles.

Asch is no angel. Because he exists in a harsh, often un-compromising world, he has had to learn to be unusually tough himself, though he never stoops to the level of Mike Hammer's cruel, sadistic behavior. In a fight, he aims for his opponent's groin, though usually only in self-defense or when provoked. When a menacing lesbian, angry at him for making eyes at her attractive female companion, comes at him with a beer mug, he doesn't hesitate to knock her cold. He has been known to slam the fingers of a reluctant subject repeatedly in a car door to make him talk, and he is also capable of actions that can only be described as mean-spirited. Irritated at his next door neighbor's habit of turning up her television to annoy him while she's out, he breaks into her apartment and pours a glass of water down the back of the set, destroying it. She later gets back at him by breaking into his apartment and returning the favor. Though ordinarily an even-tempered fellow, Asch is clearly not a person to mess with.

One shouldn't on the basis of the above conclude that Asch is a cold, unfeeling man. Unlike Spade, he is able to show his emotions. In *All God's Children* he sheds tears over the death of a girl who was murdered while in his care. And in *The Killing Floor* he reaches out and comforts a woman whose husband's body he has just discovered. He even confesses to crying during sad movies and beautiful songs. Though an early marriage ended in divorce, he also understands the importance of love and acknowledges his own need for the affection and comfort of a woman. Because of his reluctance to commit himself to a lasting relationship, the names and faces of the women he is involved with change from one novel to the next. Ironically, when in *At the Hands of Another* he finally gets up enough courage to make the commitment to tell a woman he loves her, she dumps him.

Though he's hard-boiled, Asch also possesses an engaging sense of humor which, he confesses, serves as a defense mechanism. "It's the only thing that keeps me from going completely nuts." He delights some children who watch him drive by with his head out the window because his windshield is broken by obligingly barking like a dog at them. When he flatters a dimwitted woman by telling her how intelligent she is, he sheepishly confides to us that he has to check the end of his nose to see if it is growing. His descriptive similes also attest to a kind of screwball wit. He describes one man as having more "chins than a Chinese phone book." He compares the face of a mean-looking lesbian to "a brakeshoe on a 747." And a succession of offbeat clients moves him to complain about working for a troupe of "Flying Weirdinos." Much of his humor is bawdy. He accounts for a broken hand by explaining that he got fresh with a girl who "slammed her legs shut on me." He describes a woman who tries to get him to pick her up in a bar as having a face that looks like it "had probably gone down on everything but the *Lusitania*." Though he doesn't feel compelled to turn each and every hurt into a joke or a wisecrack, such instances of humor show that one element in Asch's strategy for survival in a grim world is the ability to laugh, both at himself and at the world.

Arthur Lyons was born in Los Angeles in 1946. Following graduation from the University of California, Santa Barbara, in 1967, he opened a restaurant and since that time has successfully juggled the disparate careers of restaurant manager and writer. He currently operates two restaurant establishments in Palm Springs. Except for an early non-fiction work entitled *The Second Coming: Satanism in America* (1970), a book he says he wrote because of his interest in "the dark side of man," a theme also prominently displayed in his mystery fiction, his published writing consists entirely of his Jacob Asch novels. Though the amount of his fictional output isn't great, the quality of it is impressive. Lean yet sharply descriptive prose, crisply paced narratives, pungently realistic dialogue, a scrupulous avoidance of cliches, and unfailingly credible characters all combine to produce fiction of the highest order. The gritty tales of Jacob Asch give new meaning to terms like tough and hard-hitting when they are applied to the powerful novels of Arthur Lyons.

Matt Scudder

(Lawrence Block)

Lawrence Block's Matt Scudder is far and away the gloomiest and most guilt-ridden of all the private eyes. While many of his colleagues experience periodic bouts of depression and disillusionment—often at the end of a case when their work is over and they must return to the solitude of their lonely lives to wait until the next case comes along—Scudder is unremittingly glum. Dashiell Hammett, employing a terse, hard-boiled style, managed to produce a kind of poetry of violence; Block has instead aimed at creating in the Scudder books a kind of poetry of despair.

Unlike Pronzini's Nameless, whose life is a series of emotional crises, Scudder owes his melancholic disposition to a single tragic incident in his life. A New York City policeman for fifteen years, he was enjoying an off-duty drink in a bar one evening when two young punks entered, held up the place and killed the bartender on their way out. Scudder chased after the pair and shot them both, killing one and crippling the other. But one of his bullets went astray, ricocheted off something and struck a seven-year-old girl named Estrellita Rivera in the eye, killing her instantly. Exonerated of blame in the incident and even awarded a department commendation for his actions in apprehending the killers, Scudder's life has nevertheless been irrevocably altered by the incident. He decided he no longer wanted to be a policeman, or a husband and father for that matter. He resigned from the force, left his wife and two sons in Syosset, Long Island, and moved into a hotel on 57th Street in Manhattan, where he nurses his guilt and sorrow in lonely isolation.

Scudder is not officially a private eye. Put off by thoughts of an examination and of all the paperwork involved in keeping records and filing income tax returns, he never applied for a license. He simply does favors for people, for money. One advantage of this arrangement is that since he is never actually hired, he can never be fired. His needs are few, so he works as infrequently as he can, and the cases he agrees to take, he does so without enthusiasm. "The jobs I accept," he explains, "are ones I can't think of a way to turn down." He certainly entertains no noble notion of himself as a court of last resort for people who have exhausted every other vehicle for justice. In fact, he prefers to work for people he neither likes nor respects. That way, he says, "It pains me less to give them poor value." He also has an unorthodox way of deciding on his fee, usually settling on a figure on the spot: in *Time to Murder and Create* (1977), for example, he charges a man $320 because that is the exact amount the man had paid for the suit he is wearing.

Once he receives his fee—which he demands in advance—he routinely does two things with it: he purchases a money order and sends as much as he can spare to his ex-wife and sons on Long Island; and he stuffs ten percent of the total amount into the poor box of the nearest church as a tithe. Scudder isn't a religious man, though he does have a keen sense of sin and guilt. He confesses that if he didn't consider suicide a sin, he would have killed himself years ago. He spends a great deal of his time just sitting in churches. He claims to have no clear idea why he does this. "It seems logical to assume there's some sort of personal quest involved," he concedes, but he insists, "I've no real idea what it might be." He also has a habit of lighting candles in memory of Estrellita Rivera and other dead friends; he isn't sure what good that does either, but he's convinced it can't do any harm. His uncertain motives notwithstanding, Scudder is clearly attracted by the peace and quiet he finds in the churches he visits and his mere presence in such comforting surroundings seems to help him handle his guilt and get through the difficult ordeal of living his life from one day to the next.

The most important house of worship Scudder frequents, however, is not a church at all but a place called Armstrong's, a bar located on Ninth Avenue right around the corner from his hotel. Scudder is an alcoholic. Ever since the incident that has disrupted his life, he has come to rely more and more heavily on what he calls "maintenance drinking," usually coffee laced with bourbon. That way, he explains, "You still get drunk eventually. But you don't get tired out en route." Scudder drinks as much as or more than Jonathan Latimer's Bill Crane, the previous champion tippler among private eyes, though in Block's novels the drinking is never used for comic effect as it is in Latimer's books. It is serious business with Scudder, for it wards off pain and memory and is the only way he has found of insuring peaceful sleep at night.

But Scudder's drinking has become an increasingly serious problem. In *Time to Murder and Create,* he woke up after one of his binges in a strange hotel room and had to check his wallet to see if he had spent the night with a prostitute. Lately, however, he has twice awakened from his blackouts to find himself lying in a hospital bed. One doctor even gives him an ultimatum: stop drinking or die. And so he begins dropping into neighborhood AA meetings, though he behaves there in much the same way as when he visits churches—as a detached observer rather than an active participant. *Eight Million Ways to Die* (1982) depicts the struggle between Scudder's desire to get off the booze and his failure to understand why "anyone would think it a good idea to stay sober in this city." Fortunately for him, he has an assignment to keep his mind off drinking; he sticks with the case until he solves it, and, with the help of Jan Keane, an alcoholic sculptress who told him at the end of *A Stab in the Dark* (1981) that she needed to stop seeing him because of her desire to kick alcohol, he also manages to stop drinking for eleven days and for the first time to utter the words at an AA meeting that he had heretofore been unable to say: "My name is Matt and I'm an alcoholic." Though he may never fully overcome his guilt, it appears that he has taken the first step on the road to controlling his drinking.

Scudder's decision to assume the role if not the actual

profession of private eye was not, as is the case with many of his predecessors, prompted by disillusionment with the practices or policies of the official law enforcement agencies. Detecting is simply all he knows and all he ever did "insofar as I did anything." Even as a cop, he never had much faith in the criminal justice system. Nor was he too principled to accept his share of the graft that was rampant in the department. "I never let a man buy his way out of something I considered a serious crime," he admits, but he also concedes, "There never was a week when we lived on what the city paid me."[10] In other words, Scudder was never what you could call a romantic idealist, and since leaving the force he hasn't changed his tune. He is as cynical and as relentlessly non-idealistic as he ever was.

But he is not without a code, albeit a simple one: "It's bad for society when murders remain unpunished."[11] Scudder is no Galahad off on a crusade to save the world nor committed to rescuing damsels in distress. He walks right past a man beating a woman during an argument in *Eight Million Ways to Die,* determined not to get involved. But he cannot tolerate an unsolved murder, even one, as in *A Stab in the Dark,* that occurred nine years earlier. The thought of someone not paying for his sins nettles him, perhaps because of the high price he paid for killing Estrellita Rivera.

It isn't enough that he merely track the killer down, either; Scudder has his own personal standards of justice. In *The Sins of the Father,* for instance, after discovering that the murderer is a minister, he confronts the man and offers him a choice: either kill himself within the next forty-eight hours—he even provides the bottle of Seconal tablets—or he will go to the police with the evidence he has of the man's guilt. The minister chooses suicide. What is important to Scudder is not that society's demand for justice be satisfied, but that his own sense of justice be served. An incident which occurred while he was still a policeman reveals Scudder's attitude toward justice: he admits to planting some heroin in a murder suspect's apartment which resulted in the man's being sent to prison on a trumped-up drug charge.

The man had committed a murder, but because Scudder knew there was no way to prove it, he felt justified in framing him. Despite his confidence in this case, Scudder never fully resolves the moral dilemma that haunts him: that is, is it ever right to do the wrong thing for the right reason? Sending a guilty man to prison by illegal means is perhaps wrong, but to him justified, though he has thus far been unable in any way to justify his killing of Estrellita Rivera, even though his action in pursuing the fleeing killers was correct. Perhaps it is because there are no easy answers to such questions that Scudder has chosen to withdraw from the world to the extent that he has.

Scudder's tales are narrated in a tough, unsentimental prose with precious little levity in it, wisecracks being inappropriate for a somber man like himself. Given his bleak outlook, it's a wonder the books don't collapse under the weight of all the gloom. Block, however, does an excellent job of keeping Scudder's self-pity to a bare minimum and, especially in *Eight Million Ways to Die,* of balancing the many instances of urban horror with an equal number of hopeful tales told by the participants at the AA meetings Scudder drops in on. There are also few colorful similes or lyrical flourishes in the novels, the laconic prose perfectly suited to a man whose life has been stripped of most everything save guilt. Raymond Chandler used a rich, evocative prose to bathe Philip Marlowe in the romantic glow of the Arthurian knight errant. Block employs a much sparer style in order to present Scudder in a harsher, less flattering light, exposing all the warts and blemishes. It isn't the dashing knight on his white charger that interests Block but rather the dark night of the soul that haunts his hero.

Lawrence Block was born in Buffalo, New York, in 1938. He started writing while a student at Antioch College in Ohio, becoming a professional writer in 1958, when he began cranking out soft-core paperback sex novels at the rate of one every ten days. Since then, he has continued to be a prolific producer of fiction. The Scudder books originated as a paperback series in 1976, then moved to hardcover with the publication of *A Stab in the Dark* in 1981. The series also includes two novelettes published in *Alfred Hitchcock's Mystery Magazine* in 1977. Block has created several other series: one features Evan Tanner, a free-lance secret agent who never sleeps, his sleep center having been destroyed during the Korean War; another features Bernie Rhodenbarr, a bookstore owner who is also a professional thief. The Burglar books—so-called because each title contains the word burglar—have a light breezy tone and a comic touch that provides a nice contrast to the more somber Scudder books. Block also wrote an entertaining series of four novels under the name Chip Harrison, the latter two of which, *Make Out with Murder* (1974) and *The Topless Tulip Caper* (1975), are mystery parodies. He is the author as well of two books of helpful practical advice about writing, *Writing the Novel: From Plot to Print* (1979) and *Telling Lies for Fun and Profit* (1981), based on his columns about writing which appeared regularly in *Writer's Digest*. Divorced and the father of three daughters, Block, like Scudder, currently lives and works in New York City.

Like many of his fellow writers, Block uses the private-eye genre as a vehicle for examining the evil and corruption of modern society, but his primary interest is in laying bare the tortured soul of his hero. It is a tribute to his skill that he has made the morose Scudder such a compelling figure, for though he depicts him without sentimentality, he views him with compassion. Perhaps because he seems more in need of help than those who seek his assistance, we find ourselves caring about him, rooting for him to make it, especially during his struggle to climb out of the bottle. Scudder may not be the most likable or most engaging private eye ever to have been created, but in his troubled ordeal he is one of the most human.

The preceding are by no means the only contemporary private-eye writers worthy of serious consideration, though collectively they represent the best work done in the genre

during the 1970s. Already under way, however, are several
promising new series, any one of which has the potential to
dominate the genre in the 1980s and beyond. The group includes a number of talented young writers: Stephen
Greenleaf, who introduced San Francisco-lawyer-turned-
private-detective John Marshall Tanner in *Grave Error* in
1979; Jonathan Valin, whose Cincinnati-based private eye
Harry Stoner made his debut in *The Lime Pit* in 1980;
Richard Hoyt, creator of John Denson, a Seattle private eye
who made his initial appearance in *Decoys* in 1980; Loren
Estleman, whose Detroit private eye Amos Walker was introduced in *Motor City Blue* in 1980; and Max Byrd, whose
series of novels about San Francisco private eye Mike Haller
was launched with *California Thriller* in 1981.

Also worthy of mention are the DKA File novels of Joe
Gores, beginning with *Dead Skip* in 1972, which report the
activities of San Francisco private eye Dan Kearny and his
associates, and the two genuinely original works of James
Crumley, whose *The Wrong Case* (1975) and *The Last Good
Kiss* (1978) were among the finest private-eye novels to appear during the 1970s. Milo Milodragovitch, the Montana
private eye who was introduced in *The Wrong Case,* returned for a second appearance in 1983 with the publication
of *Dancing Bear.* In a far lighter vein, there are the Toby
Peters novels of Stuart Kaminsky, an entertaining mixture of
mystery and old movie stars, which began with *Bullet for a
Star* in 1977, and the linguistically zany Chance Purdue
burlesques of Ross H. Spencer, which originated in 1978
with *The Dada Caper.*

The impressive individual talents of each of these writers,
their imaginative approaches to the genre and their success
in fashioning fresh versions of the familiar private-eye hero
offer convincing evidence of the vitality and flexibility of
this most authentic of American genres as it continues, as it
has uninterruptedly for over sixty years, to entertain each
successive generation of readers.

7

An Enduring Hero

The title of a recent study of the hard-boiled detective novel by Edward Margolies, *Which Way Did He Go?*, gives the mistaken impression that the private eye has faded from the American scene. But even a quick glance at the number of talented contemporary writers working in the genre, turning out fresh new versions of the traditional hard-boiled mystery, suggests the opposite—that the private eye is in fine shape. The real question is not, "Where did he go?" but rather, "Why has he lasted so long?"

One can offer several reasons for his continuing popularity:

1. The private eye is an archetypal hero who embodies certain basic features of the American character. Brave, courageous, resourceful, decisive, incorruptible, fiercely independent, he is a solitary individual, poor but honest, who follows the rigorous demands of his own personal code in fighting for truth, justice, and what is right. A doer not a thinker, an adventure hero rather than a puzzle solver, he willingly risks his life in championing justice, pursuing truth and upholding his principles. In short, he personifies the

same qualities Americans admired in their earliest hero, the frontiersman. But when the frontier disappeared at the end of the nineteenth century, the wilderness hero was forced to relocate to the city. Though he may have traded his buckskin for a trenchcoat, his Winchester for a snub-nosed .38, and his palomino for a Plymouth, he never relinquished those virtues that had set him apart as someone special on the frontier. As American society has grown increasingly industrialized and bureaucratized, the private eye has continued to celebrate the importance of the individual in mass society, and though he can never perhaps fully restore justice and order to a corrupt society, his actions proclaim the value of honorable behavior in a world which too often rewards dishonorable activities.

2. The private eye is a protean hero. Although all private detectives share certain common features to one degree or another, the range of individual differences within the broad outlines of the archetype is considerable. In previous chapters we have met private eyes who differ widely in age, personality, background, habitat, and even profession—such as photographers, taxi drivers and insurance investigators. In addition to these examples of his diversity, over the years there have been numerous other attempts to extend the outlines of the hero even more dramatically: for instance, there have been dwarf private eyes (Dr. Robert Frederickson, a.k.a. "Mongo the Magnificent," created by George C. Chesbro), identical twin private eyes (Alan Riefe's Huntington and Hadley Case, who pose as a single detective), elderly private eyes (seventy-eight-year-old Jake Spanner in L. A. Morse's *The Old Dick*), black private eyes (Ernest Tidyman's John Shaft, John B. West's Rocky Steele and J. F. Burke's Sam Kelly), private eyes who live in the old West (Chad Calhoun's Brad Spear) and those who inhabit the distant future (William F. Nolan's Sam Space and Mike McQuay's Matthew Swain). There has even been a six-foot-tall rabbit private eye in Gary Wolf's *Who Censored Roger Rabbit?* And though the private eye is usually thought of as a masculine hero, there have also been several female versions

of the hero—G. G. Fickling's Honey West, Walter Wager's A. B. Gordon, and Marcia Muller's Sharon McCone. The fact that the private eye can assume such a wide variety of shapes and forms without suffering undue damage to his essential character is ample evidence of his adaptability. One might well borrow the title of Joseph Campbell's classic study of the mythic hero, *The Hero with a Thousand Faces,* as an apt description of the American private-eye hero.

3. The narrative conventions of the genre itself have contributed to its lasting appeal. Ever since Mark Twain demonstrated the rich possibilities of the American vernacular language in the first-person narration of Huck Finn, writers (and readers) have been drawn to the sound of the American voice in fiction. Beginning with Race Williams and continuing on into the present, with a few notable exceptions like Sam Spade, the private eye has generally chosen to tell his own tale in language that is tough and hard-hitting, punctuated by colorful slang, irreverent wisecracks, rude wit, and iconoclastic humor. This style has kept its freshness by adapting to changes in colloquial speech, and it has proven to be flexible enough to include everything from the terse, laconic prose of the Continental Op to the evocative, simile-laden accounts of Philip Marlowe. No one would mistake Race Williams for Philip Marlowe or Lew Archer for Mike Hammer, yet though they don't all speak with the same voice, they are all members of the same American colloquial chorus.

4. The genre offers the novelist an ideal opportunity to mirror his society. The private eye is a cultural middleman, a common man of uncommon virtue, one whose efforts are dedicated to the pursuit of the noblest ideals of his society but whose instincts are those of the streets and alleys. To achieve his ends, he thus roams freely across all classes of society, from the dingiest slums to the most affluent suburbs, and his investigations bring him into contact with characters that include bank presidents and dope pushers, housewives and hookers, saints and sinners. Also, because he is an out-

sider and ordinarily lives alone, is not affiliated with any official law enforcement agency, and stubbornly clings to a rigorously personal code that is not widely shared by the majority of his countrymen, the private eye is in an excellent position to comment on the manners and morals of his society, to assess the strengths and weaknesses of its organizations, to judge its values and priorities, and to expose its flaws and failures. Consequently, the genre has proven itself to be an unusually effective vehicle for social commentary. One seeking insight into American society in the twentieth century would be well advised to examine closely the private-eye novels written since the 1920s, for, beginning with Hammett, writers in the genre have aimed at depicting realistically the society in which they lived rather than follow the example of the classic whodunit tradition they rejected and create a safe cozy world that offers a temporary escape from reality and its actual concerns and problems.

5. The private-eye genre is a dynamic genre, capable of changing with the times, of adapting to everything from the Depression and World War II to the social and sexual revolution of the 1960s. The Prohibition hoodlums and underworld gangsters who were the private eye's main adversaries in the early hard-boiled tales have largely been replaced by perpetrators of more private and personal crimes. The private eye himself has also kept up with the times: he is more likely to be dressed in running shoes and a jogging outfit than in a trenchcoat and rumpled business suit, and his girlfriend is more apt to be an independent professional woman than a brainless secretary.

In fact, the private eye is seldom portrayed any longer as a simple tough guy fighting violence with violence, a tradition that reached its apogee with Mike Hammer. Thanks to the efforts of Raymond Chandler, the private eye was transformed from a tough guy into a knight errant who fights corruption and the forces of evil with the authority of his moral ardor rather than with a loaded gun. Violence has never entirely disappeared from the private-eye genre, though it has been reduced to the point where many private detectives no longer feel obliged to carry a gun. The contemporary private eye is generally more introspective, more compassionate, more altruistic, and often more complex, than his ancestors, his actions aimed more at protecting the innocent than punishing the guilty. Though he has admittedly softened, especially where his heart is concerned, and no longer relies on an unbreakable skull to the extent he once did, he has remained tough where it counts—in the force of his convictions, the steadfastness of his integrity, the unflagging dedication to his mission. It is still some violation of the criminal law that ordinarily prompts his involvement, but it is now more often the restoration or reaffirmation of the moral law than vengeance that is his aim.

To dismiss the private eye, as some have done, as an anachronism in the contemporary world is beside the point, for from the very beginning he has been portrayed as one who celebrates virtues associated with an earlier, more heroic past. It is perhaps more instructive to see him as a Janus figure, an individual who looks backwards to a more noble past while at the same time staring open-eyed at the world before him. He is thus both a romantic idealist spurred by dreams of how things once were—and in his mind should still be—and a pragmatic realist aware of the difficulty of the task facing him and of the very real possibility of failure. Though he remains committed to rescuing damsels in distress, he also knows he will likely continue to get knocked in the head for his efforts.

This duality is especially appealing, for the private eye caters to our nostalgic urges, reminding us of a simpler time when decisive, heroic action mattered, while also offering us a relevant model of conduct in our own age, reminding us that decent and honorable behavior is still possible in a world that often seems inhospitable to such notions. The fantasy that lay behind the Holmesian detective—that a man of superior intellect can, by applying logic, restore order to a temporarily disordered world—was rejected by the writers who created the private eye. In its place they substituted a new fantasy—that a man of superior honor, decency, and courage can bring a measure of truth and justice to an imperfect world. As long as man cherishes that belief, there will undoubtedly be private eyes to embody it.

Notes

Chapter 1

1. Arthur Conan Doyle, *The Complete Sherlock Holmes* (Garden City: Doubleday, 1930), 23.
2. George Grella, "Murder and Manners: The Formal Detective Novel," in *Detective Fiction,* ed. Robin W. Winks (Englewood Cliffs, N. J.: Prentice-Hall, 1980), 101.
3. Dashiell Hammett, "The Black Hat That Wasn't There," *Ellery Queen Mystery Magazine,* June 1951, 140.
4. John McAleer, "The Game's Afoot: Detective Fiction in the Present Day," *Kansas Quarterly* 10 (Fall 1978): 30.
5. Edmund Wilson, "Why Do People Read Detective Stories?", in *Classics and Commercials* (New York: Vintage, 1962), 235.
6. Raymond Chandler, "The Simple Art of Murder," in *The Art of the Mystery Story,* ed. Howard Haycraft (New York: Simon and Schuster, 1946), 232.
7. Ibid., 230.
8. Ibid., 234.
9. Elaine Bander, "Dorothy L. Sayers and the Apotheosis of Detective Fiction," *The Armchair Detective* 10 (October 1977): 363.
10. Carroll John Daly, *The Snarl of the Beast* (New York: Edward J. Clode, 1927), 12.

11. Michael S. Barson, " 'There's No Sex in Crime': The Two-Fisted Homilies of Race Williams," *Clues* 2:2 (Fall/Winter 1981): 110.
12. G. A. Finch, "A Fatal Attraction," *The Armchair Detective* 13 (Spring 1980): 112.
13. Ibid., 123.
14. Quoted in Richard Layman, *Shadow Man; The Life of Dashiell Hammett* (New York: Harcourt Brace Jovanovich, 1981), 46.
15. Joe Gores, "Hammett the Writer," *Xenophile,* no. 38 (1978), 9.
16. William F. Nolan, *Dashiell Hammett: A Casebook* (Santa Barbara: McNally & Loftin, 1969), 7.
17. Dashiell Hammett, *Red Harvest* (New York: Vintage, 1972), 145.
18. Philip Durham, "The *Black Mask* School," in *Tough Guy Writers of the Thirties,* ed. David Madden (Carbondale: Southern Illinois Press, 1968), 69.
19. Dashiell Hammett, "From the Memoirs of a Private Detective," in Haycraft, *Art of the Mystery Story,* 417–18.

Chapter 2

1. Raymond Chandler, *Selected Letters of Raymond Chandler,* ed. Frank MacShane (New York: Columbia University Press, 1981), 333.
2. Tony Goodstone, *The Pulps* (New York: Chelsea House, 1970), xii.
3. Joseph T. Shaw, ed., *The Hard-Boiled Omnibus* (New York: Simon and Schuster, 1946), vi.
4. Ibid., viii.
5. Quoted in Thomas Sturak, "Horace McCoy, Captain Shaw, and the *Black Mask,*" in *The Mystery and Detection Annual, 1972,* ed. Donald Adams (Beverly Hills: Castle Press, 1972), 157.
6. Frank Gruber, "The Life and Times of the Pulp Story," in *Brass Knuckles* (Los Angeles: Sherbourne Press, 1966), 23.
7. Stephen Mertz, "W. T. Ballard: An Interview," *The Armchair Detective* 12 (Winter 1979): 16.
8. Chandler, *Selected Letters,* 68.
9. Quoted in Frank Gruber, *The Pulp Jungle* (Los Angeles: Sherbourne Press, 1967), 145.
10. Quoted in Nolan, *Dashiell Hammett: A Casebook,* 67.
11. Frederick Nebel, "Spare the Rod," in *Six Deadly Dames* (Boston: Gregg Press, 1980), 97.
12. Frederick Nebel, "Rough Justice," *Black Mask,* November 1930, 17.
13. George Harmon Coxe, "Portrait of Murder," *Black Mask,* February 1936, 62.

14. Dashiell Hammett, *The Maltese Falcon* (New York: Vintage, 1972), 195.

15. Chandler, *Selected Letters,* 68.

16. Stephen Mertz, "Captain Shaw's Hard-Boiled Boys," *The Armchair Detective* 12 (Summer 1979): 265.

17. S. J. Perelman, "Somewhere a Roscoe," in *The Best of S. J. Perelman* (New York: Modern Library, 1947), 10.

18. Stephen Mertz, "Robert Leslie Bellem: The Great Unknown," *Xenophile,* no. 21 (1976), 49.

19. Perelman, "Somewhere a Roscoe," 10.

20. Bill Pronzini, "Ante-Bellem Days: Or, 'My Roscoe Sneezed *Kachee!*'," *Clues* 2:2 (Fall/Winter 1981): 42.

21. Stephen Mertz, "Investigating Dan Turner," *The Not So Private Eye,* no. 5 (1979), 12.

Chapter 3

1. Quoted in David Wilson, "The Hardboiled Comedians," *Mystery,* April 1982, 23.

2. Geoffrey O'Brien, *Hardboiled America; The Lurid Years of Paperbacks* (New York: Van Nostrand Reinhold, 1981), 111.

3. Jim McCahery, "Jonathan Latimer's William Crane—Part Two," *The Not So Private Eye,* no. 2 (1978), 7.

4. Jim McCahery, "Jonathan W. Latimer: An Interview," *Megavore,* no. 11 (1980), 17.

5. Wilson, "Hardboiled Comedians," 24.

6. Quoted in Chris Steinbrunner and Otto Penzler, eds., *Encyclopedia of Mystery and Detection* (New York: McGraw-Hill, 1976), 108.

7. Quoted in Frank MacShane, *The Life of Raymond Chandler* (New York: E. P. Dutton, 1976), 51.

8. Chandler, "The Simple Art of Murder," 237.

9. Raymond Chandler, *The Long Goodbye* (New York: Ballantine Books, 1973), 229.

10. Chandler, *Selected Letters,* 43.

11. Ibid., 483.

12. Chandler, "The Simple Art of Murder," 237.

13. Raymond Chandler, "Introduction," *Trouble Is My Business* (New York: Ballantine Books, 1977), ix.

14. Robert B. Parker, "Raymond Chandler," in *Twentieth-Century Crime and Mystery Writers,* ed. John M. Reilly (New York: St. Martin's, 1980), 286.
15. MacShane, *Life of Raymond Chandler,* 70.
16. Philip Durham, *Down These Mean Streets a Man Must Go* (Chapel Hill: University of North Carolina Press, 1963), 92.
17. Max Byrd, "The Detective Detected," *Yale Review,* October 1974, 83.
18. Robert B. Parker, "The Violent Hero, Wilderness Heritage and Urban Reality: A Study of the Private Eye in the Novels of Dashiell Hammett, Raymond Chandler and Ross Macdonald" (Unpublished doctoral dissertation, Boston University, 1970), 123.
19. Raymond Chandler, *The High Window* (New York: Ballantine Books, 1973), 161.
20. William Ruehlmann, *Saint with a Gun: The Unlawful American Private Eye* (New York: New York University Press, 1974), 76.
21. Jon Tuska, *The Detective in Hollywood* (Garden City: Doubleday, 1978), 307.
22. Cleve F. Adams, "Motivation in Mystery Fiction," *The Writer,* May 1942, 142.
23. Cleve F. Adams, *Decoy* (New York: E. P. Dutton, 1941), 187.
24. Cleve F. Adams, *Murder All Over* (New York: Signet, 1950), 150.
25. Adams, "Motivation in Mystery Fiction," 142.
26. Brett Halliday, *Dividend on Death* (New York: Dell, 1939), 8.
27. Brett Halliday, *Bodies Are Where You Find Them* (New York: Dell, 1959), 66.
28. Brett Halliday, *The Uncomplaining Corpses* (New York: Dell, 1940), 146.
29. Brett Halliday, "Michael Shayne as I Know Him," in *Bodies Are Where You Find Them,* 183–88.
30. Dennis Lynds, "Brett Halliday," in Reilly, *Twentieth-Century Crime and Mystery Writers,* 718.
31. Michael Avallone, *The Armchair Detective* 10 (April 1977): 160.

Chapter 4

1. O'Brien, *Hardboiled America,* 38.
2. Howard Browne, *The Taste of Ashes* (New York: Simon and Schuster, 1957), 122.
3. Ibid., 53.
4. John Evans [pseud.], *Halo in Brass* (New York: Pocket Books, 1950), 88.
5. Browne, *The Taste of Ashes,* 23.
6. John Evans [pseud.], *Halo in Blood* (New York: Bantam, 1958), 161.

7. Howard Browne, letter to author, 12 October 1982.
8. Ibid.
9. Unless otherwise noted, all Browne's quotes in this paragraph come from Caleb A. Lewis, "Interview with Howard Browne," *The Armchair Detective* 11 (April 1978): 173–74.
10. Browne, letter to author.
11. Wade Miller, *Guilty Bystander* (New York: Signet, 1948), 14.
12. Wade Miller, *Fatal Step* (New York: Signet, 1948), 30.
13. Ibid., 69.
14. Wade Miller, *Calamity Fair* (New York: Signet, 1951), 107.
15. Miller, *Fatal Step,* 102.
16. Wade Miller, *Shoot to Kill* (New York: Signet, 1954), 7.
17. Bart Spicer, *The Golden Door* (New York: Bantam, 1952), 121.
18. Anthony Boucher, *New York Times Book Review,* 18 November 1951, 50.
19. Richard S. Prather, *Darling, It's Death* (New York: Fawcett, 1952), 95.
20. Richard S. Prather, *Take a Murder, Darling* (Greenwich, Conn: Fawcett, 1958), 96.
21. Prather, *Darling, It's Death,* 169.
22. Richard S. Prather, Introduction to *The Comfortable Coffin* (Greenwich, Conn: Fawcett, 1960).
23. Alice Payne Hackett, *70 Years of Best Sellers, 1895–1965* (New York: R. R. Bowker Co., 1967), 12.
24. Chandler, *Selected Letters,* 310.
25. George P. Elliott, "Country Full of Blondes," *Nation,* 23 April 1960, 355.
26. Richard W. Johnston, "Death's Fair-Haired Boy," *Life,* 23 June 1952, 95.
27. Russel Nye, *The Unembarrassed Muse: The Popular Arts in America* (New York: The Dial Press, 1973), 263.
28. George Grella, "Murder and the Mean Streets," *Contempora,* March 1970, 14.
29. John G. Cawelti, *Adventure, Mystery, and Romance* (Chicago: University of Chicago Press, 1976), 183.
30. Anthony Boucher, *San Francisco Chronicle,* 3 August 1947, 19.
31. Malcolm Cowley, "Sex Murder Incorporated," *New Republic,* 11 February 1952, 18.
32. Grella, "Mean Streets," 14.
33. Julian Symons, *Mortal Consequences* (New York: Schocken Books, 1973), 215.

34. Mickey Spillane, *I, The Jury* (New York: Signet, 1968), 11.
35. Ibid., 7.
36. Mickey Spillane, *The Twisted Thing* (New York: Signet, 1980), 15.
37. Mickey Spillane, *One Lonely Night* (New York: Signet, 1980), 102.
38. Mickey Spillane, *Vengeance Is Mine* (New York: Signet, 1964), 155.
39. Michael Barson, "Just a Writer Working for a Buck," *The Armchair Detective* 12 (Fall 1979): 294.
40. Chandler, *Selected Letters,* 246.
41. Quoted in Barson, "Just a Writer," 293.
42. Ibid., 299.
43. Quoted in Christine Nasso, ed., *Contemporary Authors* (Detroit: Gale Research, 1977), Vol. 25–28, 683.
44. Quoted in Ruehlmann, *Saint with a Gun,* 98.
45. Quoted in Johnston, "Death's Fair-Haired Boy," 127.
46. Ayn Rand, *The Romantic Manifesto* (Cleveland: The World Publishing Co., 1969), 55.
47. Michael Avallone, "The 11 Best Private Eye Novels of Them All," *Xenophile,* no. 38 (1978), 130.
48. *Newsweek,* 19 June 1961, 104.
49. Quoted in "It's Mickey Spillane All Right!," *Writer's Digest,* September 1976, 18.
50. Quoted in Barson, "Just a Writer," 295.
51. Quoted in Johnston, "Death's Fair-Haired Boy," 128.
52. Quoted in Barson, "Just a Writer," 298.

Chapter 5

1. Raymond A. Sokolov, "The Art of Murder," *Newsweek,* 22 March 1971, 108.
2. Ross Macdonald, "The Writer as Detective Hero," in *Self-Portrait: Ceaselessly into the Past,* ed. Ralph B. Sipper (Santa Barbara: Capra Press, 1981), 160. Unless otherwise indicated, all Macdonald's quotes in this chapter come from this book, a collection of his essays.
3. Ross Macdonald, *The Far Side of the Dollar* (New York: Bantam, 1966), 154.
4. Quoted in John Leonard, "Ross Macdonald, His Lew Archer and Other Secret Selves," *New York Times Book Review,* 1 June 1969, 2.
5. Ibid., 19.
6. Ibid., 2.
7. Ross Macdonald, *The Barbarous Coast* (New York: Bantam, 1966), 87.
8. Eudora Welty, "The Stuff That Nightmares Are Made Of," *New York Times Book Review,* 14 February 1971, 30.

9. Thomas B. Dewey, *Every Bet's a Sure Thing* (New York: Simon and Schuster, 1953), 101.

10. Thomas B. Dewey, *Draw the Curtain Close* (New York: Pocket Books, 1968), 55.

11. Thomas B. Dewey, *Don't Cry for Me* (New York: Simon and Schuster, 1964), 107.

12. Thomas B. Dewey, *The Mean Streets* (New York: Permabooks, 1956), 139.

13. William Campbell Gault, *Dead Hero* (New York: E. P. Dutton, 1963), 73.

14. William Campbell Gault, *Day of the Ram* (New York: Bantam, 1957), 69.

15. William Campbell Gault, *Vein of Violence* (New York: Award Books, 1965), 82.

16. William Campbell Gault, *The Convertible Hearse* (New York: Bantam, 1959), 22.

17. Ibid., 14.

18. William Campbell Gault, *Come Die with Me* (New York: Random House, 1959), 181.

19. Quoted in Reilly, *Twentieth-Century Crime and Mystery Writers,* 647.

20. Michael Collins, *Blue Death* (New York: Playboy Paperbacks, 1979), 138.

21. Michael Collins, *The Brass Rainbow* (New York: Playboy Paperbacks, 1980), 66.

22. Michael Collins, *Freak* (New York: Dodd, Mead, 1983), 2.

23. Michael Collins, *Shadow of a Tiger* (Chicago: Playboy Press, 1978), 137.

24. Quoted in Reilly, *Twentieth-Century Crime and Mystery Writers,* 342.

25. Ann Evory, ed., *Contemporary Authors,* New Revision Series (Detroit: Gale Research, 1982), Vol. 6, 310.

26. Quoted in Reilly, *Twentieth-Century Crime and Mystery Writers,* 342.

27. Quoted in Evory, *Contemporary Authors,* 310.

28. Michael Collins, *The Nightrunners* (New York: Playboy Paperbacks, 1981), 63.

29. Michael Collins, "About the Author," in *Night of the Toads* (New York: Bantam, 1971).

Chapter 6

1. Bill Pronzini, "Preface," *Case File* (New York: St. Martin's, 1983), xi.

2. Ibid., xii.

3. Alan Forrest, "Gay Eye," *Books and Bookmen,* August 1973, 6.

4. Quoted in Ann Evory, ed., *Contemporary Authors* (Detroit: Gale Research, 1978), Vol. 29–32, 277.

5. "Interview: Joseph Hansen (1)," *Ellery Queen Mystery Magazine,* September 1983, 69.

6. "Interview: Joseph Hansen (2)," *Ellery Queen Mystery Magazine,* October 1983, 90.

7. Quoted in Jeff Pierce, "The Hard-Boiled Paladin," *Willamette Week's Fresh Weekly,* 20–26 January 1981, 7.

8. Arthur Lyons, *The Killing Floor* (New York: Holt, Rinehart and Winston, 1982), 194.

9. Ross Macdonald, *The Far Side of the Dollar* (New York: Bantam, 1966), 154.

10. Lawrence Block, *In the Midst of Death* (New York: Jove, 1982), 35.

11. Lawrence Block, *The Sins of the Fathers* (New York: Jove, 1982), 181.

Bibliography

I. Novels and Short Story Collections

The following bibliography is not intended to be all-inclusive. When a writer's published output is not extensive, the listing is complete, but in the case of writers like Richard Prather and Brett Halliday, who published dozens of novels, only a selected list is given. No attempt has been made to include all paperback editions. If a reprint is commonly available, that information is provided. Individual short stories are not listed. Entries are given in the order of their original publication.

CLEVE F. ADAMS

Sabotage. New York: Dutton, 1940.
And Sudden Death. New York: Dutton, 1940.
Decoy. New York: Dutton, 1941.
Up Jumped the Devil. New York: Reynal & Hitchcock, 1943; also published as *Murder All Over.* New York: Signet, 1950.
The Crooking Finger. New York: Reynal & Hitchcock, 1944.
Shady Lady. New York: Ace Books, 1955.

ROBERT LESLIE BELLEM

Robert Leslie Bellem's Dan Turner, Hollywood Detective. Edited by John Wooley. Bowling Green, Ohio: Bowling Green State University Popular Press, 1983. Short Stories.

LAWRENCE BLOCK

The Sins of the Fathers. New York: Dell, 1976; reprint ed., New York: Jove, 1982.

In the Midst of Death. New York: Dell, 1976; reprint ed., New York: Jove, 1982.

Time to Murder and Create. New York: Dell, 1977; reprint ed., New York: Jove, 1983.

A Stab in the Dark. New York: Arbor House, 1981; reprint ed., New York: Jove, 1982.

Eight Million Ways to Die. New York: Arbor House, 1982; reprint ed., New York: Jove, 1983.

RAYMOND CHANDLER

The Big Sleep. New York: Alfred A. Knopf, 1939; reprint ed., New York: Ballantine, 1971.

Farewell, My Lovely. New York: Alfred A. Knopf, 1940; reprint ed., New York: Ballantine, 1971.

The High Window. New York: Alfred A. Knopf, 1942; reprint ed., New York: Ballantine, 1971.

The Lady in the Lake. New York: Alfred A. Knopf, 1943; reprint ed., New York: Ballantine, 1971.

The Little Sister. Boston: Houghton Mifflin, 1949; reprint ed., New York: Ballantine, 1971.

The Long Goodbye. London: Hamish Hamilton, 1953; reprint ed., New York: Ballantine, 1971.

Playback. Boston: Houghton Mifflin, 1958; reprint ed., New York: Ballantine, 1977.

The Simple Art of Murder. New York: Ballantine, 1972. Short Stories.

Trouble Is My Business. New York: Ballantine, 1972. Short Stories.

Killer in the Rain. New York: Ballantine, 1972. Short Stories.

Pickup on Main Street. New York: Ballantine, 1972. Short Stories.

MICHAEL COLLINS

Act of Fear. New York: Dodd, Mead, 1967; reprint ed., New York: Playboy Paperbacks, 1980.

The Brass Rainbow. New York: Dodd, Mead, 1969; reprint ed., New York: Playboy Paperbacks, 1980.

Night of the Toads. New York: Dodd, Mead, 1970; reprint ed., New York: Playboy Paperbacks, 1980.

Walk a Black Wind. New York: Dodd, Mead, 1971; reprint ed., New York: Playboy Paperbacks, 1978.

Shadow of a Tiger. New York: Dodd, Mead, 1972; reprint ed., New York: Playboy Paperbacks, 1978.

The Silent Scream. New York: Dodd, Mead, 1973; reprint ed., New York: Playboy Paperbacks, 1979.

Blue Death. New York: Dodd, Mead, 1975; reprint ed., New York: Playboy Paperbacks, 1979.

The Blood-Red Dream. New York: Dodd, Mead, 1976; reprint ed., New York: Playboy Paperbacks, 1981.

The Nightrunners. New York: Dodd, Mead, 1978; reprint ed., New York: Playboy Paperbacks, 1981.

The Slasher. New York: Dodd, Mead, 1980; reprint ed., New York: Playboy Paperbacks, 1981.

Freak. New York: Dodd, Mead, 1983.

GEORGE HARMON COXE

Silent Are the Dead. New York: Alfred A. Knopf, 1942.

Murder for Two. New York: Alfred A. Knopf, 1943.

Flash Casey, Detective. New York: Avon, 1946. Short stories.

Error of Judgment. New York: Alfred A. Knopf, 1961.

The Man Who Died Too Soon. New York: Alfred A. Knopf, 1962.

Deadly Image. New York: Alfred A. Knopf, 1964.

CARROLL JOHN DALY

The Snarl of the Beast. New York: Clode, 1927; reprint ed., Boston: Gregg Press, 1981.

The Hidden Hand. New York: Clode, 1929.

The Tag Murders. New York: Clode, 1930.

Tainted Power. New York: Clode, 1931.

The Third Murderer. New York: Farrar and Rinehart, 1931.

The Amateur Murderer. New York: Ives Washburn, 1933.

Murder from the East. New York: Frederick A. Stokes, 1935; reprint ed., New York: International Polygonics, 1978.

NORBERT DAVIS

The Mouse in the Mountain. New York: Morrow, 1943; also published as
  Dead Little Rich Girl. New York: Handi-Books, 1945.
Sally's in the Alley. New York: Morrow, 1943.
Oh, Murderer Mine. New York: Handi-Books, 1946.

THOMAS B. DEWEY

Draw the Curtain Close. New York: Morrow, 1947.
Every Bet's a Sure Thing. New York: Simon and Schuster, 1953.
Prey for Me. New York: Simon and Schuster, 1954: also published as *The
  Case of the Murdered Model.* New York: Avon, 1955.
The Mean Streets. New York: Simon and Schuster, 1955.
The Brave, Bad Girls. New York: Simon and Schuster, 1956.
You've Got Him Cold. New York: Simon and Schuster, 1958.
The Case of the Chased and the Unchaste. New York: Random House,
  1959.
How Hard to Kill. New York: Simon and Schuster, 1962.
A Sad Song Singing. New York: Simon and Schuster, 1963.
Don't Cry for Long. New York: Simon and Schuster, 1964.
Portrait of a Dead Heiress. New York: Simon and Schuster, 1965.
Deadline. New York: Simon and Schuster, 1966.
Death and Taxes. New York: Putnam, 1967.
The King Killers. New York: Putnam, 1968.
The Love-Death Thing. New York: Simon and Schuster, 1969.
The Taurus Trip. New York: Simon and Schuster, 1970.

JOHN EVANS

Halo in Blood. Indianapolis: Bobbs-Merrill, 1946.
Halo for Satan. Indianapolis: Bobbs-Merrill, 1948.
Halo in Brass. Indianapolis: Bobbs-Merrill, 1949.
The Taste of Ashes. New York: Simon and Schuster, 1957 [As Howard
  Browne].

WILLIAM CAMPBELL GAULT

Ring Around Rosa. New York: Dutton, 1955; also published as *Murder in
  the Raw.* New York: Dell, 1956.
Day of the Ram. New York: Random House, 1956.
The Convertible Hearse. New York: Random House, 1957.
Come Die with Me. New York: Random House, 1959.
Vein of Violence. New York: Simon and Schuster, 1961.

County Kill. New York: Simon and Schuster, 1962.
Dead Hero. New York: Dutton, 1963.
The Bad Samaritan. Toronto: Raven House, 1982.
The Cana Diversion. Toronto: Raven House, 1982.

BRETT HALLIDAY

Dividend on Death. New York: Holt, 1939; reprint ed., Toronto: Raven
    House, 1982.
The Private Practice of Michael Shayne. New York: Holt, 1940.
The Uncomplaining Corpses. New York: Holt, 1940.
Tickets for Death. New York: Holt, 1941.
Bodies Are Where You Find Them. New York: Holt, 1941.
The Corpse Came Calling. New York: Dodd, Mead, 1942.
Murder Is My Business. New York: Dodd, Mead, 1945.
A Taste for Violence. New York: Dodd, Mead, 1949.
Call for Michael Shayne. New York: Dodd, Mead, 1949.
When Dorinda Dances. New York: Dodd, Mead, 1951.
She Woke to Darkness. New York: Torquil/Dodd, Mead, 1954.
A Redhead for Mike Shayne. New York: Torquil/Dodd, Mead, 1964.

DASHIELL HAMMETT

Red Harvest. New York: Alfred A. Knopf, 1929; reprint ed., New York:
    Vintage, 1972.
The Dain Curse. New York: Alfred A. Knopf, 1929; reprint ed., New
    York: Vintage, 1972.
The Maltese Falcon. New York: Alfred A. Knopf, 1930; reprint ed., New
    York: Vintage, 1972.
The Big Knockover. Edited by Lillian Hellman. New York: Vintage, 1972.
    Short stories.
The Continental Op. Edited by Steven Marcus. New York: Random
    House, 1974; reprint ed., New York: Vintage, 1975. Short stories.

JOSEPH HANSEN

Fadeout. New York: Harper & Row, 1970; reprint ed., New York: Owl
    Books, 1980.
Death Claims. New York: Harper & Row, 1973; reprint ed., New York:
    Owl Books, 1980.
Troublemaker. New York: Harper & Row, 1975; reprint ed., New York:
    Owl Books, 1981.

The Man Everybody Was Afraid Of. New York: Holt, Rinehart and Winston, 1978; reprint ed., New York: Owl Books, 1981.

Skinflick. New York: Holt, Rinehart and Winston, 1979; reprint ed., New York: Owl Books, 1980.

Gravedigger. New York: Holt, Rinehart and Winston, 1982.

Nightwork. New York: Holt, Rinehart and Winston, 1984.

JONATHAN LATIMER

Murder in the Madhouse. New York: Doubleday, Doran and Co., 1934.

Headed for a Hearse. New York: Doubleday, Doran and Co., 1935; reprint ed., Boston: Gregg Press, 1980.

The Lady in the Morgue. New York: Doubleday, Doran and Co., 1936.

The Dead Don't Care. New York: Doubleday, Doran and Co., 1938.

Red Gardenias. New York: Doubleday, Doran and Co., 1939: also published as *Some Dames Are Deadly.* New York: Jonathan Press, 1955.

MICHAEL Z. LEWIN

Ask the Right Question. New York: Putnam, 1971; reprint ed., New York: Berkley, 1979.

The Way We Die Now. New York: Putnam, 1973; reprint ed., New York: Berkley, 1979.

The Enemies Within. New York: Alfred A. Knopf, 1974; reprint ed., New York: Berkley, 1979.

The Silent Salesman. New York: Alfred A. Knopf, 1978; reprint ed., New York: Berkley, 1981.

Missing Woman. New York: Alfred A. Knopf, 1981; reprint ed., New York: Berkley, 1982.

ARTHUR LYONS

The Dead Are Discreet. New York: Mason & Lipscomb, 1974; reprint ed., New York: Owl Books, 1983.

All God's Children. New York: Mason/Charter, 1975; reprint ed., New York: Owl Books, 1982.

The Killing Floor. New York: Holt, Rinehart and Winston, 1976; reprint ed., New York: Owl Books, 1982.

Dead Ringer. New York: Mason/Charter, 1977; reprint ed., New York: Owl Books, 1983.

Castles Burning. New York: Holt, Rinehart and Winston, 1980; reprint ed., New York: Owl Books, 1982.

Hard Trade. New York: Holt, Rinehart and Winston, 1981; reprint ed., New York: Owl Books, 1983.

At the Hands of Another. New York: Holt, Rinehart and Winston, 1983.

ROSS MACDONALD

The Moving Target. New York: Alfred A. Knopf, 1949; reprint ed., New York: Bantam, 1970.

The Drowning Pool. New York: Alfred A. Knopf, 1950; reprint ed., New York: Bantam, 1970.

The Way Some People Die. New York: Alfred A. Knopf, 1951; reprint ed., New York: Bantam, 1971.

The Ivory Grin. New York: Alfred A. Knopf, 1952; reprint ed., New York: Bantam, 1971.

Find a Victim. New York: Alfred A. Knopf, 1954; reprint ed., New York: Bantam, 1972.

The Name Is Archer. New York: Bantam, 1955. Short Stories.

The Barbarous Coast. New York: Alfred A. Knopf, 1956; reprint ed., New York: Bantam, 1957.

The Doomsters. New York: Alfred A. Knopf, 1958; reprint ed., New York: Bantam, 1959.

The Galton Case. New York: Alfred A. Knopf, 1959; reprint ed., New York: Bantam, 1960.

The Wycherly Woman. New York: Alfred A. Knopf, 1961; reprint ed., New York: Bantam, 1963.

The Zebra-Striped Hearse. New York: Alfred A. Knopf, 1962; reprint ed., New York: Bantam, 1964.

The Chill. New York: Alfred A. Knopf, 1964; reprint ed., New York: Bantam, 1965.

The Far Side of the Dollar. New York: Alfred A. Knopf, 1965; reprint ed., New York: Bantam, 1966.

Black Money. New York: Alfred A. Knopf, 1965; reprint ed., New York: Bantam, 1967.

The Instant Enemy. New York: Alfred A. Knopf, 1968; reprint ed., New York: Bantam, 1969.

The Goodbye Look. New York: Alfred A. Knopf, 1969; reprint ed., New York: Bantam, 1970.

The Underground Man. New York: Alfred A. Knopf, 1971; reprint ed., New York: Bantam, 1972.

Sleeping Beauty. New York: Alfred A. Knopf, 1973; reprint ed., New York: Bantam, 1974.

The Blue Hammer. New York: Alfred A. Knopf, 1976; reprint ed., New York: Bantam, 1977.

Lew Archer, Private Investigator. New York: Mysterious Press, 1977. Short stories.

WADE MILLER

Guilty Bystander. New York: Farrar, Straus, 1947.

Fatal Step. New York: Farrar, Straus, 1948.

Uneasy Street. New York: Farrar, Straus, 1948.

Calamity Fair. New York: Farrar, Straus, 1950.

Murder Charge. New York: Farrar, Straus, 1950.

Shoot to Kill. New York: Farrar, Straus, 1951.

FREDERICK NEBEL

Six Deadly Dames. New York: Avon, 1950; reprint ed., Boston: Gregg Press, 1980. Short Stories.

ROBERT B. PARKER

The Godwulf Manuscript. Boston: Houghton Mifflin, 1974; reprint ed., New York: Dell, 1983.

God Save the Child. Boston: Houghton Mifflin, 1974; reprint ed., New York: Dell, 1983.

Mortal Stakes. Boston: Houghton Mifflin, 1975; reprint ed., New York: Dell, 1983.

Promised Land. Boston: Houghton Mifflin, 1976; reprint ed., New York: Dell, 1983.

The Judas Goat. Boston: Houghton Mifflin, 1978; reprint ed., New York: Dell, 1983.

Looking for Rachel Wallace. New York: Delacorte, 1980; reprint ed., New York: Dell, 1983.

Early Autumn. New York: Delacorte, 1981; reprint ed., New York: Dell, 1983.

A Savage Place. New York: Delacorte, 1981; reprint ed., New York: Dell, 1983.

Ceremony. New York: Delacorte, 1982; reprint ed., New York: Dell, 1983.

The Widening Gyre. New York: Delacorte, 1983; reprint ed., New York: Dell, 1984.

Valediction. New York: Delacorte, 1984.

RICHARD S. PRATHER

Case of the Vanishing Beauty. Greenwich, Conn.: Fawcett, 1950.
Bodies in Bedlam. Greenwich Conn.: Fawcett, 1951.
Way of a Wanton. Greenwich, Conn.: Fawcett, 1952.
Darling, It's Death. Greenwich, Conn.: Fawcett, 1952.
Strip for Murder. Greenwich, Conn.: Fawcett, 1955.
Take a Murder, Darling. Greenwich, Conn.: Fawcett, 1958.
Kill the Clown. Greenwich, Conn.: Fawcett, 1962.
The Cockeyed Corpse. Greenwich, Conn.: Fawcett, 1964.
The Trojan Hearse. New York: Pocket Books, 1964.
The Sure Thing. New York: Pocket Books, 1975.

BILL PRONZINI

The Snatch. New York: Random House, 1971.
The Vanished. New York: Random House, 1973.
Undercurrent. New York: Random House, 1973.
Blowback. New York: Random House, 1977.
Twospot. New York: Putnam, 1978 [Coauthored with Collin Wilcox].
Labyrinth. New York: St. Martin's, 1980.
Hoodwink. New York: St. Martin's, 1981.
Scattershot. New York: St. Martin's, 1982.
Dragonfire. New York: St. Martin's, 1982.
Case File. New York: St. Martin's, 1983. Short Stories.
Bindlestiff. New York: St. Martin's, 1983.
Quicksilver. New York: St. Martin's, 1984.

BART SPICER

The Dark Light. New York: Dodd, Mead, 1949.
Blues for the Prince. New York: Dodd, Mead, 1950.
The Golden Door. New York: Dodd, Mead, 1951.
Black Sheep, Run. New York: Dodd, Mead, 1951.
The Long Green. New York: Dodd, Mead, 1952.
The Taming of Carney Wilde. New York: Dodd, Mead, 1954.
Exit, Running. New York: Dodd, Mead, 1959.

MICKEY SPILLANE

I, The Jury. New York: Dutton, 1947; reprint ed., New York: Signet, 1948.

My Gun Is Quick. New York: Dutton, 1950; reprint ed., New York: Signet, 1950.

Vengeance Is Mine. New York: Dutton, 1950; reprint ed., New York: Signet, 1951.

The Big Kill. New York: Dutton, 1951; reprint ed., New York: Signet, 1951.

One Lonely Night. New York: Dutton, 1951; reprint ed., New York: Signet, 1951.

Kiss Me, Deadly. New York: Dutton, 1952; reprint ed., New York: Signet, 1952.

The Girl Hunters. New York: Dutton, 1962; reprint ed., New York: Signet, 1963.

The Snake. New York: Dutton, 1964; reprint ed., New York: Signet, 1964.

The Twisted Thing. New York: Dutton, 1966; reprint ed., New York: Signet, 1966.

The Body Lovers. New York: Dutton, 1967; reprint ed., New York: Signet, 1967.

Survival . . . Zero! New York: Dutton, 1970; reprint ed., New York: Signet, 1971.

RAOUL WHITFIELD

Death in a Bowl. New York: Alfred A. Knopf, 1931; reprint ed., New York: Avon, 1970.

II. Anthologies of Pulp Stories

Goulart, Ron, ed. *The Hardboiled Dicks.* Los Angeles: Sherbourne Press, 1965.

Kittredge, William, and Steven M. Krauzer, eds. *The Great American Detective.* New York: Signet, 1978.

Pronzini, Bill, ed. *The Arbor House Treasury of Detective and Mystery Stories from the Great Pulps.* New York: Arbor House, 1983.

Ruhm, Herbert, ed. *The Hard-Boiled Detectives: Stories from Black Mask Magazine (1920–1951).* New York: Vintage, 1977.

Shaw, Joseph T. *The Hard-Boiled Omnibus: Early Stories from Black Mask.* New York: Simon and Schuster, 1946.

III. General Works about the Private Eye

Cawelti, John G. *Adventure, Mystery, and Romance.* Chicago: University of Chicago Press, 1976.

———. "The Gunfighter and the Hard-Boiled Dick: Some Ruminations on American Fantasies of Heroism." *American Studies,* Fall 1975, 49-63.

Estleman, Loren. "Plus Expenses: The Private Eye as Great American Hero." *Alfred Hitchcock's Mystery Magazine,* September 1983, 64-72.

———. "No Trap So Deadly: Recurring Devices in the Private Eye Story." *Alfred Hitchcock's Mystery Magazine,* December 1983, 69-76.

Geherin, David. *Sons of Sam Spade.* New York: Frederick Ungar, 1980.

Grella, George. "Murder and the Mean Streets." *Contempora,* March 1970, 6-15; reprinted as "The Hard-Boiled Detective Hero." In *Detective Fiction,* 103-120. Edited by Robin W. Winks, Englewood Cliffs, N. J.: Prentice-Hall, 1980.

Kittredge, William, and Steven M. Krauzer. Introduction to *The Great American Detective.* New York: Signet, 1978, x–xxxiv.

Landrum, Larry, Pat Browne, Ray B. Browne, eds. *Dimensions of Detective Fiction.* Bowling Green, Ohio: The Popular Press, 1976.

Madden, David, ed. *Tough Guy Writers of the Thirties.* Carbondale: Southern Illinois Press, 1968.

Margolies, Edward. *Which Way Did He Go?: The Private Eye in Dashiell Hammett, Raymond Chandler, Chester Himes, and Ross Macdonald.* New York: Holmes & Meier, 1982.

Nye, Russel. *The Unembarrassed Muse: The Popular Arts in America.* New York: The Dial Press, 1973.

O'Brien, Geoffrey. *Hardboiled America: The Lurid Years of Paperbacks.* New York: VanNostrand Reinhold, 1981.

Parker, Robert B. "The Violent Hero, Wilderness Heritage and Urban Reality: A Study of the Private Eye in the Novels of Dashiell Hammett, Raymond Chandler and Ross Macdonald." Unpublished doctoral dissertation, Boston University, 1970.

Paterson, John. "A Cosmic View of the Private Eye." *Saturday Review,* 22 August 1953, 7.

Ruehlmann, William, *Saint with a Gun: The Unlawful American Private Eye.* New York: New York University Press, 1974.

Schopen, Bernard A. "From Puzzles to People: The Development of the American Detective Novel." *Studies in American Fiction,* Autumn 1979, 175-188.

Tuska, Jon. *The Detective in Hollywood.* Garden City: Doubleday, 1978.

Index